Eriugena: East and West

Papers of the Eighth International Colloquium
of the Society for the Promotion of Eriugenian Studies
Chicago and Notre Dame
18–20 October 1991

EDITED BY
BERNARD McGINN AND WILLEMIEN OTTEN

University of Notre Dame Press
Notre Dame   London

Copyright © 1994 by
University of Notre Dame Press
Notre Dame, Indiana 46556
All Rights Reserved

Manufactured in the United States of America

Library of Congress Cataloging-in-Publication Data

Internationales Eriugena-Colloquium (8th : 1991 : Chicago, Ill., and
Notre Dame, Ind.)
    Eriugena : papers of the eighth international colloquium of the
Society for the Promotion of Eriugenian Studies, Chicago and
Notre Dame, 18–20 October 1991 / edited by Bernard McGinn
and Willemien Otten.
        p.   cm.
    Includes bibliographical references and index.
    ISBN 0-268-00929-5
    1. Erigena, Johannes Scotus, ca. 810–ca. 877—Congresses.
    2. Religious thought—Middle Ages, 600–1500—Congresses.
    I. McGinn, Bernard, 1937–   .   II. Otten, Willemien.   III. Society
for the Promotion of Eriugenian Studies.   IV. Title.
    B765.J34I58   1991
    189—dc20   93-42514
                                                            CIP

∞ *The paper used in this publication meets the minimum requirements*
of the American National Standard for Information Sciences—Permanence of Paper
for Printed Library Materials, ANSI Z39.48-1984.

Contents

Part 3
EASTERN SOURCES AND INFLUENCES

Contributors

WERNER BEIERWALTES, Institute for Philosophy, University of Munich

OLEG BYCHKOV, Pontifical Institute of Mediaeval Studies, University of Toronto

DEIRDRE CARABINE, Department of Philosophy, University College, Dublin

GIULIO D'ONOFRIO, History of Medieval Philosophy, University of Salerno

DONALD F. DUCLOW, Humanities Faculty, Gwynned-Mercy College

MICHAEL McCORMICK, Department of History, Harvard University

JAMES McEVOY, Faculty of Philosophy, University of Louvain-la-Neuve

BERNARD McGINN, Divinity School, University of Chicago

J. C. MARLER, Department of Philosophy, St. Louis University

JOHN MEYENDORFF, Late Professor and Dean, St. Vladimir's Seminary

WILLEMIEN OTTEN, Department of Theology, Loyola University of Chicago

JEAN PÉPIN, Ecole Pratique des Hautes Etudes, Paris

ERIC D. PERL, Department of Philosophy, University of Dallas

Abbreviations

CCCM   Corpus Christianorum, Series Latina, Continuatio Medi-
aevalis. Turnhout: Brepols, 1966–.

CCSG   Corpus Christianorum, Series Graeca. Turnhout:
Brepols, 1977–.

CCSL   Corpus Christianorum, Series Latina. Turnhout:
Brepols, 1953–.

P   *Periphyseon.* Eriugena's major work is cited by book in roman numerals (e.g., book I), by chapter, when needed, in
arabic numerals (I, 1), according to the following: Books
I–III: *Iohannes Scotti Eriugenae Periphyseon (De diuisione naturae),* ed. I. P. Sheldon-Williams (Dublin: Dublin Institute
for Advanced Studies, 1968, 1972, 1981), with page number and line numbers when needed. And Books IV–V:
Ed. H. J. Floss, PL 122, with column number.

PG   Patrologiae Cursus Completus, Series Graeca. Ed. J. P.
Migne (Paris, 1857–66). 161 vols.

PL   Patrologiae Cursus Completus, Series Latina. Ed. J. P.
Migne. 221 vols.; 4 index vols. Paris, 1844–64.

PLS   PL Supplement. 5 vols. Paris, 1958–74.

SC   Sources chrétiennes. Ed. H. de Lubac, J. Daniélou et al.
Paris: Editions du Cerf, 1942–.

Note: Because there is no universally recognized form of his name, the editors have left the contributors free to use Eriugena, John the Scot, John Scottus Eriugena, Johannes Scottus Eriugena.

Introduction
Eriugena: East and West

Bernard McGinn

THE EIGHTH INTERNATIONAL COLLOQUIUM of the Society for the Promotion of Eriugenian Studies (SPES), which met at the University of Chicago and the University of Notre Dame from 18 through 20 October 1991, was devoted to how the great Irish scholar of the ninth century represented a special, even a unique, meeting place between eastern and western Christian thought during the early Middle Ages. Held under the auspices of the Institute for the Advanced Study of Religion of the Divinity School of the University of Chicago, the Medieval Institute of the University of Notre Dame, and the Department of Theology of Loyola University of Chicago this international meeting was designed to bring the best modern scholarship to bear on a crucial moment in the history of Christian ecumenism. On behalf of the planning committee for the colloquium, which consisted of John Contreni of Purdue University, Stephen Gersh and John Van Engen of the University of Notre Dame, and Willemien Otten of Loyola University, as well as myself, I would like to thank the three institutional sponsors and all our contributors for their efforts in making the meeting a productive one and in facilitating the publication of this volume. This introduction is based upon remarks delivered at the opening of the colloquium, but it has been considerably revised in the light of the issues raised by the papers and discussed during the meeting.

One of Eriugena's most profound readers of the Middle Ages provides us with an image that may suggest the purpose of the following volume. At some time during his intellectually and personally adventurous life, Nicholas of Cusa found himself "at sea" between East and West, an experience he described in the letter to his patron Giuliano Cardinal Cesarini appended to the *De docta ignorantia:*

> Now, Reverend Father, receive what I long wanted to attain through various doctrinal paths, but never could before I was at sea returning from Greece. I believe that it was by a heavenly gift from the Father of Lights who gives every best gift (see James 1:17) that I was led to embrace incomprehensible things in an incomprehensible way through learned ignorance by surpassing those incorruptible truths that can be known in human fashion.[1]

Whether or not this reflects a real event that took place during Cusa's return voyage from Constantinople as papal legate during the winter months of 1437–38, or whether it symbolizes in good Neoplatonic fashion the human condition awash in the sea of mutability,[2] is not of ultimate importance here. The issue is rather that Cusa, a western thinker like John Scottus Eriugena, was given—by divine gift, be it noted—incomprehensible comprehension of the incomprehensible while returning from Greece. Poised between East and West, he received the gift of *docta ignorantia.*

The scholarly papers gathered in this volume investigate Eriugena's role as a bridge between East and West. Though they make no claims for divine insight, nor for incomprehensible comprehension, they do, I think, leave us less at sea about some of the most intriguing aspects of the Irishman's contribution. Both Eriugena and Nicholas of Cusa were deeply concerned with the relation of Greek and Latin theology in the history of Christianity. Both, in their own time, sought to heal the fissures that had opened up between the eastern and western communions. These divisions, though shorn of much of their acrimony, are still with us today. John Scottus Eriugena was unique among early medieval Latin thinkers for the magisterial optimism with which he felt that East and West could be integrated into a higher theological synthesis. Even if we cannot share the full measure of his optimism, it is instructive to investigate how so great a thinker pursued so hopeful a solution.

This introduction has two goals: first, to provide a sketch of the historical developments that even in Eriugena's day made the conciliation of East and West a difficult task; and second, to reflect on how the essays in this volume illuminate various aspects of the Irish scholar's attempt to reconcile Latins and Greeks.

Though born among Aramaic-speaking Jews, Christianity was spread by Greek-speaking Jews through the cities of the Mediterranean world in the first century of the common era. It was not until towards the end of the second century that we have evidence of the rise of a distinctively Latin-speaking Christianity in North Africa and Italy. For the next two centuries Greek and Latin Christianity remained in open and familiar dialogue, despite the diverse forms of acculturation that the differing languages expressed. In the late fourth century, a Hilary of Poitiers or an Ambrose of Milan, educated Roman gentlemen and bishops, read and used Greek with ease and fought shoulder-to-shoulder with the Athanasians of the East against Arianism. What is surprising is how rapidly this situation changed after the year 400.[3]

Debate still exists about how much Greek Augustine actually knew, but all would agree that he did not have the easy command of Hilary, Ambrose, or Jerome. All during Augustine's long episcopacy (396–430), the inroads of the barbarian invasions, along with many other less visible factors, were taking their toll on the interchange between eastern and western Christianity, especially with regard to knowledge of the Greek language. Let me cite just one telling example. In 430, the year of Augustine's death, Pope Celestine complained that his delay in reacting to the teaching of Nestorius had been caused by the difficulty of finding anyone in Rome who could translate the relevant documents sent him into Latin.[4]

The linguistic and cultural separation that become evident in the fifth century was to have many unfortunate effects. It was towards the end of that century that the first of the doctrinal disputes between Rome and Constantinople, the chapter in the Monophysite controversy known as the Acacian schism, divided East and West for almost forty years. Neither the Acacian schism nor any of its successors can be blamed on language differences alone, but the increasing theological divergences between East and West were inextricably connected with the language issue.

Despite the efforts of many over the next three and a half centuries, from the perspective of the history of Christian thought it is growing separation rather than ongoing collaborative understanding which is the dominant note. Early in the sixth century, Boethius sought to make the riches of Greek philosophy available in translation to the West but died before the project was complete. His contemporary, Dionysius Exiguus, translated some important Greek patristic works, but only a handful.[5] A century later, the Roman church still maintained some contact with the East. In this era we find the imposing figure of Maximus Confessor, who spent a number of years in Rome, and who can justly be considered the last common Father in the sense of one whose experience and teaching reflected both parts of Christendom. But Maximus never learned Latin and his Greek writings were not accessible to most of his Latin contemporaries. Indeed, what later became available of Maximus did so through the translating efforts of John the Scot.

It is not so much a lack of continuing contacts as it was a developing difference of viewpoint between two theological worlds that made it difficult for each side to understand the other. The history of this mutual incomprehension has often been told and need not be repeated here. The schisms of the ninth century and the eleventh century, the fateful crusade of the thirteenth century, and the failure of the attempted reunion councils of the thirteenth century and the fifteenth century, altogether form one of the saddest chapters in the history of Christianity.

It is surprising how powerful this incomprehension was to remain, even into the modern era. Adolf Harnack read as much and thought as creatively about the development of Christian doctrine as any scholar of the past century, which makes it all the more puzzling to conceive how just over a hundred years ago Harnack could have claimed that from the seventh century on "independent theology had been extinguished in the churches of the East," and that "the history of dogma came to an end in the Greek Church a thousand years ago."[6] More recent histories of doctrine by western theologians, such as that of Jaroslav Pelikan, have tried to redress the balance.[7]

When we look back at the history of so many centuries of misunderstanding, however, we are occasionally confronted by moments of light—events, discussions, personalities on both sides of the divide that form exceptions to the tide of growing separation and lack of comprehension between East and West. John Scottus Eriugena is one of these exceptions. The purpose of this volume is to investigate why John thought it important to bring East and West together and how he actually went about the task. In discussing this important topic, especially in relation to a thinker as difficult as Eriugena, we cannot but expect to find different perspectives, divergent evaluations, and sometimes even direct disagreements among the interpreters. This is as it should be. What unifies this volume is not a set of common answers, but the conviction on the part of all the contributors of the centrality of the issue of East-West dialogue, both for Eriugena and for the history of Christian thought.

The essays in the volume fall into three parts. While the major theme obviously implies a concentration on the history of medieval theology and philosophy, theologians as influential as Ernst Troeltsch and Marie-Dominique Chenu have reminded us that ideas never live in a vacuum. For this reason, the first part of *Eriugena: East and West* is devoted to a paper by Michael McCormick on the topic "Diplomacy and the Carolingian Encounter with Byzantium down to the Accession of Charles the Bald." McCormick sets the stage for Eriugena's remarkable accomplishment by a careful investigation of the concrete and documented bridges between the Byzantine Empire and the Carolingian West, showing that the Frankish court into which the Irish scholar was received was indeed a center of cultural receptivity and innovation, especially through its Roman and Venetian contacts and its direct diplomatic relations with the East.

The second and longest section of the volume, "Themes of the East-West Encounter," contains seven essays dealing with crucial issues that emerge from Eriugena's attempt to synthesize Greek and Latin thought. The first of these is by our much-lamented friend and colleague, the Orthodox theologian John Meyendorff. Father Meyendorff's contribution to this volume goes far beyond this typically wide-ranging evaluation of Eriugena's agreement with his major Greek sources, especially in the area of theocentric anthropology, and his differences from the Greeks, which Meyendorff argues rests in his lack of a clear distinction between nature (*physis*) and will (*thelēma*) in God. By means of his valuable comments during the course of the colloquium, but especially through his presence as a living embodiment of the kind of open and honest ecumenical discussion to which this volume was dedicated, John Meyendorff's role in our meeting was a central one. When word of his untimely death reached us in the summer of 1992, it was the unanimous decision of the contributors that the volume be dedicated to the memory of this great scholar and ecumenist.

In the second essay in this part, Willemien Otten explores Eriugena's contribution to the theological tradition from a western perspective. Otten, like Meyendorff, finds anthropology a key to Eriugena's thought. Her analysis of the "textual genre" and the "textual method" of *Periphyseon* in comparison with the earlier *On Divine Predestination* argues that the Irishman's distinctive thought-pattern was already present in the early work and was not produced by his encounter with Greek patristic authors, as important as this was for him. Among the many key principles used by Eriugena in his attempt at synthesizing the tradition available to him none were more important than those concerning the nature and function of *auctoritas* and its relation to *recta ratio*, or *vera ratio*. Two important essays take up that theme, J. C. Marler's "Dialectical Use of Authority in the *Periphyseon*," and Giulio d'Onofrio's "The *Concordia* of Augustine and Dionysius: Toward a Hermeneutic of the Disagreement of Patristic Sources in John the Scot's *Periphyseon*." *Auctoritas* in Eriugena is a complex topic that has been investigated before and will doubtless be investigated again, but these two complementary essays constitute the most detailed treatments currently available on this crucial theme.

The three remaining essays of the second section of the volume explore particular aspects of Eriugena's thought that illustrate how he sought to "create a consensus" (*consensum machinari*) between East and West.[8] Deirdre Carabine studies Eriugena's use of the symbolism of light, cloud, and darkness, showing that while the Irish scholar does not differ much from Gregory of Nyssa and Dionysius in his use of light and dark, his adaptation of the cloud symbol in book V of *Periphyseon* has important Augustinian elements. James McEvoy's essay on "Biblical and Platonic Measure in John Scottus Eriugena" demonstrates the creative fecundity of Eriugena in relation to both his biblical and Greek heritage, particularly in the way in which he fused Augustinian and Dionysian insights in his use of the famous text of Wisdom 11:21—"God created all things in measure, number, and weight"—as a key for understanding creation as a dialectical theophany.[9] Finally, Jean Pépin, with his characteristic breadth of learning, explores how Eriugena utilized an impressive range of eastern and western sources in studying the role of humanity in genus *animal*, especially in book IV of *Periphyseon*.

The third part of *Eriugena: East and West,* "Eastern Sources and Influences," deals with specific comparisons between John Scottus Eriugena and thinkers of the eastern Christian tradition. Three of the essays concern John's use of Greek Fathers; the final essay studies his appropriation by a modern Orthodox thinker. Werner Beierwaltes continues his long line of distinguished contributions to Eriugenian studies with "Unity and Trinity in East and West," dealing primarily with Dionysius and Eriugena in the light of the long-lasting "serious game" between philosophy and theology in the development of trinitarian thought. If Dionysius's bringing together of the Relationless One and Related One for the understanding of trinitarian faith was a crucial source for Eriugena, Beierwaltes goes on to show how the Irishman made a contribution of his own through his understanding of the Trinity as causal self-explication. Donald F. Duclow also takes up the relation between Dionysius and Eriugena, specifically on their understanding of the role of the angels. Duclow shows how for all his reverence for the Areopagite, Eriugena broke with the Dionysian view of necessary angelic mediation due to his understanding of humanity as created equal to the angels. Once again, anthropology emerges as a key element in Eriugena's thought.

Eric D. Perl's essay on "Metaphysics and Christology in Maximus Confessor and Eriugena" takes up another key theological encounter between the Carolingian scholar and Byzantine thought. Perl's essay, not unlike John Meyendorff's, shows how Eriugena both adopted and departed from his eastern sources, this time in the area of Christology. Though the Irishman was much influenced by Maximus in working out his notion of the Cosmic Christ, by separating creation and incarnation into two events (the standard western pattern), he did not advance a fully "pan-Christic" ontology in the manner of the Greek monk.

If the first essay in this collection deals with the historical contextualization of Eriugena's meeting of East and West, the final piece by Oleg Bychkov reminds us that the Irish thinker's special contribution to ongoing ecumenism has continued to be a source of inspiration for others. At the end of the nineteenth century, the Russian scholar Alexander Brilliantov wrote one of the first major modern studies of Eriugena, arguing that his combination of eastern and western views of humanity as *imago Dei* showed him to be an admirable example of the type of "East-West" thinker needed for the future of Christianity. While the contemporary scholars who have contributed to this volume might not agree with all the aspects of Brilliantov's reading, they certainly share his hope for the emergence of such "East-West" views of the Christian tradition.

I would like to close this introduction with a few general comments on the theme of East-West views, comments which in no way either set the agenda for what the reader will find in the individual essays nor decide any of the important issues. They are meant only to express my own perspective on two sets of underlying issues: those that concern how John the Scot actually tried to relate eastern and western traditions; and those that involve what we might learn from this example.

It has been said that John the Scot attempted to fuse the largely Augustinian theology of the early medieval West with the Dionysianism that he learned from his epoch-making translations of that most mysterious of eastern Fathers. This statement is at best a half-truth, and one that probably raises more questions than it answers. For one thing, from the eastern perspective it neglects the important role that so many other Greek patristic sources, such as Origen, Gregory Nazianzen, Basil, Gregory of Nyssa, Epiphanius, and especially Maximus, had upon the Irishman's thought. From the Latin side, the difficulty is perhaps even greater, because Augustinianism can scarcely be said to be one thing. The towering genius of the bishop of Hippo left not only a vast corpus to his followers, but also a corpus that reflected a moving viewpoint on almost every aspect of Christian teaching. The history of western Christian thought down through the Reformation could be written as the history of competing understandings and misunderstandings of Augustine.

According to the figures compiled by Goulven Madec, John the Scot refers explicitly to Augustine some 119 times in his *Periphyseon*, as compared with 82 citations from Gregory of Nyssa, 83 of Dionysius, and 80 for Maximus.[10] But in order to understand what Augustine meant for the Irishman, we need to engage in careful study of which works of Augustine he prefers and how he uses them. I have no intention of trying here to add to the many valuable studies devoted to Eriugena's use of Augustine, beyond noting that in *Periphyseon* at least it is largely from certain sections in the *City of God* (23 citations) and the *Literal Commentary on Genesis* (33 citations) that Eriugena extracted the Augustinian element in his great synthesis.[11] In other words, it is a particular aspect of Augustine, largely cosmological and anthropological, and heavily Neoplatonic, that the Irishman mined for his speculation.

Quellenforschung, or the hunt after sources, is an important beginning, but never the end of attempts to penetrate the mind of a great thinker. An alternative, and perhaps preferable, approach to the investigation of the relation between East and West in Eriugena's thought would be to begin from a broad characterization of his system which could serve as the basis for showing how he utilized different elements in both the Greek and Latin traditions to help in its elucidation. From this perspective, I would argue that John Scottus Eriugena is the first major western representative of a dialectical form of Platonic Christian theology created by some of the Greek Fathers. This form of speculation is a *Christian* theology, because its primary intention was the elucidation of faith in Jesus Christ as savior. It is also a *Platonic* theology because its proponents found in the ancient tradition that had developed from Plato a systematic and speculative language which could be adapted and transformed for the deeper penetration and expression of their belief. Finally, it is *dialectical* theology (as many of the essays contained herein, such as those of d'Onofrio, McEvoy, and Beierwaltes, demonstrate) because at its heart stood a particular form of Platonism ultimately based on the *Parmenides* that found in the higher unity of mutually opposed predications the most adequate expression of what could be said of God and everything else, the totality Eriugena called *natura.*

Eriugena's thought is among the most powerful and subtle of the varieties of dialectical Platonic Christian theology. It is difficult to think that he could have worked out his understanding of it without his knowledge of Gregory, Dionysius, and Maximus. But the way in which he actually did develop it shows, I believe, important differences from them precisely because of how he integrated aspects of Augustine and the western tradition into the whole.[12]

Any great system, however, cannot be reduced to its component parts. Insofar as it succeeds, at least as a resource for further reflection, it does so on the basis of the new viewpoint it brings to perennial problems and issues. That Eriugena did so succeed is ev-

ident as much from the thought of subsequent dialectical Platonic
Christians, like Meister Eckhart and Nicholas of Cusa, who were
inspired by his insights, as by the increasing number of modern
scholars who have found in his writings not only monuments of
the past but challenges for present reflection.

It is this last point which brings me to the final aspect of these
remarks, that is, what we might be able to learn from a thinker
separated from us in so many ways and by so many centuries. The
term "challenge" is crucial. I doubt if any one of the contributors
to *Eriugena: East and West* would want to argue that Eriugena's solution to a question is necessarily the only one, or even the best
one, and some would doubtless think that questions of correctness, adequacy, or truth should have only historical application.
But John the Scot did make theological claims and the study of
theological systems does not end, at least for all of us, in the historical determination of what a particular thinker did and said.
Eriugena is one of those rare speculators who invites us to think
along with him, even when we recognize that we may no longer
share his views. He does this with regard to issues relating to
purely theological and philosophical concerns, but also, I believe,
with regard to the question of the *catholicity* of the Christian
tradition.

Eriugena as a translator made available to the new Carolingian
world of medieval Europe many of the riches of Greek Orthodox
theology, especially the Dionysian corpus. Though later translations superseded his, this was a decisive intervention. Latin theology would have looked different in ways we probably cannot
conceive without these writings. But the Irishman also challenged
the growing separation and incomprehension between the eastern
and western Christian communities by his bold rethinking of *both*
Greek and Latin sources in the construction of his synthesis. The
catholicity of his view of Christian truth was to grow increasingly
rare as East and West grew more and more estranged, and later as
the fabric of western Christianity unraveled in the Reformation
disputes. Lady Theology was eventually to be left, much like Lady
Philosophy at the opening of Boethius's *Consolation,* bewailing her
dress torn by the marauders who had each carried off whatever
piece they could get their hands on.

There are many challenges facing Christian theology today, and
it would be foolish to suggest that Eriugena has answers for them

all, even implicitly. But among these problems not the least is the presence of the great theological division between East and West that for all our ecumenicity still remains so real. Here, the example of John Scottus Eriugena is of real importance, not as providing us with any immediate and easy solution to this division, but at least as reminding us that no solution will ever be forthcoming unless we begin once again to break out of the narrow confines into which a sad history has bound us and to enter into an honest conversation without prejudging the conclusions. Whatever contribution this volume can make, directly or indirectly, to that endeavor will be continuing proof of Eriugena's special role in the history of Christian thought.

NOTES

1. Nicholas of Cusa, "Epistola auctoris ad dominum Iulianum cardinalem," in *Nicholai de Cusa, De docta ignorantia: Die belehrte Unwissenheit Buch III* (Hamburg: Felix Meiner, 1977), 98–100: "Accipe nunc, pater metuende, quae iam dudum attingere variis doctrinarum viis concupivi, sed prius non potui, quousque in mari me ex Graecia redeunte, credo superno dono a patre luminum a quo datum optimum, ad hoc ductus sum, ut incomprehensibilia incomprehensibiliter amplecterer in docta ignorantia per transcensum veritatum incorruptibilium humaniter scibilium."

2. See Marjorie O'Rourke Boyle, "Cusanus at Sea: The Topicality of Illuminative Discourse," *Journal of Religion* 71 (1991): 180–201.

3. For a survey, see Adalbert Hamman, "I. The Turnabout of the Fourth Century," in *Patrology*, vol. 4, ed. Angelo di Berardino with an introduction by Johannes Quasten (Westminster, Md.: Christian Classics, 1986), 1–32.

4. See Celestine's *Epistola* 13, cited in Hamman, 6.

5. For a helpful list of Greek works available in Latin, see J. T. Muckle, "Greek Works Translated Directly into Latin before 1350," *Mediaeval Studies* 4 (1942): 33–43, and 5 (1943): 102–115. See also the ongoing project of the Union Académique Internationale, the *Catalogus Translationum et Commentariorum: Mediaeval and Renaissance Latin Translations and Commentaries* (7 volumes to date).

6. Adolph Harnack, *History of Dogma* (reprint, New York: Dover, 1961), 4:352.

7. See Jaroslav Pelikan, *The Christian Tradition*, vol. 2, *The Spirit of Eastern Christendom (600–1700)* (Chicago: University of Chicago, 1974).

8. The phrase is taken from the noted passage in P IV, 11 (804D) where Eriugena confronts the disagreement between Augustine and Gregory of Nyssa on whether Adam was created with a body. See the treatment of this theme in G. d'Onofrio's essay.

9. See the passage in P III, 58, 12–22 (633A–B).

10. See Goulven Madec, "Jean Scot Erigène et ses auteurs," in *Jean Scot écrivain: Actes du IVe collogue international de SPES, Montréal,* ed. Guy Allard (Montréal-Paris: Bellarmin-Vrin, 1986), 143–186. Also useful for tracking down references and citations is the "Index Auctorum" in G. H. Allard, *Johannis Scoti Eriugenae Periphyseon: Indices Generales* (Montréal-Paris: Institut d'Etudes Mediévales and J. Vrin, 1983), 619–624.

11. The other works frequently cited also conform to a strong Neoplatonist current: the *Confessions* (7 references); *On True Religion* (6); *The Trinity* (5); and *On Music* (4).

12. The differences between Eriugena and his Greek sources are highlighted in almost all of the essays here; see especially those of Meyendorff, Otten, d'Onofrio, Duclow, and Perl.

Part 1

HISTORICAL BACKGROUND

Diplomacy and the Carolingian Encounter with Byzantium down to the Accession of Charles the Bald

Michael McCormick

The carolingian context of eriugena's thought continues to pose problems for the historian. After Maïeul Cappuyns, the studies of John Contreni on Laon or Edouard Jeauneau on Eriugena's Hellenism have done much to illuminate the immediate cultural background of John the Scot's achievement.[1] And yet, Eriugena's broader historical setting as an early medieval intellectual working to interpret and interrelate two cultures lying at opposite ends of the Mediterranean Sea continues to pose a profound historical enigma.

Since the time of Henri Pirenne, economic historians have usually admitted that the Mediterranean changed from the Roman Empire's royal road of commerce and therefore communication into a war-ravaged no-man's-land, with the result that direct contacts between Byzantium and the early medieval West withered to minimal levels. Cultural historians have documented a shrinking knowledge of Greek which seems to fit the overall reduction of contacts. Against this vision, how was it possible that an Irishman should discover in Frankland a talent for studying Byzantine thinkers like Ps.-Dionysius, Maximus Confessor, and Gregory of Nyssa? And even more remarkable perhaps, that he should find there the means to accomplish that study: the Greek manuscripts, the linguistic tools, the economic support of a patron willing and able to further the study of abstruse theological masterpieces of Byzantine high culture?[2]

It seems unlikely that we will ever identify precisely from whom Eriugena learned his Greek, or how exactly he was bitten by the Byzantine bug. The best efforts of accomplished historians have turned up only a few, fugitive traces of Eriugena's physical presence.[3]

A better hope for deepening our understanding of Eriugena as a historical actor on the Carolingian stage may lie in seeking out the broader historical processes and societal dynamics within which recent work has situated John. Recovering another facet of the Carolingian encounter with Hellenism may prove fruitful to the Eriugenian enterprise, even if this discussion focuses on the years before Charles the Bald's accession and Eriugena's first documented appearance on the Continent. This means that my contribution aims to describe the immediate legacy within which John, his friends and rivals, his enemies and patrons, operated. And this study has a provisional character, since it must lean on early results of an ongoing investigation into patterns of cross-cultural contacts in the early Middle Ages.

Against the broader historical stage on which Eriugena strode, his achievement appears remarkable indeed. Outside of the Islamic world, Mediterranean commerce and travel between regions had diminished and, it is argued, practically disappeared. One of Pirenne's essential conclusions contended that the rise of Islam blockaded western Europe from its ancient center of gravity in the Mediterranean. This forced Europe to shift its attention northwards and triggered a radically new pattern of geographic, economic, and cultural development centering around the North Sea.

To be sure, a half-century of challenge and reexamination has altered many facets of the Belgian historian's initial formulation. Archaeologists and numismatists in particular have disclosed new and surprising links between Europe and modern-day Iraq along a northern arc, via the Vikings, the Baltic, and Russia. Excavations have delineated how shipping developed across the western zone of this route, as Frisian and Anglo-Saxon sailors plied the North Sea and Channel between England and the newly exhumed Frankish trade emporia of Dorestad on the old Rhine or Quentovic on the Canche River. It was this North Sea shipping that provided the infrastructure which brought so many insular scholars and pilgrims to the Continent, and it is by this route that Eriugena likely reached West Francia. The written sources are in harmony with what has emerged from the earth. In the 880s, Notker of St. Gall imagined that Irish scholars came to Charlemagne's court aboard these ships. His testimony surely reveals more about his own era than that of Charlemagne. Earlier, however, Alcuin him-self—and he should have known, since he certainly did not walk on water during his several trips between York and Frankland—shows other Irish holy men active in the coastal region between the Somme and the Canche Rivers, and St. Richarius appears as traveling from that region to England and back.[4]

Scholarly opinion on the subject of transmediterranean contacts in the Carolingian period remains uncertain. Excellent scholars like R. S. Lopez or F. Gabrieli have rejected Pirenne's conclusions in whole or in part. Many others have accepted them in modified form, so that Pirenne's fundamental views on the economic di-vorce of Charlemagne's Europe from the Mediterranean still command widespread adherence. As two noted specialists have trenchantly formulated it: "Between the reign of Heraclius and the Arab raids of the ninth century internal relations within the Mediterranean were reduced to an almost 'prehistoric' scale."[5]

In the face of such a verdict, the enigma of Eriugena's Helle-nism—and of a Frankish court society which fostered, financed, and rewarded it—looms ever larger. One begins once again to wonder whether Eriugena was not some historical fluke, entirely independent of the Frankish or Byzantine societies between which he appears to us as a privileged intermediary. And it is a fact that more than physical distance separated Byzantium from the Franks. The Frankish kingdoms were essentially land-based net-works of extended kinships originally rooted in the Rhine-Meuse basin. Like the society they encompassed, these kingdoms and their power networks were an affair of persons, not institutions. Literacy was more markedly ecclesiastical than in the East. By the time Eriugena appears on the scene, the hybrid Germano-Latin aristocracy known as the Franks were beginning to lose control over much of the western Europe which they had conquered in the last three generations.

Over the last thirty years, new insights have transformed the modern view of early medieval Byzantium. No longer is Byzan-tium viewed complacently as the unchanging heir and reservoir of an urbanized, classicizing, Hellenic civilization.[6] Archaeology has now made clear that Byzantium's early medieval cities fared little better than those of Merovingian Gaul, and there too the wither-ing of urban society brought with it an impoverishment and ru-ralization of culture.[7] Over a century of catastrophe had reduced the old empire to a shade of its former self, but the imperial capital of Constantinople still controlled much of the Balkan coast and large parts of Asia Minor; it was losing Sicily, the sheet-anchor of Byzantine power in Italy, but fighting gamely to defend Calabria and clinging still to its nominal overlordship of the Campanian seaports, Venice, and outposts along the eastern Adriatic coast. Newly reorganized institutions bound this Greek-speaking empire together: a relatively strong monarchy; an army, navy, and officer corps; and the bureaucracy required to finance and run them. Indeed the institutions which structured Byzantine society were beginning to make a remarkable comeback, after narrowly escaping annihilation at the hands of the Arabs and, later, the Bulgars.

The crises had helped to produce successive shifts in the ruling faction's view of the cult of icons and its christological implications. In turn these doctrinal shifts produced political and cultural stress even as they sparked renewed theological investigation.[8] In fact, Byzantine literary culture which, in the eighth century, had flourished really only on the empire's fringes and beyond its frontiers—John of Damascus's family worked for the Caliph, not the Basileus—was now, in Eriugena's lifetime, stirring anew in an imperial city whose tattered urban fabric was itself showing signs of recovery.[9] The Irish scholar's contemporaries in Constantinople were only the second or third generation of a nascent revival of Greek letters, members of a small coterie of scholar-bureaucrats struggling to find, compare, gloss, and transliterate old works. Their efforts would launch the "Macedonian renaissance," more aptly dubbed the "encyclopedic movement."[10] Although the rebirth of high culture, wealth, and power in Byzantium is every bit as exciting as the western revival, the new vision of Byzantium underscores that Frankish fascination with Constantinople and its culture was anything but obvious.

Given the cultural and physical distance separating the centers of Frankish and Byzantine culture and the apparent absence of the commercial relations that might have encouraged interaction, one might expect little or no cross-cultural exchange between them. And yet, it is not only Eriugena who tells a different story.

The last two generations of scholars have uncovered much of Byzantium's impact on Carolingian Europe. Byzantine "influence" has been detected in the Frankish monarchy, art, liturgy, and literature. In 813, Charlemagne staged the final political act of his long reign by crowning his sole surviving son Louis as co-emperor in his palace chapel at Aachen. The Frankish ceremony seems to derive directly from the Byzantine emperor's coronation of his heir two years before.[11] Byzantine artists or inspiration have been invoked to explain some aspects of Carolingian court art.[12] Greek liturgical chants like the great Akathistos hymn to the Virgin were translated and ultimately adapted into the purified Latin liturgy propagated by the Carolingians.[13] This seems all the more remarkable in view of the liturgy's central role in early medieval culture and the Carolingian family's obsession with purging it of "foreign" accretions.

To this more traditional kind of Byzantine influence, I would add a more novel variety: information. Occasional but remarkable bits of information concerning Constantinople crop up in the oddest places in Carolingian literature. For example, the eighth-century Chronicle of Moissac interrupts its usual court fare of births, deaths, and battles to mention, quite out of the blue, the harsh weather conditions which prevailed one winter in the Gauls, Illyricum, and *in Byzantine Thrace.*[14]

Clearly, Eriugena's Hellenism was not a totally isolated phenomenon. Yet, for all the distinguished scholarship devoted to this theme, little evidence has hitherto been adduced to explain how, in concrete historical terms, borrowings from a distant Byzantium occurred if most long-distance contacts in the Mediterranean world had in fact ground to a halt.

One important reason behind this dilemma lies in the very notion of Byzantine "influence." For the conceptual connotations of "influence" supply a metaphor which misleads historical analysis.[15] To speak of Byzantine "influence" is implicitly to suggest that Constantinople was a kind of medieval volcano actively spewing forth its culture across thousands of miles onto an inert, passive Frankish West. Yet historical observation suggests that just the opposite is true: when one culture encounters another, the receiving culture takes the initiative of appropriating something from the donor culture. But before the borrowing can occur, the two civilizations must meet somewhere, there must be sufficient contact for the donor culture to be available to the borrowing culture. This is the historical dilemma: historians of all obediences have detected not a few cross-cultural borrowings between the two empires at the same time that other historians have observed the shrinking of relations between them. If contacts between Byzantium and the Franks shared the presumed fate of long-distance commerce, how could the Franks know enough about Byzantine civilization to appropriate it for themselves?

To answer this historical riddle means approaching it in terms that meant something in the eighth and ninth centuries. We should examine our assumptions about Mediterranean commerce even as we seek out other opportunities for interaction between Constantinople and the West. Abstractions like "influence" and even "appropriating milieux" are less helpful than specific people and places, the documented bridges between the two worlds. And there is a common thread to many Frankish borrowings from Byzantium which helps to guide the inquiry. That thread leads precisely to Eriugena's historical milieu: the Carolingian court.

The royal court's role in launching the Carolingian renaissance is well known. Key features of Carolingian society like kingship, personal bonds of kinship and friendship, patronage, gift-giving, and a lust for authenticity helped shape and structure this remarkable social group.[16] The court fostered Charlemagne's efforts to improve education, foreign scholars' integration into the Frankish empire, and the introduction of rare works into northern libraries. We need think only of Charlemagne's library and its rare classical texts, including perhaps a unique translation of Euclid or, closer to Eriugena, the Byzantine-Frankish dossier on iconoclasm that may have belonged to Charles the Bald's library. In sum the Frankish royal court represented a highly charged locus of cultural receptivity and innovation. It boasted the greatest concentration of talented intellectuals, resources, and patrons of culture.[17]

The structures of Frankish society conditioned how this milieu fastened onto Byzantine culture. Given the predominance of person-to-person ties over institutional ones, long-distance relations involving individuals associated with the court should be very revealing.

Personal contacts with merchants may have been of limited importance. Even if ongoing research were to revise the current assessment of "stone-age" levels of Mediterranean commerce—my own work suggests a view which differs somewhat from the conventional wisdom outlined above—economic historians have challenged anachronistic assumptions about the importance of trade in ancient times. On present evidence, early medieval economies were likely to be even more agrarian than ancient ones.[18] In the best of times, that is, trade was a limited phenomenon, so that effective media for cross-cultural exchange should be sought outside or alongside of commerce. Where else should one look?

The reality of Byzantine provincial culture lay in the Franks' own backyard. Scholars are increasingly uncovering the role of border provinces in diffusing Byzantine civilization.[19] For the Carolingians, this meant Italy, much of which was just leaving the Byzantine world in the eighth and ninth centuries.[20] Charlemagne was a child when the imperial administration finally abandoned Ravenna, and he later went to war with Constantinople for control of Byzantine outposts on the Adriatic, including Venice.[21]

Then as now, loss of political control coincided only roughly with cultural reorientation. Though the most recent research has tended to minimize Greek culture at contemporary Ravenna, the Lombards who attempted to absorb the Exarchate show signs of indebtedness to Byzantine military ritual, chancery practices, and court entertainment. When the Franks annexed northern Italy in 774, the last Lombard king fled to Constantinople where he joined the Byzantine aristocracy as a patrician.[22] And the impact of Byzantine culture is clear on the imperial borders in the southern Lombard duchy of Benevento, where one duke founded a convent dedicated to "Sancta Sophia" and another, who had lived at Charlemagne's court as a hostage, married Evanthia, sister-in-law of emperor Constantine VI.[23]

Byzantium's hand had once weighed even more heavily in Rome. When Charlemagne took the throne, the papacy was just emerging from its century-long "Byzantine period," during which most popes had been recruited from the Greek-speaking elites who had fled Byzantium's catastrophes in the East. Pope Zachary, who ruled the see of Peter in Charlemagne's childhood and underwrote St. Boniface's mission in Germany, translated the Latin dialogues of Gregory the Great into his own native Greek—quite possibly so that they could be read in the monasteries of Rome.[24] For the paradox is often forgotten that precisely when Monte Cassino's Benedictine rule was conquering abbeys north of the Alps, Byzantine monasticism prevailed at Rome itself. In fact a list of Roman monasteries drawn up in 807 reveals that Saint Sabas, Saint Anastasius, and Saint Silvester's were the city's three most important abbeys, and all three were Greek. Four other Byzantine monasteries and convents figure in the list and, in 818/819, Pope Paschal I would found an eighth, Saint Praxedis.[25] Little wonder then that Rome ceased recognizing eastern sovereignty only late in the eighth century.[26]

Thus Carolingian Rome and its inhabitants, like other areas of Italy, offered a complex cultural picture in which Byzantium figured prominently. Franks who traveled to Italy, and particularly to Rome, encountered Byzantine provincial civilization at firsthand. Byzantines also encountered Franks. It may have been Byzantine residents of Rome who coined the variant on a traditional Greek proverb cited by Einhard: "If you have a Frank who is a friend, you don't have him for a neighbor."[27]

In addition to frequent pilgrimage south to Rome, six times in the eighth century's last forty-five years, the Frankish king, his court, and some thousands of his military followers crossed the Alps and campaigned in Italy. Charles the Bald would himself head south twice at the close of his reign, although after we lose certain sight of Eriugena. Indeed, Charles the Bald's famous experiment in Byzantine ceremony came hard on the heels of an expedition to Italy.[28]

Firsthand experience of Mediterranean civilization must have made a profound impression on the Frankish aristocrats who constituted the army, and the results of these massive movements of men and material are reflected in the transfer of books, artworks, and people across the Alps. The surviving manuscripts which actually made the trip northward show how much more intensive this movement was under the Carolingians than in the tenth century.[29] Even more consequential, given the nature of Frankish society, was Charlemagne's systematic replacement of Lombard officials by northern aristocrats. This administrative policy insured an enduring transalpine presence in Italy and, for the first time since the Roman Empire, created a powerful, permanent medium for diffusing ideas and customs from the south: extensive aristocratic kinship networks now spanned the Alps and would endure over a century.[30] A splendid example from Eriugena's time is Charles the Bald's own sister Gisla and her cultivated husband, Eberhard, margrave of Friuli, who left a much-discussed library to his heirs. Although their hereditary properties lay chiefly in Charles the Bald's kingdom and Gisla would retire there, these aristocrats spent most of their active lives overseeing the Frankish

frontier of Byzantine Venice.[31] Eberhard was well-enough connected with Irish circles north of the Alps that Sedulius Scottus
celebrated him in panegyrics and composed his son's epitaph.[32] It
was in their household that the Saxon noble Godescalc—whose
controversial ideas on predestination first bring John the Scot
clearly into view—found temporary refuge en route to Byzantine
Dalmatia. There, presumably, Godescalc learned the technical terminology which the Venetians used to describe their relations with
the Byzantine emperor.[33]

Early in its relationship with the Carolingians, the Roman
church had played a key role as intermediary between Constantinople and the Franks: in the mid-eighth century, the popes had
supplied the Frankish court with the experts on Byzantium that
it so urgently needed.[34] Later on, the popes used their eastern
connections to furnish Charlemagne with news bulletins on events
in Constantinople.[35] And it is well known that Rome supplied the
northern court with Latin books, but Greek ones also crossed the
Alps.[36]

There were more casual contacts too. For example, in Rome,
Einhard's secretary Ratleic met and was inspired to pious theft by
Basilius the monk who, with four disciples, had emigrated from
Constantinople two years before entering the brand-new Greek
monastery of St. Caesarius.[37] By the time Eriugena appears at
Charles the Bald's court, Ratleic had succeeded Einhard as abbot
of Seligenstadt and ascended to a key position at the court of Louis
the German, where he would serve as head of the royal writing
office until 854.[38]

In the second half of the ninth century, however, the situation
may have been changing. Every passing decade since the end of
the doctrinal controversies at Constantinople and the later waves
of immigration that they had triggered may have diluted the Byzantine component of local Roman culture. Certainly the city's
Greek monasteries declined in the last quarter of the ninth
century.[39] By then a cultural intermediary like Anastasius Bibliothecarius appears as a towering and, seemingly, rather isolated
figure.[40] Since Latin into Greek may be a better gauge of an important Hellenic presence than the inverse, it is probably significant that the latest securely documented ninth-century translation
at Rome from Latin into Greek dates from 824.[41] But if Rome's
connections with Byzantium did slacken somewhat as the ninth

century progressed, those of Venice intensified and opened a new set of possibilities. Already Louis the Pious had turned to Venice to find someone who could build a Byzantine organ for court cere-monies at the Aachen of Charles the Bald's childhood.[42]

And so Frankish Italy defines one zone in which Byzantine and Carolingian cultures overlapped and created the person-to-person contacts which, in an early medieval society, were particularly pro-pitious to cross-cultural exchange. Although far more distant, a second area linked Byzantine civilization beyond the imperial bor-ders with the Frankish elite and deserves at least passing mention.

Jerusalem fascinated and attracted Christians from around the world, despite its distant location within the political boundaries of the Islamic caliphate. The Frankish court had connections there. These personal relations illuminate the unlikely fact that the most detailed description of Christian institutions in the Holy Land between the Arab conquest and the Crusades occurs in a Carolingian financial document. It instructed Charles the Great that seventeen women from his dominions lived in a convent at-tached to the Holy Sepulcher, that thirty-five monks inhabited the Frankish monastery on the Mount of Olives, and that the patri-arch of Jerusalem spent 630 gold pieces on his clergy every year.[43] And it was the liturgical practice of the Franks in reciting their Creed at Jerusalem that first spotlighted the *filioque* formula and its rejection by the Byzantine—and papal—church.[44] Similar con-tacts continued into Eriugena's time, as we know from the lively account that a monk has left of his trip to Jerusalem and its Frank-ish establishment in the reign of Charles the Bald.[45] Like Byzan-tine Italy, in other words, Jerusalem promises some surprising rewards to further research.

A third "zone" for direct personal contact between eastern and western elites might appear, at first glance, quantitatively insignif-icant. With more insight than evidence, Maïeul Cappuyns, for in-stance, argued that Eriugena found his Greek at the royal court.[46] Whether or not that was the case, Jeauneau is surely right to em-phasize that the prestige Byzantium enjoyed at court conditioned the context of Eriugena's activity.[47] This raises the problem of di-rect contacts between the Frankish court and Constantinople, that is, the place of diplomacy in the cultural encounter between East and West. Now it might be objected that diplomatic relations are

not a promising place to seek significant cultural exchange. But
was that true in the early Middle Ages? Certainly Frankish-
Byzantine relations were rocky, swinging—literally—from near
honeymoon idyll to war and back again. It might be observed too
that dark-age diplomats had little time for the niceties of cross-
cultural exchange and, even had they had the time, the rarity of
diplomatic contacts and tiny numbers of persons involved in a
Mediterranean reduced to "stone-age" relations could scarcely reward detailed scrutiny. And what substance could there be to such
exchanges between societies so different and so distant?

Even a quick glance at the diplomatic record demonstrates that
substance was not lacking. Byzantine diplomacy was a prized instrument of power, and Constantinople initiated relations as soon
as the Franks intervened in the sphere of Byzantine interests in
Italy. Down to 840, diplomats negotiated four or five marriage
contracts between the ruling dynasties and—a not unconnected
fact—concluded two wars. This suggests substantive diplomatic
relations.[48]

Several factors make these contacts a privileged path for uncovering the early medieval dynamics of cross-cultural exchange. The
naked fact of the embassies is often, if not invariably, attested
in the scanty surviving sources; we can sometimes identify the
ambassadors themselves and so analyze their social and cultural
profile. And, most importantly, the legations concerned and connected the summits of the two societies, their courts. Given the
Carolingian court's cultural vigor, even the most limited contact
here could work far broader consequences than comparable encounters between private individuals.

How many people were involved? Diplomatic exchanges between the Carolingian court and Constantinople from the beginning in 756 to 840, over the three generations of Carolingian
power represented by Pippin, Charlemagne, and Louis the Pious,
comprised some nine embassies sent by the Frankish king to Constantinople and at least twenty-one Byzantine legations in the
opposite direction for a total of about thirty missions over eighty-
four years.[49] By the most conservative count the nine western
embassies involved more than seventeen documentable ambassadors, while the twenty-one eastern legations included thirty-eight
officials of status exalted enough to be named in the surviving

sources. This total of over fifty-five officials very likely underrepresents the real number of ranking ambassadors, irrespective of how many legations actually took place.[50]

More than fifty-five persons physically linking the two early medieval courts over nine decades seems a surprisingly high number, given conventional wisdom on the state of Mediterranean-borne traffic between Byzantium and the West. But even this intriguing figure fails to convey how many people were directly involved. It does not take into account an essential historical characteristic of early medieval society, when power was reckoned not so much in how many pieces of silver one owned but in the number of men that one commanded. True to their laconic and aristocratic slant, the same Carolingian historical records which virtually ignore the Irish court teacher without Frankish kin, bishopric, or abbey, mention only the heads of embassies.[51] Yet in the early Middle Ages, people were power, and every grandee, in both societies, prided himself on the size and impressiveness of his personal retinue.[52] What is more, a Frankish bishop or a Byzantine patrician could hardly be expected to cook for himself, write his own letters, or feed his own horses, and the legations needed to protect their precious gifts. So purely practical concerns combined with prestige to force ambassadors to surround themselves with grooms, soldiers, secretaries, priests, interpreters, and cooks. Earlier and slightly later sources clearly attest that embassies and their personnel were structured along these lines; a few stray allusions from our period confirm the pattern.[53]

How large were the retinues? The only precise and certain figure I have found for a western ambassador's entourage to Constantinople in the early Middle Ages comes from the tenth century. But surely it furnishes a good idea of the order of magnitude of such expeditions: the legation which Liutprand led to Constantinople in 968 included the bishop's personal retinue of twenty-five followers.[54] That this figure is valid and even on the low side for our period is suggested by a Carolingian capitulary regulating the daily supplies furnished to envoys on royal business. A bishop's *per diem* included forty loaves of bread, three suckling piglets, one young pig, three measures of drink, three chickens, and fifteen eggs, while the supplies furnished to a count, an abbot, or a royal vassal are only slightly lower, starting with thirty loaves of bread. The amounts are specifically earmarked for each envoy.

The conclusion is inescapable: each grandee traveled with his own personal retinue. One loaf per day per person was the usual Carolingian rule of thumb for calculating food rations. This means that Louis the Pious's court presumed that bishops' retinues on government business numbered around forty persons, while those of abbots and counts counted around thirty, and royal vassals traveled with seventeen followers.[55]

While the actual attested size of Liutprand's entourage may be on the low side, it is certainly believable. Using Liutprand's escort to remain on the safe side, and multiplying it by the seventeen Frankish ambassadors, we are forced to reckon that some 425 followers accompanied the ambassadors to Constantinople. In all probability, then, a minimum of 442 Franks traveled to the Byzantine court on official business over three generations. If roughly the same figures hold for Byzantine embassies to the Frankish court—and several Byzantine sources suggest they do—we must assess their total numbers at somewhere around 936 Byzantines traveling to Aachen and the other Carolingian palaces.[56]

And so, well over one thousand persons from Constantinople and the Carolingian courts seem to have traveled across the length and breadth of each other's empire to visit their respective courts in the eighty-four years preceding Charles the Bald's accession. Even allowing for overlapping due to individuals who may have repeated the journey, the general order of magnitude offers a startling challenge to received wisdom about the levels of direct interaction between the two early medieval court societies. Clearly, it is time to start revising our assumptions about dark-age diplomacy.

Nonetheless, this figure of many hundreds of travelers says little about their social status and therefore cultural weight. This is fundamental in an era when, in the West at least, aristocratic kindreds set the tone for civilization. Many of the travelers must have been subordinates, and some were probably even of servile status.[57] In any case, we can usually verify the backgrounds of known ambassadors. Thirteen of seventeen Frankish ambassadors are identified by name. Typically, these men came from the most influential and aristocratic kinship groups of their time. One example may speak for all: Count Hugh the Timid served as ambassador to Constantinople in 811–812. Hugh came from an Alemannian family which was prominent throughout the empire, and Hugh himself was a dominant personality at the court into which Charles the Bald was

born. The man's nobility and political status enabled him to marry
one daughter to Lothar I, while a second daughter married
Charles the Bald's maternal uncle.[58] When kinship networks of
this prominence and power are implicated in the journey to Constantinople, the potential cultural consequences among the Carolingian elite are great indeed. It bears remembering that the
records usually mention only the heads of embassies. Yet the nature of Carolingian society dictated that, wherever they went
on the king's business, Frankish aristocrats were accompanied by
their kinsmen and their closest associates. So, over a decade after
the fact, we learn quite incidentally that another of Charlemagne's
ambassadors to Constantinople, Haito, bishop of Basel and abbot
of Reichenau, had taken his future successor at Reichenau with
him on his voyage to Constantinople.[59] And in this society of blood
bonds and feuds, some followers were probably close relatives of
the noble ambassadors themselves.[60] Nor were intellectuals missing
from the ranks of Carolingian ambassadors: the famous liturgical
commentator Amalarius of Metz, the moral theologian Halitgar,
bishop of Cambrai, and the great translator Anastasius Bibliothecarius, who criticized Eriugena's Greek, all sailed to Byzantium as
ambassadors of Frankish emperors.[61]

How long did these large parties of aristocrats and their retain-
ers spend at each other's courts? The ninth-century infrastructure
of travel dictated the rhythm of contacts. Since the Mediterranean
was closed for travel between November and March, Frankish
legations of this era usually left for Byzantium in the spring or
summer and returned to the Frankish court at the same time
of the following year. Six of the nine documented Frankish embassies certainly wintered in the Byzantine empire, and Amalarius,
who, Eriugenists will recall, was consulted along with John the
Scot about the Godescalc affair, complains that his embassy
spent eighty days at Constantinople awaiting the return of Emperor Leo V.[62] This pattern provides an intriguing correlation
with what we know of the annual rhythms of the Byzantine court,
which tended to cluster key social, ceremonial, and political activities around the great liturgical feasts of Christmas, Epiphany, and
Easter.[63] In other words, the Frankish missions tended to spend
several months in the Byzantine capital, and they were just the
months that corresponded to the imperial court's greatest activity.

Data on eastern ambassadors is less complete, which is not surprising given the scarcity of Byzantine sources of the eighth and ninth centuries. On general grounds, however, it is probably safe to assume that after two or three months of arduous travel, tired Byzantine ambassadors usually did not do an abrupt about face as soon as they had reached their goal. Since the ceremonial audience granted ambassadors sometimes coincided with the annual general assemblies of the Frankish aristocracy and their king, ambassadors would have had to wait at court until that date, a point which is explicitly confirmed for the Byzantine embassy of 765. Moreover, the itinerant style of Carolingian rulership meant envoys sometimes arrived at one of the main palaces only to find that the king was absent, forcing them to remain there until his return. This explains why a familiar figure at the court both of Louis the Pious and Charles the Bald later insisted that a senior official should constantly remain at the palace in case any delegations might arrive in the prince's absence.[64] Finally, a late report which seems reliable claims that the Byzantine embassy of 812 spent the winter holidays, including Epiphany, with Charlemagne at Aachen.[65] We may therefore lend some credence to the sources' implication that an eastern legation usually stayed longer than a few days and less than three months.[66] And to the temporary sojourn of the Greek ambassadors themselves must be added the long-term presence of Byzantine eunuch teachers and etiquette experts who certainly arrived with eastern legations but who were left at the Frankish court to prepare Carolingian princesses for the weddings arranged between the courts, even though unbeknownst to the principals those marriages were destined never to occur.[67] In other words, ample time was available to both parties for deepening their acquaintance with the other's culture.

A full description of the cultural characteristics of Byzantine ambassadors who visited the Frankish court must await another venue. But the fact that lay ambassadors tended to be high-ranking bureaucrats and that, beginning in 798, secular clergy were well represented, supplies an important clue: they correspond closely to the contemporary social profile of Byzantine literacy and litterati.[68] This observation is comforted by the fact that one of Byzantium's greatest intellects, Photius, seems actually to have participated in a diplomatic mission around 845.[69] Even

though this was to the caliphate and even though the most cultivated aristocrat could scarcely approach the achievement of Photius, it warns against underestimating the cultural level one might
encounter among Byzantine diplomats.

The Byzantine ambassadors who visited the court of Charles
the Bald's father and grandfather in fact confirm this impression.
Michael, metropolitan of Synada, was sent to Charlemagne and
Pope Leo III with Count Hugh in 812 and looks like a learned
theologian by contemporary Byzantine lights. At a young age he
played an important role in the deliberations of the Second Council of Nicaea in 787/788, and he would figure again in the conference on icons convened by Emperor Leo V at Constantinople
some years later.[70] Theodore Krithinos, a high official in the administration of the Hagia Sophia, had participated in the embassy
to Louis the Pious in 824 and, it has been thought, led that of 827.
These embassies' theological concerns, Theodore's role in spon-
soring translation from Latin into Greek, his subsequent career as
archbishop of Syracuse, and the fact that he was remembered as
the arch-heretic of iconoclasm all suggest an intellectual background.[71] A final case from Frankish Italy which may be of interest to specialists of Eriugena merits mention. In 867, Photius
selected his childhood friend Zachary, metropolitan of Chalcedon,
as his ambassador to the court of Louis II, emperor of Italy.
Though Zachary's mission was never completed, in this instance
the patriarch actually chose a philosopher for an exceedingly del-
icate mission to a western court.[72] Zachary authored one of the
rare Byzantine philosophical treatises contemporary with Eriugena. This work on time and the soul reflects an Aristotelian background and, quite probably, the teaching of Zachary's mentor
Photius. Even more interesting: this treatise's textual transmission
links Zachary to the group of mid–ninth-century Greek manuscripts from the "Allen" scriptorium which constitute a key witness
to the text of Plato, and also transmit Ps.-Dionysius.[73]

These then are some preliminary indications on the conditions
which fostered cultural interaction between Byzantium and the
Franks down to the accession of Charles the Bald. Yet the opportunities for person-to-person contact between Franks and Byzantines were wider still. An exhaustive account would have to
include Byzantine servants at the Frankish court, the forgotten
Greek eunuch chamberlains who attended to Charlemagne, Louis

the Pious, or their families.[74] And other Byzantines of higher status lurked there as well, like Photius's kinsman Sisinnius who spent a decade of his life as a Frankish hostage.[75] But these individuals and the cross-cultural contacts they provided are better left for another occasion.

Whatever further research may reveal about the state of transmediterranean commerce, in the three generations preceding Eriugena's appearance at the court of Charles the Bald, person-to-person relations, precisely the kind of contacts that counted in Frankish society, were not infrequent and they were of significant duration. They concerned hundreds of individuals, some of whom represented the social and cultural apex of their respective civilizations. And these personal encounters occurred at the court, that is, in the most propitious context possible for affecting a civilization in the making. Here at last the certain historical context which has been so often postulated begins to emerge. But did cross-cultural exchange actually occur there?

A full response would detail the cultural artifacts transmitted by diplomatic exchange, of which the best-attested are diplomatic gifts. The earliest surviving middle-Byzantine bureaucratic memorandum on gifts comes only in 935 and concerns a rather low-level delegation to King Hugh of Provence. But it does provide two key insights. On one hand, the inclusion of objets d'art like an onyx chalice, glassware, and gilded silverware confirms the contention of some scholars that Byzantine diplomatic gifts familiarized foreign elites with Constantinopolitan art. On the other, the memorandum specifies who should get what among the seven counts and six bishops associated with Hugh's court. This is essential: it reveals Constantinople's shrewd understanding of the diffuse structure of power that typified an early medieval court, and shows that gifts were tailored to prospective recipients.[76] Both points were no less true of earlier Byzantine dealings with the Franks.

Frankish sources often allude to diplomatic gifts and occasionally mention the most spectacular by name. The freshly copied Greek manuscript of the works of Ps.-Dionysius presented to Louis the Pious's court at Compiègne in September 827 reveals the subtlety with which such gifts were chosen. One of Constantinople's primary diplomatic objectives in this period was negotiating the unification of the eastern and western churches.[77] In contemporary Byzantine terms this could only mean the adoption of icon-oclasm in the West. Now Theodore Krithinos had gotten to know Louis's entourage during his visit to Rouen in 824. The ambassa-dors of 827 capitalized on that experience by astutely exploiting Frankish court politics. Negotiations aiming to unite the western and eastern churches would inevitably have involved Hilduin, one of Louis's chief advisors. As head of the imperial chapel, Hilduin coordinated ecclesiastical affairs in Frankland. He also happened to be abbot of St. Dionysius or St. Denis in Paris, where he was leading a campaign to prove that the disciple of Saint Paul and pu-tative author of those Neoplatonic treatises was in fact the patron saint of his abbey. Now, thanks to Greeks bearing gifts, Hilduin could claim that the presentation of the book to him in Com-piègne set off a series of miracles in Paris, thereby proving the identity of the two Dionysii to any but the most vile unbeliever.[78] It was, presumably, this precise historical situation that explains why one of Hilduin's closest and most faithful proteges, a young canon of St. Denis named Hincmar, was rummaging in the palace ar-chives for the original manuscript of Charlemagne's refutation of icon veneration, the *Libri Carolini.*[79]

And it is no less significant that this same Byzantine embassy reveals the lesser-known phenomenon of Frankish influence on Byzantium. For the cross-cultural exchange fostered by such dip-lomatic contacts was no one-way street. Hilduin's preposterous claim and the Parisian legend of St. Denis entered Byzantine lit-erature on the return trip, since it shows up at Constantinople al-most immediately in Greek hagiography.[80]

As the cult of St. Denis shows, more than just books moved be-tween the two courts and their cultures. In a famous anecdote, Charlemagne is reported to have been so moved by the beauty of the Greek chant he heard coming from a Byzantine ambassador's retinue that he ordered a Latin translation of the same text set to the same music. Liturgists and musicologists have demonstrated that these Latin antiphons for the octave of Epiphany, *O veterem hominem,* do indeed preserve an archaic Byzantine chant.[81] What is more, and this underscores the enduring relevance of the events of the first half of the ninth century to the precise historical con-text of Eriugena, the early textual transmission of the piece turns precisely on a manuscript somehow connected with the court of Charles the Bald, the Antiphonary of Compiègne.[82] In fact, the saints mentioned in it seem to suggest that the manuscript was originally copied for the monastery of St. Médard of Soissons, one of the places where scholars have located John the Scot.[83] Whether in the chapel of his royal patron or at St. Médard, in other words, Eriugena could well have listened to Byzantine chant which had reached the West with ambassadors to Charlemagne. It is symbolically significant that these cross-cultural transfers center on the things that really counted for the ninth century, both Greek and Latin. Whatever we moderns may feel about them, saints and the liturgy lay close indeed to the hearts of early medieval men and women.

The unparalleled mention of winter conditions in Byzantine Thrace in 763 from the Chronicle of Moissac was mentioned above as a kind of random fact of Carolingian court literature. But it too calls out for explanation, and diplomatic relations clarify it. To explain the Chronicle of Moissac's sudden interest in Byzantine weather conditions requires only a fact which the Chronicle does not mention: that a Carolingian legation to Emperor Constantine V was caught outside of Constantinople precisely by the terrible early winter of autumn 763.[84]

This case and others like it begin to suggest that not only objects, like organs or books, but information too is trackable. And this suggests an exciting perspective: because material on Byzantium is proportionally uncommon in the abundant literary production of the Carolingian renaissance, it is identifiable and manageable. In a sense, it resembles a trace element injected into Frankish literature which, because of its unique character, can sometimes be correlated with a limited number of individuals and kinship networks. In other words, the ongoing analysis of early medieval cultural borrowing and diffusion in its authentic social dimension promises to show how, in concrete historical terms, ideas, books, information, in a word, how culture, disseminated. In some privileged cases at least, this promises to illuminate not only what happened in one sector of the Carolingian renaissance but how and why it happened, with whom and where it happened. It promises to move from the cataloguing of literary production to the historical explanation of one facet of literary production.

Though this essay has only begun to sketch the role of dark-age diplomacy in precipitating cross-cultural exchange, even this first approach has pointed to a remarkable number and range of personal contacts between the western and eastern courts. It begins to hint that the human and historical channels of communication may be recoverable to a degree hitherto unsuspected. The developments I have sketched, though they directly affect only the years preceding Eriugena's documented appearance on the Continent, give an idea of the atmosphere at the court at which his great patron grew up and which supplied the early entourage of Charles the Bald, the entourage to which Eriugena himself belonged.

Imperfect and rough though they are, these observations mark the path to a clearer, more precise understanding of the Carolingian elite's cultural encounters and attitudes. Expanding scholarly horizons to tracking the movement of people as well as books, ideas, and pictures, and correlating the results with contemporary social structures may cast some new light on the early medieval interaction of Byzantium and the West. In so doing we may hope better to grasp how early medieval diplomacy helped foster the encounter of East and West in the cultural context which prevailed when John the Scot first set foot on the European continent.

NOTES

1. J. J. Contreni, *The Cathedral School of Laon from 850 to 930*, Münchener Beiträge zur Mediävistik und Renaissance-Forschung, no. 29 (Munich, 1978); E. Jeauneau, "Jean Scot Erigène et le grec," *Archivum Latinitatis Medii Aevi* 41 (1977–1978 [1979]): 5–50 is the indispensable introduction to the problem treated here; P. Riché, "Le grec dans les centres de culture d'Occident," in *The Sacred Nectar of the Greeks: The Study of Greek in the West in the Early Middle Ages*, ed. M. W. Herren and S. A. Brown (London, 1988), 143–168, here 147–153, provides a quick overview. The present study originated in a broader research project on personal contacts and cross-cultural exchange in early medieval Christendom and was launched under the excellent conditions provided by support from the John Simon Guggenheim Memorial Foundation. I am now preparing a monograph based on that research.

2. For a list of Greek manuscripts which Eriugena would have needed, see Jeauneau, "Erigène et le grec," 28–29; for the kind of linguistic tools he might have had, ibid., 26–40, and, in particular, A. C. Dionisotti, "Greek Grammars and Dictionaries in Carolingian Europe," in *Sacred Nectar*, 1–56, esp. 13.

3. See M. Cappuyns, *Jean Scot Erigène, sa vie, son oeuvre, sa pensée* (Louvain, 1933); for recent overviews: J. J. O'Meara, *Eriugena* (Oxford, 1988); and G. Schrimpf, "Johannes Scottus Eriugena," *Theologische Realenzyklopädie*, vol. 17 (1988), 156–172, esp. 160–161, for the evidence suggesting John's stay at Soissons. For what his poems suggest, see P. E. Dutton, "Eriugena, the Royal Poet," in *Jean Scot écrivain*, ed. G. H. Allard (Montreal, 1986), 51–80. On the question of his trace in the manuscripts: T. A. M. Bishop, "Autographa of John the Scot," in *Jean Scot Erigène et l'histoire de la philosophie* (Paris, 1977), 89–94; J. Vezin, "A propos des manuscrits de Jean Scot: Quelques remarques sur les manuscrits autographes du haut moyen âge," in *Erigène et l'histoire*, 95–99. For his life in Ireland, P. P. Onéill, "The Old-Irish Words in Eriugena's Biblical Glosses," in *Jean Scot écrivain*, 287–297.

4. On the archaeological evidence: R. Hodges, "Trade and Market Origins in the Ninth Century: Relations between England and the Continent," in *Charles the Bald: Court and Kingdom*, ed. M. T. Gibson and J. L. Nelson, 2d ed. (London, 1990), 202–223. Notker, *Gesta Karoli magni imperatoris*, 1, 1, ed. H. F. Haefele, MGH Scriptores Rerum Germanicarum n.s. 12 (Berlin, 1959), 1. On Irish holymen and St. Richarius (Riquier): Alcuin, *Vita Richarii*, 2 and 8–9, ed. B. Krusch, MGH Scriptores Rerum Merovingicarum 4 (Hanover, 1902), 390–391 and 393–394. Cf. Alcuin's eighth-century source: *V. Richarii*, 2 and 7, ed. B. Krusch, MGH Scriptores Rerum Merovingicarum 7 (Hanover, 1920), 445 and 448.

5. H. Pirenne, *Mohammed and Charlemagne* (1937; reprint, Cleveland, 1959); further reprinted with valuable essays as H. Pirenne, B. Lyon et al., *Mahomet et Charlemagne: Byzance, Islam et Occident dans le haut moyen âge* (Antwerp, 1987). Cf. L. Genicot, "Mahomet et Charlemagne après 50 ans," *Revue d'histoire ecclésiastique* 82 (1987): 277–281. Cf. R. S. Lopez, "The Trade of Medieval Europe: The South," in *Cambridge Economic History of Europe*, vol. 2, *Trade and Industry in the Middle Ages*, 2d ed., ed. M. M. Postan and E. Millar (Cambridge, 1987), 306–401, esp. 316ff. and 320ff.; and F. Gabrieli, "Effets et influences de l'Islam sur l'Europe occidentale," in *Mahomet et Charlemagne*, 195–247, esp. 199. For a selection of the extensive reactions to Pirenne's thesis, see *Bedeutung und Rolle des Islam beim Übergang vom Altertum zum Mittelalter*, ed. P. E. Hübinger (Darmstadt, 1968); and esp. R. Hodges and D. Whitehouse, *Mohammed, Charlemagne, and the Origins of Europe: Archaeology and the Pirenne Thesis* (Ithaca, 1983), from which the quotation is taken, p. 75. The written evidence has been reexamined by D. Claude, *Der Handel im westlichen Mittelmeer während des Frühmittelalters*, Abhandlungen der Akademie der Wissenschaften in Göttingen, Phil.-hist. Kl. 3d ser., no. 144 (Göt-

tingen, 1985), who concludes that long-distance shipping involving the western Mediterranean reached a nadir c. 700.

6. The chief architect of this new view of Byzantium is A. P. Kazhdan, beginning with his study of Byzantine cities, "Vizantyskie goroda v VII–IX vv.," *Sovetskaya arckeologiya* 21 (1954): 164–188; cf. more recently A. P. Kazhdan and A. Cutler, "Continuity and Discontinuity in Byzantine History," *Byzantion* 52 (1982): 429–478.

7. For a recent survey of the transformations of the urban landscape in the East, see J. F. Haldon, *Byzantium in the Seventh Century* (Cambridge, 1990), 92–124.

8. C. Mango, "The Availability of Books in the Byzantine Empire," in *Byzantine Books and Bookmen: A Dumbarton Oaks Colloquium* (Washington, 1975), 30–45, here 44–45, observes the bibliographic impulse generated by the controversy. On the roots of iconoclasm in the crises of the seventh and early eighth centuries, see C. Mango, "Historical Introduction," in *Iconoclasm*, ed. A. Bryer and J. Herrin (Birmingham, 1977), 1–6, here 2–3.

9. On the geographical marginalization of Byzantine culture, see C. Mango, "La culture grecque et l'Occident au VIIIe siècle," in *I problemi dell'Occidente nel secolo VIII*, Settimane di studio del centro italiano di studi sull'alto medioevo, no. 20 (Spoleto, 1973), 683–721; and R. Blake, "La littérature grecque en Palestine au VIIIe siècle," *Le Muséon* 78 (1965): 367–380, which needs updating. Cf. N. G. Wilson, *Scholars of Byzantium* (Baltimore, 1983), 69 and 76–78; as well as R. Browning and A. P. Kazhdan, "Greek outside the Empire," *Oxford Dictionary of Byzantium*, 3 vols. (Oxford, 1991), 2:873–874 (hereafter cited as *ODB*). On Constantinople: C. Mango, *Le développement urbain de Constantinople (IVe–VIIe siècles)* (Paris, 1985), 51–62. For the reemergence of Constantinopolitan literary culture, see P. Lemerle, *Le premier humanisme byzantin* (Paris, 1971), 108ff. Immigration to the capital may have played a role in this reemergence and, in any case, suggests increasing opportunities there: cf. the careers of Michael Syncellus, Theophanes Graptus, and Patriarch Methodius, on whom see the relevant articles in the *ODB*. The incorporation of Palestinian usages into the Constantinopolitan liturgy was perhaps part of this broader centripetal movement of culture and people: see, e.g., R. Taft, "Byzantine Rite," *ODB* 1:343–344.

10. Lemerle, *Premier humanisme*, 268. Cf. A. Kazhdan, "Encyclopedism," *ODB* 1:696–697.

11. Michael I's coronation of Theophylactus: W. Wendling, "Die Erhebung Ludwigs d. Fr. zum Mitkaiser im Jahre 813 und ihre Bedeutung für die Verfassungsgeschichte des Frankenreiches," *Frühmittelalterliche Studien* 19 (1985): 210–238, esp. 217–223.

12. E.g., Wien, Schatzkammer s.n.: Cautiously: W. Koehler, *Die karolingischen Miniaturen* 3, 1 (Berlin, 1960), 49–51, esp. 51. More emphatically: J. Beckwith, "Byzantine Influence on Art at the Court of Charlemagne," in *Karl der Grosse: Lebenswerk und Nachleben*, vol. 3 (Düsseldorf, 1965): 288–300, here 297–299; but cf. the more careful and convincing appraisal of F. Mütherich, "Die Buchmalerei am Hofe Karls des Grossen," in *Karl der Grosse* 3:9–53, here 45–53.

13. The exact circumstances of the translation remain unclear, although part of the text occurs in a s. ix MS (Zurich C 78). M. Huglo, "L'ancienne version latine de l'hymne Acathiste," *Le Muséon* 64 (1951): 27–61, argues for the Frankish court and Hilduin of St. Denis's milieu. G. G. Meersseman, *Der Hymnos Akathistos im Abendland*, vol. 1, *Akathistos-Akolutie und Grusshymnen*, Spicilegium Friburgense, no. 2 (Fribourg, 1958), 49–57, attributed it to a Venetian bishop in exile at Charlemagne's court. A. Pertusi, "Episodi culturali tra Venezia e il Levante nel medioevo e nell' Umanesimo fino al sec. XV," in *Venezia e il Levante fino al secolo XV*, ed. A. Pertusi, vol. 2 (Florence, 1974), 331–360, here 332–334, rightly rejects Meersseman's reasoning as fragile; he also hesitates to accept Huglo's arguments. Cf., too, M. Huglo, *Scriptorium* 37 (1983): 4*–5*, no. 10. For further liturgical borrowing attested in Eriugena's circle, see Jeauneau, "Erigène et le grec," 38.

14. *Chronicon Moissacense*, a. 762, ed. G. H. Pertz, MGH Scriptores 1 (Hanover, 1826), 294. On this work's connections with the court: W. Wattenbach, W. Levison, and H. Löwe, *Deutschlands Geschichtsquellen im Mittelalter: Vorzeit und Karolinger*, vol. 2 (Weimar, 1953), 265–266.

15. P. E. Schramm, *Herrschaftszeichen und Staatssymbolik*, Schriften der MGH no. 13, 3 (Stuttgart, 1956), 1068–1072; cf. P. Brown, *Society and the Holy in Late Antiquity* (Berkeley, 1982), 171–172.

16. Although much has been written about its activities and personnel, this key institution still awaits a general study. See, e.g., J. Fleckenstein, *Die Hofkapelle der deutschen Könige*, Schriften der MGH no. 16, 1 (Stuttgart, 1959); S. Airlie, "Bonds of Power and Bonds of Association in the Court Circle of Louis the Pious," in *Charlemagne's Heir: New Perspectives on the Reign of Louis the Pious (814–840)*, ed. P. Godman and R. Collins (Oxford, 1990), 191–204; R. McKitterick, "The Palace School of Charles the Bald," in *Charles the Bald*, 326–339. Cf., too, next note.

17. See, for instance, Charlemagne's *Epistola de litteris colendis*, ed. A. Boretius, MGH Capitularia 1 (Hanover, 1883), 79. On the courts and scholars, see, e.g., F. Brunhölzl, *Geschichte der lateinischen Literatur des Mittelalters*, vol. 1 (Munich, 1975), 244–249; for Charlemagne's

court and MS traditions, B. Bischoff, *Mittelalterliche Studien,* vol. 3 (Stuttgart, 1981), 149–169; on the fragmentary Euclid translation copied c. 800 (Munich, Univ. B. 2° 757), Bischoff, *Mittelalterliche Studien* 3:158, n. 43. The iconoclast dossier of 825 is in Paris, B.N. lat. 1597A, from a scriptorium which did work for Charles the Bald, according to Bernhard Bischoff as cited by R. McKitterick, "Charles the Bald (823–877) and His Library: The Patronage of Learning," *English Historical Review* 95 (1980): 28–47, here 40, n. 3.

18. A. H. M. Jones, *The Later Roman Empire, 284–602: A Social, Economic, and Administrative Survey,* vol. 1 (1964; reprint, Baltimore, 1986), 465, and 2:864–872; cf. M. Hendy, *Studies in the Byzantine Monetary Economy, c. 300–1450* (Cambridge, 1985), 157.

19. *Eternal Victory: Triumphal Rulership in Late Antiquity, Byzantium, and the Early Medieval West,* 2d ed. (Cambridge, 1990), 232.

20. P. Classen, *Ausgewählte Aufsätze,* ed. J. Fleckenstein et al. (Sigmaringen, 1983), 85–115.

21. The best overall study of Charlemagne's relations with Constantinople remains P. Classen, *Karl der Grosse, das Papsttum und Byzanz,* 3d ed., ed. H. Fuhrmann and C. Märtl (Sigmaringen, 1985).

22. On Greek at Ravenna, see, e.g., T. S. Brown, *Gentlemen and Officers: Imperial Administration and Aristocratic Power in Byzantine Italy A.D. 554–800* (Rome, 1984), 66–69. For Byzantium and the Lombard royal court milieux, see *Eternal Victory,* 287–294. For the Byzantine jester Gregorius at the court of king Liutprand (ob. 744), see Charlemagne's diploma, ed. E. Mühlbacher et al., MGH Diplomata Karolinorum 1 (Hanover, 1906), 247, no. 183. On Adalgis, king of the Lombards, son and co-ruler of Desiderius, who changed his name in Byzantium to Theodotos, see *Annales Einhardi,* a. 774, ed. F. Kurze, MGH Scriptores Rerum Germanicarum (Hanover, 1895), 62; Theophanes, *Chronographia,* a.m. 6281, ed. C. De Boor, vol. 1 (Leipzig, 1883), 464.2–8.

23. See H. Belting, "Studien zum Beneventanischen Hof im 8.Jh.," *Dumbarton Oaks Papers* 16 (1962): 141–194. On Evanthia's marriage to Grimald: Nicetas, *Vita Philareti,* ed. M. H. Fourmy and M. Leroy, "La Vie de S. Philarète," *Byzantion* 9 (1934): 85–170, here 143.20–35. For the identification: A. A. Vasiliev, "Zhitie Philareta Milostivago," *Izvestiya Russkago arkheologischeskago instituta v Konstantinople* 5 (1900): 49–86, here 58–61, accepted by Fourmy and Leroy, 105–108.

24. On Zachary's translation and Roman monasteries, see J. M. Sansterre, *Les moines grecs et orientaux à Rome aux époques byzantine et carolingienne,* Académie Royale de Belgique: Mémoires de la classe des lettres 8, 2d ser., vol. 66, nos. 1–2 (Brussels, 1982), here 1:75.

25. Sansterre, *Les moines grecs,* 1.32–33 and 90–91.

26. *Eternal Victory*, 385.

27. Einhard, *Vita Karoli*, 16, 6th ed., ed. O. Holder-Egger and G. Waitz (Hanover, 1911), 20; the suggestion of Rome was made by Classen, *Karl der Grosse*, 23. The proverb looks to be an authentic middle-Byzantine utterance. It is closely linked to an adage about Armenians which is preserved in the collection of Maximus Planudes (ob. c. 1305), ed. E. Kurtz, *Die Sprichwörtersammlung des Maximus Planudes* (Leipzig, 1886), 20, no. 53: "Armenon echeis philon, cheiron' echthron me thele"; cf. K. Krumbacher, "Mittelgriechische Sprichwörter," *Sitzungsberichte, Bayerische Akademie der Wissenschaften*, Phil.-hist. Kl., 1893, no. 2: 1–272, here 246–248. The proverb, in various forms and applied to various ethnic groups, was still alive in the nineteenth century, if not later: N. G. Polites, *Meletai peri tou biou kai tes glosses tou ellenikou laou: Paroimiai*, vol. 2 (1900; reprint, Athens, 1965), 465–466.

28. *Annales Fuldenses*, a. 876, ed. F. Kurze, MGH Scriptores Rerum Germanicarum (Hanover, 1891), 86. Cf., e.g., Jeauneau, "Erigène et le grec," 17, with n. 47.

29. For the movement of MSS, see, e.g., D. Bullough, "Roman Books and Carolingian *renovatio*," in *Studies in Church History*, 14 (1977): 23–40. On the comparison with the tenth century: B. Bischoff, "Italienische Handschriften des neunten bis elften Jahrhunderts in frühmittelalterlichen Bibliotheken ausserhalb Italiens," in *Il libro e il testo*, ed. C. Questa and R. Raffaelli (Urbino, 1984), 171–194, here 193–194.

30. G. Tellenbach, "Der grossfränkische Adel und die Regierung Italiens in der Blütezeit des Karolingerreiches," in *Studien und Vorarbeiten zur Geschichte des grossfränkischen und frühdeutschen Adels*, ed. G. Tellenbach, Forschungen zur oberrheinischen Landesgeschichte, no. 4 (Freiburg, 1957), 40–70; and E. Hlawitschka, *Franken, Alemannen, Bayern und Burgunder in Oberitalien (774–962)*, Forschungen zur oberrheinischen Landesgeschichte, no. 8 (Freiburg, 1960).

31. On Eberhard and his career from 828 to 866: Hlawitschka, *Franken*, 169–172. By one hypothesis he was the son of Beggo, count of Paris; see F. Vianello, "Gli Unruochingi e la famiglia di Beggo, conte di Parigi," *Bullettino dell'Istituto storico italiano per il medio evo* 91 (1984): 337–369. On his will and books: R. McKitterick, *The Carolingians and the Written Word* (Cambridge, 1989), 245–248. For Gisla's presence in West Francia in, e.g., 869 and 870: see her acts, ed. I. De Coussemaker, *Cartulaire de l'abbaye de Cysoing et des dépendances* (Lille, 1886), 7–9.

32. See, e.g., the poem ed. E. Dümmler, MGH Poetae 3 (Berlin, 1896), 220–221, no. 67; or the epitaph about little Eberhard, ibid.

201, no. 37. Cf. R. Düchting, *Sedulius Scottus: Seine Dichtungen* (Munich, 1968), 181–184 (possibly 860 A.D.), and 125–128. On Sedulius and the dispatch of a copy of Vegetius to Eberhard: Düchting, *Sedulius Scottus*, 158–159.

33. On Godescalc's stay with Eberhard: Hrabanus Maurus, Ep. 42, ed. E. Dümmler, MGH Epistolae 5 (Berlin, 1899), 481–487, esp. 481: "...constat quendam sciolum nomine Gotescalcum, apud vos manere..."; and 487: "...et si quis iuxta te manens inpudenter docet... prohibeas eum...." His travels on the Byzantine frontier are documented by the battle near his villa between a Byzantine patrician and the Slavic king: *Responsa de diuersis*, ed. C. Lambot, *Oeuvres théologiques et grammaticales de Godescalc d'Orbais*, Spicilegium Sacrum Lovaniense, no. 20 (Louvain, 1945), 169. For his knowledge of Venetian and Dalmatian terminology for the Byzantine emperor: *De praedestinatione*, 6, ed. Lambot, *Oeuvres*, 208.

34. It is possible to identify some of them by name. For instance, Marinus, a Roman priest resident at Pippin III's court, was of sufficient stature that his mother had daily access to the pope (*Codex Carolinus* [= *C.C.*] 29, ed. W. Gundlach, MGH Epistolae 3 [Berlin, 1892], 535). He received the titular church of St. Chrysogonus from Pope Paul I at Pippin's request (*C.C.* 24, p. 529). Emperor Constantine V's accusations against him prove that he advised Pippin on relations with Constantinople (*C.C.* 25, p. 529).

35. "Codex Carolinus," *ODB* 1:473.

36. Latin books: Bullough, "Roman Books." Greek books in 758–763: *C.C.* 24, p. 529 (liturgy, grammar, Ps.-Dionysius, etc.), on which see Sansterre, *Moines grecs* 1:182–183. This isolated mention could be supplemented by careful analysis of the actual surviving Greek books or texts known to have existed in ninth-century libraries, on which some preliminary indications may be had from Jeauneau, "Erigène et le grec," 6–7; W. Berschin, *Griechisch-lateinisches Mittelalter* (Bern, 1980), 137ff.; Dionisotti, "Greek Grammars," 24–31.

37. Einhard, *Translatio Marcellini et Petri*, 1, 5, ed. G. Waitz, MGH Scriptores 15, 1 (Hanover, 1887) [hereafter *Trans. Marc. et Petri*], 242. Sansterre, *Moines grecs* 1:48, identifies the monastery.

38. H. Bresslau, *Handbuch der Urkundenlehre für Deutschland und Italien*, 2d ed., vol. 1 (1912; reprint, Berlin, 1958), 431.

39. J. M. Sansterre, "Le monachisme byzantin à Rome," *Bisanzio, Roma e l'Italia nell'alto medioevo*, Settimane di studio del centro italiano di studi sull'alto medioevo, no. 34 (Spoleto, 1988), 701–746, here 709.

40. On Anastasius and Byzantium, see *ODB* 1:89–90. The case of one of his most cultivated contemporaries, John Hymmonides, may be illustrative: according to G. Arnaldi, "Giovanni Immonide e la cul-

tura a Roma al tempo di Giovanni VIII," *Bullettino dell'Istituto storico italiano per il medio evo* 68 (1956): 33–89, here 35–36, he did not know Greek, although Sansterre, *Moines grecs* 1:70–71, believes that he had at least some acquaintance with the language. For the study of Greek in a private Roman household in the late ninth century, as well as the generally provincial graphic level of contemporary Greek inscriptions, see G. Cavallo, "Le tipologie della cultura nel riflesso delle testimonianze scritte," in *Bisanzio*, 467–516, here 490–492. T. F. X. Noble, "The Declining Knowledge of Greek in Eighth- and Ninth-Century Rome," *Byzantinische Zeitschrift* 78 (1985): 56–62, surveys the evidence.

41. *Passio Anastasiae,* ed. F. Halkin, *Légendes grecques des "martyres romaines,"* Subsidia Hagiographica, no. 55 (Brussels, 1973), 89–131; translator's epilogue, 131. On Theodore: J. Gouillard, "Deux figures mal connues du second iconoclasme," *Byzantion* 31 (1961): 371–401, here 387ff.; cf. R. Loenertz, "La légende parisienne de S. Denys l'Aréopagite: Sa genèse et son premier témoin," *Byzantion* 69 (1951): 217–237, here 233.

42. The Venetian priest George entered Louis's service in June 826 and received the abbey of St. Saulve near Valenciennes as his reward; *Annales regni Francorum,* s.a., ed. F. Kurze, MGH Scriptores Rerum Germanicarum (Hanover, 1895) [hereafter *Ann. regni Franc.*], 170; cf. Astronomer, *Vita Hludowici imperatoris,* 40, ed. G. H. Pertz, MGH Scriptores 2 (Hanover, 1829), 629–630; and Einhard, *Trans. Marc. et Petri,* 4, 8, and 10, p. 258 and 259–260. On the organ at Aachen, cf. Ermold Nigellus, *In honorem Hludowici,* ed. E. Faral, *Ermold le Noir, Poème sur Louis le Pieux et épîtres au roi Pépin,* lines 2519–2525 (Paris, 1932), 192. For Venice's ninth-century contribution to relations between Byzantium and the West, see in general Pertusi, "Episodi."

43. *Breve commemoratorii,* ed. T. Tobler and A. Molinier, *Itinera hierosolymitana* 1, 2 (Geneva, 1880), 301–305; cf. K. Schmid, "Aachen und Jerusalem: Ein Beitrag zur historischen Personenforschung der Karolingerzeit," in *Das Einhardkreuz: Vorträge und Studien der Münsteraner Diskussion zum arcus Einhardi,* ed. K. Hauck, Abhandlungen der Akademie der Wissenschaften in Göttingen, Phil.-hist. Kl. 3d ser., vol. 87 (Göttingen, 1974), 122–142, esp. 138, n. 57, for B. Bischoff's paleographical expertise (upper Rhineland, 2d quarter of s. ix); and M. Borgolte, *Der Gesandtenaustausch der Karolinger mit den Abbasiden und mit den Patriarchen von Jerusalem,* Münchener Beiträge zur Mediävistik und Renaissance-Forschung, no. 25 (Munich, 1976), 45ff.

44. See V. Peri, "Leone III e il 'filioque': Echi del caso nell'agiografia greca," *Rivista di storia della chiesa in Italia* 25 (1971): 3–58.

45. Bernard the Monk, *Itinerarium*, ed. T. Tobler and A. Molinier, *Itinera hierosolymitana* 1, 2 (Geneva, 1880), 309–320.

46. Cappuyns, *Erigène, sa vie,* 135–137.

47. Jeauneau, "Erigène et le grec," 16–22.

48. The best study of the technical aspects of Carolingian diplomacy to date remains F. L. Ganshof, "The Frankish Monarchy and Its External Relations from Pippin III to Louis the Pious," in *The Carolingians and the Frankish Monarchy,* trans. J. Sondheimer (London, 1971), 162–204 (originally published in 1964). A more detailed account will be supplied in my monograph. See also the following notes.

49. For Byzantine embassies to the Franks, see F. Dölger, *Regesten der Kaiserurkunden des oströmischen Reiches von 565–1453* 1 (Munich, 1924), nos. 318 (756 A.D.), 320 (757), 322 (pre-764), 325 (c. 765), 326 (766), 339 (781), 345 (787), 350 (797), 353 (798), 354 (799), 357 (802), 361 (803), 371 (810), 385 (811/812), 391 (814), 397 (816), 398 (817), 408 (824), 413 (827), 429 (833), 438 (838). Cf. the useful material in T. C. Lounghis, *Les ambassades byzantines en Occident depuis la fondation des Etats barbares jusqu'aux croisades* (Athens, 1980), here 143–168. For Frankish embassies: J. F. Böhmer, E. Mühlbacher et al., *Die Regesten des Kaiserreiches unter den Karolingern, 751–918,* 2d ed., ed. C. Brühl and H. Kaminsky, Regesta Imperii, 1 (Hildesheim, 1966) [hereafter cited as B.M.], no. 84a (756?); *C.C.* (above, n. 34) 28 and 29, pp. 533 and 534–535 (762/764 A.D.); *C.C.* 37, p. 549 (764/766 A.D.; possibly identical with preceding); *C.C.* 36, p. 544–545 (766/767); B.M. 282c (786/787 A.D.); B.M. 379b (802); B.M. 459a (811); B.M. 476 (813); B.M. 528a (814); B.M. 844a (828). These figures may underrepresent the actual total, since the Carolingian court annals suppress all reference to certain Frankish missions: 763/764 A.D.: *C.C.* 28–29, p. 533 and 534–535; 787/788: *Gesta sanctorum patrum Fontanellensis coenobii,* 12, 1, ed. F. Lohier and J. Laporte (Rouen, 1936), 85. On tactful omissions in the royal annals, see *Les annales du haut moyen âge,* Typologie des sources du moyen âge occidental, no. 14 (Turnhout, 1975), 40.

50. Whenever the sources mention only an abstract collective noun like *legatio,* I have counted only one ambassador, and whenever the ancient records refer only to anonymous ambassadors in the plural, I have counted only two, even though a legation led by only one ambassador was exceptional and embassies involving three or four ambassadors, not unknown. Here is the reckoning: at least four anonymous western ambassadors: one for 756? ("legatio"), *Fredegarius Continuatus,* 40 (123), ed. B. Krusch, MGH Scriptores Rerum Merovingicarum 2 (Hanover, 1888) [hereafter *Fred. Cont.*], 186; one for 762/764, *C.C.* 28–29, pp. 533 and 534–535; two for 766/767 ("cum vestris missis"), *C.C.* 36, p. 545. For the thirteen named western ambassadors

from 786/788 to 828, see the references above, n. 49. Ten anonymous Byzantine ambassadors: one (757) "legatio" (*Fred. Cont.* loc. cit.); two (766) "Graecos" (*Ann. regni Franc.*, a. 767, p.24); two (787) "cum missis imperatoris" (*Ann. regni Franc.*, a. 786, p. 72); two (817) "legatos" (*Ann. regni Franc.*, a. 817, p. 146); three (827) "echonomus . . . et ceteri missi" (Hilduin of St. Denis, *Epistolae variorum* 20, 4, ed. E. Dümmler, MGH Epistolae 5 [Hanover, 1899], 330). There were twenty-eight or thirty named Byzantine ambassadors, depending on the identity of ambassadors with the same name. For the references, see above, n. 49. Full details on eastern and western ambassadors will be supplied in my monograph.

51. As Ganshof, "Relations," 166–167, has also noted.

52. On western retinues, e.g., W. Schlesinger, "Herrschaft und Gefolgschaft in der germanisch-deutschen Verfassungsgeschichte," in *Herrschaft und Staat im Mittelalter,* ed. H. Kämpf (Darmstadt, 1956), 135–190. In the East, precisely an aristocrat's desire to surround himself with a large number of impressive physical specimens and so outshine his peers introduced the future Emperor Basil I to Byzantine high society: H. G. Beck, "Byzantinisches Gefolgschaftswesen," *Sitzungsberichte, Bayerische Akademie der Wissenschaften,* Phil.-hist. Kl. no. 5 (1965), esp. 6ff.

53. Thus a Frankish embassy to Constantinople was sizable enough to become involved in a pitched battle with "two or three thousand" Byzantines at Carthage in the 580s, lose several members, and survive: Gregory of Tours, *Historiarum libri x,* 2d ed., ed. B. Krusch and W. Levison, MGH Scriptores Rerum Merovingicarum 1 (Hanover, 1951), 482; cf. 486f.; Liutprand of Cremona incidentally sheds some light on the structure of a tenth-century legation. His retinue was too big to fit into two boats: *Legatio,* 58–59, ed. J. Becker, MGH Scriptores Rerum Germanicarum (Hanover, 1915), 207; it included five *milites* from Cremona (*Legatio* 6, p. 179; 24, p. 188), an interpreter (46, p. 200; cf. 54, p. 204), a western cook (46, p. 200), and unidentified companions of his own exalted social status, since he was displeased that they could not accompany him to an imperial banquet (11, p. 181), not to mention the four live-in Byzantine guards assigned to him (39, p. 193.7–8), a *diasostes,* and two imperial *mandatores* who escorted his party from Constantinople (58–59, p. 207). His party must have included clergy to aid Liutprand in his liturgical duties, and this would have been even truer in the Carolingian period, before "private" Masses had developed very far.

54. *Legatio,* 34, p. 193, where his companions are called *asseclae* (in Liutprand's mouth, the word seems not necessarily to connote the lower social status it did in classical Latin; see index, s.v.). The figure

explicitly excludes Liutprand's four Byzantine guards, whom he was also expected to feed; these figures are judged to be on the low side by V. Menzel, *Deutsches Gesandtschaftswesen im Mittelalter* (Hanover, 1892), 196–197. The forty horses from the imperial stable sent to the papal legates of 869 do not provide clear evidence on the size of the legates' retinue, since earlier Byzantine practice suggests that the number of beasts supplied to a diplomatic mission symbolized imperial favor rather than actual need. Cf. *Le Liber pontificalis*, 2d ed., ed. L. Duchesne and C. Vogel, vol. 2 (Paris, 1955), 180; and Constantine VII, *De ceremoniis*, 1, 89, ed. J. J. Reiske (Bonn, 1829), 400.8–12.

55. Ed. A. Boretius, MGH Capitularia 1, 291, c. 29. On the loaf ration, see M. Rouche, "La faim à l'époque carolingienne: Essai sur quelques types de rations alimentaires," *Revue historique* 250 (1973): 295–320, esp. 308–309. On the fundamental similarity of *missi* sent to a foreign court and those entrusted with missions within the far-flung Frankish dominions, Ganshof, "Relations," 163–164.

56. I have found, to date, no clear statement on numbers involved in Byzantine embassies to the West from this period. Later evidence shows that they were sizable and included all manner of attendants like their western counterparts, e.g., the embassy of November 1190, when Frederick I humiliated the Byzantine ambassadors in reprisal for a perceived slight to his own envoy. Frederick seated them in his presence along with "their servants and not even allowing to stand aside the cooks, grooms, and bakers . . . to insult the Romans . . ."; N. Choniates, *Historiae*, ed. J. A. Van Dieten, Corpus Fontium Historiae Byzantinae 11, 1 (Berlin, 1975), 410.61–72. The eighth- or ninth-century *Narratio sanctae Sophiae*, 11, ed. T. Preger, in *Scriptores Originum Constantinopolitanarum* 1 (Leipzig, 1901), 88.20–89.5, describes a miraculous eunuch who appears to Justinian and receives from him three officials and their retinue of fifty servants. Although the story is fiction, the figure may reflect contemporary notions of what was appropriate. (I owe these references to the kindness of A. P. Kazhdan.) The figures for the Franks seem very low when compared to those of the chieftain Olga of Kiev in the next century. Her retinue (excluding the separate retinue of her son) included eighty-six men, six kinswomen, and eighteen ladies-in-waiting, i.e., 110 who were of status high enough to be invited to the imperial banquet: Constantine VII, *De ceremoniis*, 2, 15, 596.14–598.12; cf. A. Toynbee, *Constantine Porphyrogenitus and His World* (London, 1973), 504–505.

57. Thus the slaves (*pueri*) in the Merovingian incident at Carthage (above, n. 53).

58. G. Tellenbach, *Königtum und Stämme in der Werdezeit des Deutschen Reiches* (Weimar, 1939), 52; and F. Vollmer, "Die Etichonen: Ein

Beitrag zur Frage der Kontinuität früher Adelsfamilien," in *Studien und Vorarbeiten*, 137–184, here 163ff.

59. Erlbald: see Walafrid Strabo, *Visio Wettini*, 134–138, ed. E. Dümmler, MGH Poetae 2 (Berlin, 1884), 308.

60. For more on the individual Frankish ambassadors to the East and their social status, see my monograph (in preparation).

61. For Amalarius and Halitgar, see, e.g., B.M. 476a and 844a. Anastasius was Louis II's ambassador: see G. Arnaldi, *Dizionario biografico degli Italiani*, vol. 3 (Rome, 1961), 25–37, here 30–32.

62. Embassies which wintered in the Byzantine empire: 762/764 A.D.; 786/787; 802; 811; 813; 814 (cf. above, n. 49). For Amalarius's stay, see his *Versus marini*, 38, ed. E. Dümmler, MGH Poetae 1 (Berlin, 1881), 427.

63. The famous *mare clausum* custom virtually excluded winter travel by sea: Claude, *Handel*, 31f. L. Casson, *Ships and Seamanship in the Ancient World* (Princeton, 1971), 270–299, and J. Rougé, *Recherches sur l'organisation du commerce maritime en Méditerranée sous l'empire romain* (Paris, 1966), 99ff., suggest that with favorable winds a direct trip from Rome to Constantinople might have taken c. 20–30 days in the classical period. In the late seventh century, three months were considered the minimum for the round trip between Ravenna and Constantinople: Claude, *Handel*, 63. The problem of travel time and changing infrastructures will be treated at length in my monograph. On seasonal rhythms of Byzantine court activities, see *Eternal Victory*, 198. A somewhat different pattern emerges from an analysis of the activity of the imperial chancery which, between the eleventh and thirteenth century, peaks between March and June: M. Bartusis, "The Rhythm of the Chancery: Seasonality in the Issuance of Byzantine Imperial Documents," *Byzantine and Modern Greek Studies* 13 (1989): 1–21.

64. Hincmar, *De ordine palatii*, 25, ed. T. Gross and R. Schieffer, MGH Fontes Iuris Germanici Antiqui in Usum Scholarum 3 (Munich, 1980), 78. For the Byzantine embassy which awaited the assembly of Frankish grandees: *C.C.* 37, p. 549; cf. Ganshof, "Relations," 163.

65. Notker, *Gesta Karoli*, 2, 7, p. 58; cf. J. Lemarié, "Les antiennes 'Veterem hominem' du jour octave de l'épiphanie et les antiennes d'origine grecque de l'épiphanie," *Ephemerides Liturgicae* 72 (1958): 3–38; O. Strunk, "The Latin Antiphons for the Octave of the Epiphany," in *Mélanges Ostrogorsky*, ed. F. Barišić, vol. 2 (Belgrad, 1964), 417–426.

66. The only two occasions on which court records explicitly state how long ambassadors from distant regions stayed indicate, on one hand, "a few days" (*Ann. regni Franc.*, a. 797, p. 100) and nearly four

months, on the other (ibid., a. 800–801, p. 112), suggesting that both may have been considered exceptional enough to warrant mention and implying that embassies' sojourns at the Frankish court usually fell somewhere in between. Cf. Ganshof, "Relations," 175–177.

67. Such was certainly the case of Elissaios, eunuch and *notarius* left at the Frankish court in 782 (Theophanes, *Chronographia*, a.m. 6274, p. 455.22–25); his mission was to teach Charlemagne's daughter Rotruda "ta te ton Graikon grammata kai ten glossan, kai paideusai auten ta ethe tes Romaion basileias." It also seems to explain why another Byzantine legation left the eunuch Sinesius at Pippin III's court after the marriage agreement involving Gisela and Leo IV (*C.C.* 36, p. 545).

68. On secular clergy as ambassadors, cf. Lounghis, *Ambassades*, 320–324. This was demonstrated by C. Mango in an unpublished paper on Byzantine literacy c. 800 which he delivered at a Dumbarton Oaks symposium in 1983. His conclusions can be summarily verified by examining the addresses of Theodore Studite's letters (PG 99: 1896–1904).

69. For Photius's embassy see *Bibliotheca*, 1, 1, ed. R. Henry, 1 (Paris, 1959), 1; on the date and circumstances, W. T. Treadgold, *The Nature of the Bibliotheca of Photius* (Washington, 1980), 16–36.

70. *Ann. regni Franc.*, a. 812, p. 136. Theophanes, *Chronographia*, a.m. 6304, p. 494.20–25 (Anastasius Bibliothecarius, ibid. 2:332). Cf. Ganshof, "Relations," 190–191, n. 77; *Synaxarium Constantinopolitanum*, ed. *Acta Sanctorum*, Novembris, Propylaeum (Brussels, 1902), January 5 (Gregory of Akritas), 373.10–15; and V. Grumel, *Les regestes des actes du patriarcat de Constantinople* 1, 2 (n. pl., 1936), no. 382. Cf. J. Pargoire, "Saints iconophiles," *Echos d'Orient* 4 (1901): 347–356, here 347–350; and R. Janin, in *Bibliotheca Sanctorum* 9 (Rome, 1967): 457–458.

71. B.M. 793a; B.M. 842b; cf. Dölger, *Regesten*, nos. 408 and 413. Cf. Hilduin of St. Denis, MGH Epistolae 5:330; *Concilium Constantinopolitanum a. 869, actio* 8, ed. J. D. Mansi, *Sacrorum Conciliorum Nova et Amplissima Collectio* 16 (Florence, 1771), 139C–142E. For his seal: V. Laurent, *Le corpus des sceaux de l'empire byzantin* 5, 1 (Paris, 1963), no. 886; notwithstanding Laurent's remarks, the evidence seems less than convincing to me for *Corpus* 5, 1, no. 84. On Theodore and the two embassies, see J. Gouillard, "Deux figures," 399ff.

72. Zachary of Chalcedon's mission of 867 was interrupted by the fall of Emperor Michael III: Grumel, *Regestes*, nos. 483–484. Photius wrote several letters to Zachary; his treatise *On Time* is edited by K. Oehler, "Zacharias von Chalkedon über die Zeit," *Byzantinische Zeitschrift* 50 (1957): 31–38. Cf. H. Hunger, *Die hochsprachliche profane*

Literatur der Byzantiner, 1 (Munich, 1978): 31–32; and S. Vailhé, in *Echos d'Orient* 11 (1908): 351.

73. Wilson, *Scholars,* 86–87. Ps.-Dionysius: Vat. Gr. 2249.

74. Thus, Theodulf of Orleans's description of Charlemagne's court mentions three chamberlains. "Putifar" is explicitly identified as "Graeculus"; "Bagao" and "Egeus" are not. The pseudonyms are allusions to biblical eunuchs (e.g., Jth 12:12; Est 2:3) in keeping with Theodulf's style: *Carmen 27,* ed. E. Dümmler, MGH Poetae 1:493. Drogus (note the Slavic name), *cubicularius* of Louis the Pious, is called "natione Graecus" by Einhard, *Trans. Marc. et Petri,* 4, 1, p. 256. Sedulius Scottus, *De rectoribus christianis,* 7, ed. S. Hellmann, *Quellen und Untersuchungen zur lateinischen Philologie des Mittelalters,* 1, 1 (Munich, 1906), 41, demonstrates nothing, since it is borrowed from the *Historia Augusta, Aurelius* 43, 1, 2d ed., ed. E. Hohl and C. Samberger, 2 (Teubner, 1955), 182.

75. Sisinnius, brother of patriarch Tarasius: *Ann. regni. Franc.,* a. 798, p. 104; cf. *Ann. Ein.,* p. 105. Their relationship is confirmed by a Byzantine source that identifies Tarasius's grandfather as a high official named Sisinnius: *Catalogus patriarcharum Constantinopolitanorum,* ed. F. Fischer, "De patriarcharum Constantinopolitanorum catalogis," *Commentationes Philologicae Jenenses* 3 (1884):263–333, here 291.2–3, a reference I owe to M. Herlong. Photius himself calls Patriarch Tarasius his *patrotheios,* which usually means paternal uncle; Photius's brother was named Sisinnius. We do not certainly know the name of Photius's father, although it was very possibly Sergius. C. Mango's important contribution admits a paternal kinship tie but argues that Sergius cannot have been of the same generation as Tarasius, suggesting that the latter may have been Photius's great uncle ("The Liquidation of Iconoclasm and the Patriarch Photius," in *Iconoclasm,* 133–145, here 136–139).

76. *De cer.* 2, 44, 661.13–21.

77. This goal is implied by the phrasing of Michael II and Theophilus's letter to Louis the Pious, ed. A. Werminghoff, MGH Concilia Aevi Karolini 1, 2 (Hanover, 1908), 481. It is explicitly stated by Theodore Krithinos in his epilogue to the Greek translation of the *Passio Anastasiae,* p. 131.

78. See M. McCormick, "Byzantium's Role in the Formation of Early Medieval Civilization: Approaches and Problems," *Illinois Classical Studies* 12 (1987): 207–220, here 218–219.

79. Hincmar of Reims, PL 126:360. Cf. J. Devisse, *Hincmar: Archevêque de Reims 845–882* (Geneva, 1976), 2:1090; and esp. A. Freeman, "Carolingian Orthodoxy and the Fate of the *Libri Carolini,*" *Viator* 16 (1985): 65–108, here 96–98.

80. R. Loenertz, "Le panégyrique de S. Denis l'Aréopagite par S. Michel le syncelle," *Analecta bollandiana* 68 (1950): 94–107; cf. Loenertz, "La légende parisienne." On the authenticity of ascriptions to Michael Syncellus: H. G. Beck, *Kirche und theologische Literatur im byzantinischen Reich* (Munich, 1959), 503–505; whether one accepts this ascription or not, the text exists in a MS of s. ix (Loenertz, "Panégyrique," 106–107).

81. On the chant, see above, n. 65.

82. Its earliest witness is the Antiphonary of Compiègne (Paris, B.N. lat. 17436); for the MS's connection with the court of Charles the Bald—clearly suggested by the inclusion of antiphons "de susceptione regum" (f. 93v–94v)—see P. E. Schramm and F. Mütherich, *Denkmale der deutschen Könige und Kaiser* (Munich, 1962), 131–132. Cf. the similar conclusions of R. Jonsson, *Historia: Etudes sur la genèse des offices versifiés* (Lund, 1968), 31–32 and 54–62. More recently, J. Froger, "Le lieu de destination et de provenance du *Compendiensis*," in *Ut Mens Concordet Voci: Festschrift Eugene Cardine zum 75. Geburtstag,* ed. J. Berchmans Göschl (St. Ottilien, 1980), 338–353, concluded on the basis of the sanctorale that the MS was copied for St. Médard of Soissons. The sanctorale shows affinities as well with St. Germain des Prés and St. Denis, and, as Froger notes, this would hint at a link with Hilduin of St. Denis, who was abbot of all three and of course linked as well with the court. I owe this reference to the kindness of Prof. Ruth Steiner; cf., too, her "Antiphons for the *Benedicite* at Lauds," *Journal of the Plainsong and Mediaeval Music Society* 7 (1984): 1–17.

83. See, most recently, Schrimpf, "Eriugena," 160–161.

84. *C.C.* 28, p. 533; cf. L. Oelsner, *Jahrbücher des fränkischen Reiches unter König Pippin* (Leipzig, 1871), 383, n. 2, who documents the veracity of the report from Theophanes but never wonders how the Frankish annalist learned about it.

Part 2

THEMES OF THE EAST-WEST ENCOUNTER

Remarks on Eastern Patristic Thought in John Scottus Eriugena

JOHN MEYENDORFF

THE BIFURCATION BETWEEN THE EASTERN AND THE WESTERN theological approaches to the Christian faith did not occur instantly or through anyone's specific bad will. It was a long and slow process of estrangement. Even the schism itself between the churches cannot be dated with precision. It did not occur as other schisms *within* eastern Christianity (e.g., the christological conflict between supporters and critics of the Council of Chalcedon), or *within* western Christianity (as the Reformation of the sixteenth century). In those schisms, theologians of similar training and similar background disagreed on specific formulas or specific doctrines. East and West, on the contrary, developed different visions, different perceptions, *long before* they clashed on specific points, such as the *Filioque* dispute, or the issue of Rome's authority. When these—and a few other—specific conflicts occurred, it is the lack of a deeper, common vision which made solutions impossible.

In order to have prevented the different visions and perceptions from becoming one-sided and therefore divisive, as they eventually did, constant watchfulness, concern for communication, and dialogue between East and West would have been needed. Such concerns did actually exist, but only in the cases of some few major patristic figures. In the West, Hilary and Ambrose knew Greek and cherished connections with eastern theologians, although, by inclination and method, they anticipated the later Latin approach to the Trinity. St. Augustine knew less Greek. Using his own creative genius, he conceived a philosophical interpretation of Christianity. His thought shaped western Christendom in its distinctiveness, but nothing was further from his mind than the conscious creation of a separate tradition, distinct from the eastern one. Dominating all his Latin contemporaries intellectually,

51

he was convinced that he was defending and expressing the catholic faith common to East and West. And he really did so, in so many ways. But he was not capable of discerning the importance of the lonely voice of Cassian and the monks of Lérins, who—in the name of the East—were raising doubts about some of his positions in the anti-Pelagian polemics.

In the East, St. Basil had made unsuccessful but dedicated efforts to gain Pope Damasus and the western bishops to his understanding of the trinitarian faith which made possible the triumph of Nicaea in the East. A few decades later the Council of Chalcedon recognized the commonsense wisdom of the *Tome* of St. Leo for the solution of the Christological dilemma, in spite of terminological difficulties. And the great Maximus the Confessor established his solid partnership with Pope Martin in the seventh century, while fighting Monothelitism. However, at the time of Maximus, the intellectual, spiritual, and linguistic gap is already in evidence. Maximus lived in Africa perhaps for two entire decades, but in his voluminous writings, there is not a single reference to Augustine, and there is no evidence that he knew any Latin. Similarly, St. Gregory the Great, a papal representative in Constantinople for seven years (579–586), knew no Greek.[1]

The gradual estrangement did not, therefore, exclude much good will on both sides, but the good will of a few individuals was insufficient to fill the cultural and intellectual gap which history was creating between the sophisticated and conservative tradition of Orthodox Byzantium and the fresh dynamism of "barbarian" Europe in the Carolingian age. The political antagonism of Charlemagne himself against Byzantium added a new dimension to mutual ignorance on the intellectual level: the anti-Greek polemics of the *Caroline Books* (*Libri Carolini*) initiated the fateful controversy on the *Filioque* addition. This controversy flared up again during the struggle between Pope Nicholas I and Patriarch Photius, in the fifties of the ninth century, precisely at the time when John the Scot was active at the court of Charles the Bald, translating the works of Pseudo-Dionysius.

But even this time of crisis did not lack people of good will. The attitude towards the West adopted by Patriarch Photius, the greatest of Byzantine scholars, is a case in point. In his major work refuting the Latin doctrine of the "double procession" of the Spirit, he shows awareness of the fact that his Latin adversaries invoke texts by Jerome, Ambrose, and Augustine in favor of the *Filioque*. His reaction is characteristic: one should not deny the authority of Latin fathers, but hide their individual mistakes by "covering their nudity," as the good sons of Noah did.[2] At the same time, he shows ignorance of the Latin tradition as a whole, except for some fragmented information which reached him by hearsay. In his famous *Bibliotheca*, he discusses the question of the *sin of nature*, which he considers as a heresy introduced by a mysterious author whom he calls *Aram*, and who is obviously none other than St. Jerome, although the learned patriarch fails to identify "Aram" with the saint venerated universally, and whose authority he himself invokes elsewhere.[3] And he obviously has no knowledge at all of the real role of Augustine in shaping western views on nature, sin, and grace.

Against this background of mutual ignorance, the appearance of a person like Eriugena is truly extraordinary. His enthusiasm for Greek thought and philosophical vocabulary, and his belief in their superiority over the Latin understanding and language, could have been partly a matter of self-promotion, since he was the only available translator of Greek texts in France. Indeed, in his preamble to the translation of the *Areopagitica*, he praises Charles the Bald for "waking up" sleeping Latin scholars by calling them to the "purest and most numerous Greek sources" (*ad purissimos copiosissimosque Graium latices*),[4] of which he—John the Scot—was the interpreter.

John was aware of the *Filioque* controversy, which was embarrassing for him. His contemporaries, Ratramnus of Corbie and Aeneas of Paris, were composing polemical treatises against his beloved Greeks on that particular topic. Not willing to take sides too formally, he clearly recognizes that the Greek position is based on the original version of the creed, and that the addition provoked unnecessary controversy: "Perhaps the reason why it is declared by the Nicene synod," he writes, "that the Holy Spirit proceeds from the Father alone is to prevent public discussion of such a subject."[5] In the ninth century, the interpolated creed was in use throughout Carolingian Europe—but not in Rome—so John accepts the Latin text but regrets that one cannot consult the (anonymous) Latin fathers who introduced the interpolation to ask them why they did it.[6] He recognizes that there are scriptural prooftexts favoring the double procession of the Holy Spirit, and he is aware of the recognition, by the Greek side, of the formula *per Filium* (procession of the Spirit from the Father *through* the Son). But when he comes to a detailed discussion of the theological issue itself, he sides with the Greek position. Asked by the *Alumnus* "whether it is from the essence (οὐσία) or from the substance (ὑπόστασις) of the Father that the Son is born and the Holy Spirit proceeds," he refers specifically to the real difference accepted by the Greek fathers between the common οὐσία and the particular ὑποστάσεις, and unambiguously affirms that the generation of the Son and the procession of the Spirit are to be attributed to the *substantia* (ὑπόστασις) of the Father alone.[7] This is actually the most fundamental point maintained by Photius, and by all Eastern theologians ever since.

This position of Eriugena illustrates how deliberate was his dedication to the cause of finding the authentic Christian truth in Greek sources. Of course, at no point is he ready to discard his own western tradition, and particularly St. Augustine. Thus, he introduces the Augustinian psychological image in his discussion of the procession of the Spirit,[8] but his attempt stands rather peripherally in his overall conception of the trinitarian problem, which basically relies upon his reading of the two Gregories and Maximus the Confessor.

Thus, Eriugena was able to take the side of the East on this particular issue of the procession of the Spirit which, he knew, was already in his time a controversial issue between East and West. What is it, then, which led him to that position? What did he discover in the Greek fathers which allowed him to take some distance from the teachings of St. Augustine—not only, as we know, in the area of trinitarian theology, but even more definitely on other central philosophical and theological issues—although St. Augustine was for him, as for the entire Latin Christian world, the theological teacher *par excellence?*

Quite symptomatically, in his early treatise, *On Predestination,* composed by request of Hincmar of Rheims to refute the doctrine of double predestination proclaimed by Gottschalk, Eriugena already affirms the theocentric monism which will be at the heart of his system in the *Periphyseon.* He argues that in God there is no difference between predestination and foreknowledge. God, therefore, cannot be the cause of any evil or punishment. The evildoers are themselves their own punishment, because they separate themselves from God on their own volition. No Eastern fathers are referred to in this context, only Augustine, with the characteristic explanation that the passages where Augustine *does* allude to double predestination and *does* affirm divine retribution to sinners are pedagogical teachings for the unlearned, not the intimate circle, endowed with true spiritual knowledge of the mysteries.

Therefore, Eriugena, as he begins his translations of the *Areopagitica,* St. Maximus, and St. Gregory of Nyssa, has already taken a positive stand towards Neoplatonic monism. And it is this monism that he discovers in Greek patristics, or at least in the authors who were accessible to him. He then develops it into a philosophical system, as found in the *Periphyseon.* He must have realized that Neoplatonism had helped Augustine to overcome (at least partially) the Manichaeism of his youth, but in the Greek authors he discovered an interpretation of the Christian faith in which the Neoplatonic scheme of procession and return was even more widely used, with varied degrees of consistency, to express and interpret the biblical conceptions of creation, salvation, and restoration.

Thus, in St. Gregory of Nyssa, Eriugena found what today we call "theocentric anthropology." The doctrine of the image of God is understood by Gregory as the necessary presence of a "divine spark" in humanity, which makes it impossible to understand human nature without reference to God. It is this divine presence which makes human beings truly *human,* so that a fall from God is a form of suicide. God is the fullness of goodness ($\pi\lambda\dot{\eta}\rho\omega\mu\alpha$ $\tau\hat{\omega}\nu$ $\dot{\alpha}\gamma\alpha\theta\hat{\omega}\nu$ $\tau\dot{o}$ $\theta\varepsilon\hat{\iota}o\nu$) and the only source of goodness for humanity.[9] Furthermore, the divine image, although it is eminently present in the human $\nu o\hat{\upsilon}\varsigma$, which is called to control and to "reign over" the rest of the human being (and the created world in general), is not truly realizable in a human individual, but in all of humanity together ($\ddot{\alpha}\pi\alpha\nu$ $\tau\dot{o}$ $\alpha\nu\theta\rho\dot{\omega}\pi\iota\nu o\nu$), restored in God. Indeed, the "fullness of goodness" can only belong to the fullness of humanity ($\tau\dot{o}$ $\tau\hat{\eta}\varsigma$ $\dot{\alpha}\nu\theta\rho\omega\pi\dot{o}\tau\eta\tau o\varsigma$ $\pi\lambda\dot{\eta}\rho\omega\mu\alpha$).[10] The doctrine of the image of God thus serves as the ontological basis for the doctrine of the universal restoration, or *apokatastasis.* In his entire approach, Gregory uses the doctrine of the image of God in humanity to explain human nature itself, and not, as Augustine did, to learn about the absolute God from God's finite reflection in humanity.

What Eriugena finds in Gregory of Nyssa and Maximus the Confessor is a vision of the original humanity in paradise as a purely spiritual nature in communion with God. Humanity is called to return to that state through the process of deification, because relations between God and the world, and between all existing things, are not conceived as external contacts between self-subsisting entities but as mutual participation. For Eriugena, "Everything that is, is either participant, or participated, or participation, or [both] participated *and* participant at once."[11] There is no opposition between "nature" and "grace," because "every perfect creature *consists* of nature and grace."[12] It is also in the writings of Gregory and Maximus—not to mention the *Areopagitica*—that Eriugena found constant references to *theosis,* or "deification," expressing the goal of Christian life. "This use of this word, Deification, is very rare in the Latin books," he bemoans; ". . . I am not sure of the reason for this reticence: perhaps it is because the meaning of this word *theosis* (the term which the Greeks usually employ in the sense of the psychic and bodily transformation of the saints into God so as to become One in Him and with Him, when there will remain in them nothing of their animal, earthly and moral nature) seemed too profound for those who cannot rise above carnal speculations, and would therefore be to them incomprehensible and incredible."[13]

What Eriugena also found in Gregory of Nyssa is a specific, neoplatonizing interpretation of *theosis,* with a strong sense of incompatibility between participation in divine life and all forms of materiality and animality. This applies particularly to the conception of humanity before the fall and the ultimate return to that glorious state of "angelic" life in God. The problem here resides not in the very fact of a spiritual, transfigured existence which was prepared by God for Adam and Eve in paradise and is the future hope of Christians in heaven, but in the nature of this transfiguration. What is involved is not only the nature of matter and materiality, including human bodies, which are seen as a "concourse of accidents,"[14] and as having no substance except on the intelligible plane, but whether visible, historical existence, human achievement and creativity in *this* world has any permanent value, or whether the entire "process" out of God has no other goal and meaning than its ultimate return to exactly the same point *in God* from where it originally proceeded. The issue of human gender is the most obvious case in point, and the best illustration of the problem. Eriugena adopts from Gregory of Nyssa the notion that the gender distinction was originally created by God only *in view* of the forthcoming fall. For Gregory, man and woman possessed, in paradise, another "angelic" method of reproduction, foreign to animality.[15] Eriugena goes further. For him, the Genesis account of creation and the fall does not involve time at all, so there is no need to speculate on the matter: "When we say 'before and after sin,' we are demonstrating the multiplicity of our thought processes which is due to the fact that we are still subject to temporal conditions: but to God the foreknowledge of sin and the consequence of sin itself are contemporaneous."[16] The problem therefore is not only with sexual animality, but with the value of human qualities and achievements *in time and history*. According to the traditional teaching of eastern Christianity, those who despise marriage are condemned by the Church. The use of Ephesians 5 to justify the existence of a *sacrament* of marriage implies that the gender distinction has a content and a dimension transcending animality, that it belongs to human nature—not only to its fallen state—and that it will be maintained in the eschatological kingdom. But, beyond the specific issue of gender, the Neoplatonic understanding of deification deprives human activity, human creativity, and therefore the exercise of human freedom in *this* world of ontological meaning. Paradoxically, Neoplatonic monism, which denies an ontology of evil, and Manichaean dualism, which affirms it, practically coincide in their negative approach to the realities of history in the fallen world.

Finally, Eriugena also invokes the Greek fathers, particularly the book *On the Divine Names* of Dionysius, to justify his understanding of the doctrine of divine ideas and creation. He uses the Dionysian terminology to describe his overall conception of the relationship between the transcendent uncreated Mind of God and created realities. It is on this point that his basic monistic philosophy appears most clearly. God creates "from nothing," but, according to the apophatic theology of Dionysius, God himself "is nothing," because he is "superessential" ($\dot{\upsilon}\pi\epsilon\rho o\dot{\upsilon}\sigma\iota o\varsigma$). It is therefore possible, and even necessary, to say that God creates out of himself. Indeed, God is an absolute Intellect, who cannot be perceived through any category of cognition, but whose eternal ideas constitute the very reality of all being. Relative to God, these ideas are "created and creating nature." Relative to visible, perceptible realities, divine ideas are eternal, and, in that sense, uncreated. There is, therefore, a basic contradiction in Eriugena's view of creation, and he himself recognizes his inability to solve the dilemma created by his initial premise, that there is being only through participation in the Being:

> If all things that are, are eternal in the creative Wisdom, how are they made out of nothing? For how can that be eternal which before it was made was not, or how can that which begins to be in time [and with time] be in eternity? For nothing that participates in eternity either begins to be or desists from being, whereas that which was not and begins to be will of necessity desist from being what it is. For nothing that is not without a beginning can be without an end. Therefore I cannot discover how these opinions do not contradict each other.[17]

In any case, and in spite of his honest acknowledgment of the difficulty, Eriugena's own conviction is not only that creation is, indeed, an eternal act, inherent to the divine being, but that there is ontological continuity between God and creatures: "We should not understand God and the creature as two things removed from one another, but *as one and the same thing.* For the creature subsists in God, and *God is created in the creature* in a wonderful and ineffable way, making himself manifest, invisible making himself more visible."[18] In fact, for Eriugena, the creative act consists in making eternal, divine ideas perceptible and visible. In God's simple being, there is no difference between volition and vision. So creatures are not other than *theophanies,* and "it is from himself that God takes the occasions of his theophanies . . . since all things are from him and through him and in him and for him."[19]

These are just a few examples of how Eriugena uses the eastern patristic tradition, and how references to the *Areopagitica,* to Gregory of Nyssa, and to Maximus fit into his own original philosophical system. A discussion of how he made his selections and how he used the particular views of some eastern fathers should lead to an interesting discussion, not only about Eriugena, but also about the eastern Christian tradition itself. For Eriugena did not use Greek patristic authors simply to find prooftexts: he did understand and adopt for himself the internal logic of Christian Neoplatonism, without, however, giving full credit to the overall context of doctrinal development in the East, where the Neoplatonic vision of reality was always in the process of being qualified, critically modified, and channeled through the mainstream of a Christian tradition, defined in terms of trinitarian and christological criteria.

In the Greek fathers, Eriugena discovered what indeed constitutes a justified common ground between Christianity and Neoplatonism—that which is broadly referred to today as "theocentric anthropology." The human being simply does not exist as "pure nature"—independent and autonomous from divine presence—and that communion with God is not a mystical *donum superadditum*, but a constitutive element of true humanity, as it was originally created and as it is destined to be restored in the eschatological kingdom. This is a conception quite common in the East since Irenaeus and provides the general context for the interpretation of Genesis 1:26, on the creation of man and woman in the "image and likeness" of God. In Greek patristics, however, there was not only Neoplatonism. Side by side, and often in close conjunction with the neoplatonizing authors, who tended to identify the "image" with the intellect ($vo\hat{v}\varsigma$), monastic literature developed a conception of the "heart," as the "meadow of the Spirit." Maintaining more closely than the Neoplatonists a vision of the human being as a psychosomatic whole, this conception remained more biblical, and also more trinitarian in its spirituality, because of its pneumatological dimension. If Eriugena had had broader access to the theology of the Cappadocian fathers, he would have experienced more difficulty in using them as he did, within an exclusively Neoplatonic—and therefore somewhat biased—context. As a case in point, one can refer to the parallelism established by Werner Jaeger between Gregory of Nyssa and the writings attributed to Macarius the Great[20]—a parallelism which is not so apparent in Gregory's treatise *On the Creation of Man*, translated by Eriugena, but which is quite significant for the more general understanding of anthropology not only in Gregory but certainly also in Basil. In any case, the common Neoplatonic background of both Gregory of Nyssa and Maximus—which made those authors so particularly appealing to Eriugena—was, in fact, already very much qualified by these authors themselves, and is certainly not coextensive with the eastern spiritual tradition as a whole.

Even more significant are the basic trinitarian and christological options taken in the East, which were known and accepted by the very eastern authors used by Eriugena, particularly in their view of creation.

A first and most important point is the distinction between *nature* (φύσις) and *will* (θέλημα) in the anti-Arian argument of St. Athanasius in favor of the Nicene *homoousios*. By *nature*, God generates the Son and makes the Spirit to proceed; by *will*, God creates the world, and this creative action is conceived as *optional*, precisely because it does not involve God's nature and excludes ontological continuity between God and creation. This distinction between *nature* and *will* was a major argument against the idea that the Logos was a creature. Creation's *preexistence* in the mind of the Logos did not imply real *existence*, but was seen as a pure potentiality. Therefore, as distinct from the Son, who comes from the essence, or nature, of the Father, "the nature of creatures which came into being from nothing is fluid, impotent, mortal, and composite."[21] God, therefore, is *what he is*, and is not determined by what *he does*.[22] The familiarity of both Gregory of Nyssa and Maximus with this basic postulate of Athanasian anti-Arianism made it quite impossible for them to approach the problem of creation as Eriugena did, and indeed they both are very clear in affirming the creating act as a creation *from nothing and in time*. For God, creation was not a matter of natural necessity, but an act, in a sense arbitrary, of a loving, personal God.

The second and very significant factor which had a decisive significance, if not for Gregory of Nyssa and Dionysius, at least for Maximus, is the refinement of christological thought and christological terminology on the basis of the Chalcedonian definition and the controversies which followed it. The union of two natures in one *hypostasis*—the preexisting *hypostasis* of the Logos—implied that Jesus, being God hypostatically and fully divine in his divine nature, possessed also the fullness of a willing and dynamic humanity, without being a human *hypostasis*, or person. This doctrine implied that the *hypostasis* was neither the expression of a nature nor was it part of nature, because if *hypostasis* is a part of nature, Christ was not fully man. In the case of the humanity of Jesus, the *hypostasis* could not, for example, be identified with his human intellect, because the intellect is part of human created nature. The ultimate "self," the "actor" of his human nature, being thus the divine Logos, he nevertheless lived a fully human life and possessed "energy" and a human "will."

Eriugena seems to have understood the specific importance of the very distinct concept of *hypostasis* in trinitarian theology, as promoted by the Cappadocians. This he shows in his discussion of the procession of the Spirit, which I mentioned earlier. But his monistic approach to reality prevents him from giving full credit to the proper dynamism—we can say creativity—of created nature: the "movement" (κίνησις)—in the person of Christ and, by implication, in created nature in general. Since created nature, including the humanity of Jesus, is in fact, for Eriugena, an expression of the divine being, his Christology had necessarily a monophysitic outlook. Created history had no value in itself, except within the framework of the "procession-and-return" scheme.

It is true, however, that when he discusses the process of *return*, developing his discussion very much in accordance with Gregory of Nyssa and Dionysius, through various steps of purification and illumination, he uses a terminology which is not Augustinian, but assumes the eastern concept of "synergy" between nature and grace: "Resurrection," he writes, "is effected by the cooperation of both agents, nature and grace."[23] Indeed, "the human nature possesses naturally the power of resurrection."[24] But since "created nature" is but the manifestation of divine ideas, the significance of "synergy" in Eriugena may not be the same as in patristic authors, for whom created being is clearly distinct from God, exists only by his will, but possesses also—as Maximus shows so well—its own distinctive "movement" and "energy," which are called to act in communion with God but without ever being identified with divine energy.

A third element, certainly implied in the first two, which draws a distinctive line between Eriugena and the Greek fathers whom he admired so much, is their respective attitudes towards what can be broadly called "Origenism." In fact, it is mostly through Origen that the Cappadocian fathers appropriated their Christian Platonism. However, they were already aware of the one major issue where Origen's system could hardly be incorporated in the Christian tradition, especially the Nicene faith defended by Athanasius. This issue, as I said earlier, is the issue of creation. Indeed, for Origen—as also, in fact, for Eriugena—creation is God's *natural* act, an expression of His eternally subsisting ideas. Implicitly disavowed, on this point, by the Cappadocians, Origen was eventually condemned by the Fifth Council (553), and this condemnation, which followed specific controversies in the sixth century, was well known and fully taken into account by Maximus. In any case, no one in the East would refer to the "blessed" or "great" Origen, as Eriugena does.[25] Of course, John the Scot was not a conscious Origenist. He knew Origen only in the corrected Latin translation of Rufinus. But he liked the echoes of the Origenistic approach, which he could discern in Gregory and Maximus, without taking into account the radical modifications of Origenistic views which were introduced by the same authors in *their* version of Christian Neoplatonism. The echoes of "unredeemed" Origenism include the doctrine of "double creation" and the *apokatastasis* in Gregory of Nyssa, but both Gregory and Maximus conceive the relationship between Creator and creatures in a way clearly different from that of Origen and Eriugena.

For Eriugena, the divine *ideas*—"nature created and creating"—are coeternal with God and also constitute the real *substance* of all that is. Although he recognizes that there exists here an insoluble antinomy, he affirms: "Let us believe and, so far as it is given us, contemplate with the keenness of our mind how all things visible and invisible, eternal and temporal, and the eternal itself and time itself, and places and extension, and all things which are spoken of as substance and accident, and, to speak generally, whatever the totality of the whole creature contains, are at the same time eternal and made in the only begotten Word of God, and that in them neither does their eternity precede their making nor their making precede their eternity."[26] There is, therefore, nothing really external to God, because God not only *will be* "all in all" at the end of time, but always *was and is* "all in all," as foundation and essence of all things.

For the Greek authors, the created world is, indeed, ontologically external to God. It is rooted in his will, which is different from his nature. Therefore they recognize a distinction *within God himself* between his totally transcendent and unknowable essence and his presence *ad extra,* that is his uncreated energy and will. The personal, trinitarian, uncreated, divine being is therefore *both* totally transcendent and truly immanent. The preexisting ideas of creation were indeed in him, before time, but they did not belong to his essence. The deification of humanity and the ultimate eschatological transfiguration of the entire creation imply that God will be "all in all," but not *by essence* (κατ᾽ οὐσίαν), which would imply pantheism, but always through his will and uncreated energy, because ontologically and eternally only the Father, the Son, and the Spirit are "God by essence" (κατ᾽ οὐσίαν), whereas deification of creation, while fully real, occurs "by energy" (κατ᾽ ἐνέργειαν), or "by grace" (κατὰ χάριν), although it is a participation in the uncreated being of God. The paradox and the antinomy are, therefore, located within God himself and are not reducible to philosophical notions like the Neoplatonic Monad, or "divine simplicity."

This doctrine of "energies" appears in different contexts. In the Cappadocian fathers, it serves to formulate the Orthodox position against Eunomius: "While we affirm," writes Basil, "that we know our God in his energies, we scarcely promise that he may be approached in his very essence. For although his energies descend to us, his essence remains inaccessible."[27] And Gregory of Nyssa expresses very clearly the same antinomy of the divine being: "Wherefore it is true *both* that the pure heart sees God and that no one has ever seen God. In fact he who is invisible by nature becomes visible by his energies, appearing to us in some surroundings of his nature" (ἔν τισι τοῖς περὶ αὐτὸν καθορώμενοις).[28] In St. Maximus, the doctrine of the energies becomes a necessary aspect of Christology.[29] Each of Christ's two natures expresses itself in an "energy" and a "will." The two energies and wills remain distinct, although the human will follows the divine, and the energies are "penetrating" each other (περιχώρησις), so that on the mount of transfiguration, or after the resurrection, the humanity of Jesus appears "deified," i.e., it is penetrated with divine life, anticipating the eschatological glory of all those who are "in Christ." Both the unity of Christ's being and the distinction of natures and energies are possible because of the *hypostatic* union, i.e., the unity of the person of the incarnated Logos, who acts in both fully divine and fully human ways within the mystery of redemption. Finally, in the fourteenth century, Byzantium became the theater of a fierce debate on the reality of mystical experience, which involved different interpretations of the apophatic theology of Dionysius and of his use of symbolism. Monastic, or "hesychast" theologians, led by Gregory Palamas, affirmed the possibility of communion with God and deification, because divine transcendence, expressed through apophatic theology, applied to the divine essence (οὐσία) only, whereas the "descending" energies—uncreated and truly divine—make possible real communion with God.[30] There is no doubt that Eriugena's philosophical and religious vision would tend in the direction of Palamism in that he stood for the full reality of deification. But the absence, in his system, of the distinction between essence and energy inevitably leads him to Neoplatonic monism.

Among the other bridge builders between the eastern and the western Christian traditions, Eriugena occupies a unique position. He is different from earlier predecessors, like Jerome and Cassian, who had been in the East personally and had transmitted the ascetic traditions of eastern monks to their own Latin compatriots. In the age of Eriugena, times were different and direct communications more difficult. While we cannot be sure he had any direct contacts with living Easterners, he nevertheless became personally enthusiastic with what he found in the writings of the Greek fathers. His enthusiasm, however, was only an aspect of his broader philosophical commitment to the Neoplatonic worldview.

The question which might be tentatively asked is: What is the *major* source of his knowledge of Christian Neoplatonism? The standard answer has often been: his acquaintance with the writings of Dionysius, which he translated into Latin. One wonders, however, whether this answer is fully accurate. Eriugena's admiration for Dionysius as "the highest theologian" and "most famous bishop of Athens" (*summus theologus, praeclarissimus Athenarum episcopus*)[31] is, of course, obvious. Constant also in Eriugena is the use of the very specific Dionysian vocabulary and terminology. But the key concepts of Eriugena's system, such as his notion of an eternal creation of ideas and of creatures being thus eternal manifestations of the divine being, do not come from Dionysius but are akin to basic Origenism. It is also the more Origenistic aspects of the anthropology and cosmology of Gregory of Nyssa which are picked up by Eriugena, as I have noted earlier. It is difficult to say—because references to Origen in Eriugena are rare, though always respectful—whether there is direct inspiration, or borrowing, or whether the obvious parallelisms are to be understood in the context of a common Platonic inspiration. In using and discussing apophatic theology, Eriugena is, of course, quite dependent upon Dionysian terminology, but in substance, the apophatic approach is fully expressed in the Cappadocian fathers and Maximus as well, so Eriugena did not need Dionysius to learn about apophatic theology. But for the Cappadocian fathers and for the many later interpreters of Dionysius, starting with Maximus the Confessor, the apophatic, negative expressions in designating God mean to indicate the gap between him, as Creator or Cause of beings, from the creatures whose very existence is caused by him. This radical character of apophaticism in Dionysius is what makes his God different from the "One" of Plotinus, and allows us to classify him among those Greek fathers who hold to the idea of God as the true *Creator* from nothing, while using Greek apophatic terminology to express the Hebrew biblical idea of creation from nothing.[32] Since on this point Eriugena holds to an *ontological continuity* between Creator and creatures—following Clement and Origen—one wonders whether his apophaticism does not, rather, tend in the direction which it will acquire in Thomism, as a way of simply expressing the "more sublime" character of the divine names, or qualities, when they are compared with the lower and imperfect manifestations of the same names and qualities among creatures.

Considering the work of that extraordinary man, one can only regret that he was so lonely in his interest and commitment to the Greek Christian tradition. If knowledge of that tradition had been more widespread, Eriugena could have more easily given a more "catholic," or more "orthodox" shape to his system, without abandoning what is so precious in it: his "theocentric anthropology" and his understanding of spiritual life as a free ascent to *theosis*. He is obviously sincere when he writes, "It is most clear that our sole quest should be joy in the Truth, which is Christ; and our sole dread the deprivation of it, for that is the one and only cause of all eternal suffering. Take Christ from me, and no good is left for me, nor is there any torment left to terrify me. For I hold that the deprivation of Christ and his absence are the sole torment for every rational creature and that there is no other."[33]

In concluding, allow me to quote Etienne Gilson: "one can imagine the astonishment of contemporaries in the face of this immense metaphysical epic . . . , supported, at each step, by Dionysius, Maximus, the two Gregories, Origen, Augustine, or some other among the twenty authorities which our author could in-

66 John Meyendorff

voke with his astonishing erudition. Things happen as if Eriugena had fulfilled a pledge to affirm all the propositions, put forward by Doctors of the Church when they were *not* speaking as Doctors of the Church."[34] Thus, in Eriugena's time, his system did not succeed in bridging the intellectual and spiritual gap between the two worlds, which continued to move on their separate ways. But today, as we know more about the problems which separated them, Eriugena deserves to be rediscovered, as a lonely, but prophetic and powerful, voice, searching for the right solutions, but hardly succeeding in a task much too vast to be handled by his lonely, isolated genius.

NOTES

1. An attempt to show that he might have known *some* Greek was made by Joan M. Petersen, "Did Gregory the Great Know Greek?" in *The Orthodox Churches and the West,* ed. Derek Baker, Studies in Church History 13 (Oxford, 1976), 121–134.

2. Photius, *On the Mystagogy of the Holy Spirit* (PG 102:349–352).

3. Photius, *Biblioteca,* codex 177 (ed. R. Henry [Paris, 1960], 2:177).

4. Eriugena, *Praef. ad vers. Dionysii* (PL 122:1031C). In his preface to the translation of St. Maximus, Eriugena exalts Charles for seeking "sane doctrine" among the Greeks ("ex praeclarissimis Graecorum fontibus": PL 122:1196B).

5. P II, PL 122:611D (trans. J. O'Meara [Montreal and Washington, 1987], 233). Eriugena refers to the source of his knowledge of the original text of the creed: the *Ancoratus* "on the faith" by St. Epiphanius of Cyprus (PL 122:601C; trans. 211). He obviously had no contacts with contemporary Orthodox Greeks. The text of the *Ancoratus* is in PG 43:17–236.

6. P II, PL 122:612B (trans. 224).

7. P II, PL 122:613A–615C (trans. 225–228). For a good discussion of Eriugena's position on the *Filioque* issue, see A. Brilliantov, *Vliyanie Vostochnago bogosloviya na Zapadnoe v proizvedeniyakh Ioanna Skota Erigeny (The Influence of Eastern Theology upon the Western One in the Writings of John Scottus Eriugena;* St. Petersburg, 1898), 275–280.

8. Cf. his discussion of the relations between mind (*mens*), knowledge of itself (*notitia sui*), and love (*amor*) as a trinitarian image in P II, PL 122:610B–611A (trans. 222–223). The later Byzantine theological tradition would actually use the image within its own context, as well;

see Gregory Palamas, *The One Hundred and Fifty Chapters: A Critical Edition, Translation, and Study*, ed. and trans. R. E. Sinkewicz (Toronto, 1988), 123–125.

9. Gregory of Nyssa, *De opificio hominis* 16 (PG 44:184).

10. Ibid., 185.

11. P III, PL 122:630A (trans. 246).

12. Ibid., 631D (trans. 248).

13. P V, PL 122:1015C (trans. 706).

14. P I, PL 122:502A (trans. 96).

15. For a recent discussion of this view, see V. E. F. Harrison, "Male and Female in Cappadocian Theology," *Journal of Theological Studies*, NS, 41, 2 (October 1990): 441–471.

16. P IV, PL 122:808A–B (trans. 460–461).

17. P III, PL 122:636A–D (trans. 253).

18. Ibid., 678C (trans. 305).

19. Ibid., 679A (trans. 305).

20. Cf. W. Jaeger, *Two Rediscovered Works of Ancient Christian Literature: Gregory of Nyssa and Macarius* (Leiden, 1954).

21. Athanasius, *Contra gentes* 41 (PG 25:81C–D).

22. Cf., on that point, G. Florovsky, "The Concept of Creation in Saint Athanasius," *Studia Patristica* 6, part 6, *Texte und Untersuchungen* 81 (Berlin, 1962): 36–37; see also J. Meyendorff, "Creation in the History of Orthodox Theology," *St. Vladimir's Theological Quarterly* 27 (1983): 1, 27–30.

23. P V, PL 122:902D (trans. 574).

24. "Inest enim naturaliter humanae naturae virtus resurrectionis": Eriugena, *Comm. in John*, III, 1 (ed. E. Jeauneau [Paris, 1972], SC 180, 206 = PL 122:315D).

25. P V, PL 122:922C (trans. 596); ibid. 929A (trans. 604).

26. P III, PL 122:669A (trans. 293).

27. Basil, *Letter 234 to Amphilochios* (PG 32:869).

28. Gregory of Nyssa, *De beatitudinibus*, Oratio VI (PG 44:1269).

29. There is a profusion of studies on St. Maximus in the last decades (von Balthasar, Völker, Thunberg, Guarrigues, Léthel, and others), which differ in some of their interpretations of Maximian theology but agree on the centrality of Christology in his overcoming Origenistic metaphysics.

30. For a recent introduction to the issue, see *Gregory Palamas: The Triads*, ed. and intro. J. Meyendorff, trans. N. Gendle, preface by J. Pelikan, Classics of Western Spirituality (New York, 1983). For a more complete discussion and bibliography, see J. Meyendorff, "Palamas, Grégoire," *Dictionnaire de spiritualité* (Paris, 1983), 12:81–107; cf.

J. Meyendorff, *Introduction a l'étude de Grégoire Palamas* (Paris, 1959), English trans. (London, 1964; reprint, Crestwood, N.Y., 1974).

31. P III, PL 122:644B (trans. 263).

32. Cf. V. Lossky, *The Mystical Theology of the Eastern Church,* 2d ed. (Crestwood, N.Y., 1976), 29–43.

33. P V, PL 122:989A (trans. 674).

34. E. Gilson, *La philosophie au moyen âge* (Paris, 1952), 222.

Eriugena's *Periphyseon:*
A Carolingian Contribution
to the Theological Tradition

WILLEMIEN OTTEN

TO GIVE AN UNEQUIVOCAL INTERPRETATION of Eriugena's *Periphyseon* is not an easy task.[1] Conflicting tendencies seem to underlie this work, as it displays not only an eclectic configuration of topics but also an unusual variety of genres. Such conflicting tendencies have complicated the analysis of the *Periphyseon* as an original and important work in the history of Christian thought. To explain the work's complexity, scholars have often pointed to the fact that in it Eriugena uniquely employs eastern theological sources. Consequently, the *Periphyseon* became seen not just as a complex work but also as an anomalous one, since it appears to fall outside the scope of the early medieval West.[2] Precisely this presumption has inspired me to study the *Periphyseon*'s place in the theological tradition.

My inquiry will begin with some observations about the *Periphyseon*'s compositional structure in order to show that Eriugena's position can be seen as one of intellectual integrity. Since the work's integrity is not always matched by equal consistency, I shall refrain from judging either the value of its ideas or the success of its integration of eastern sources. My procedure in this first stage is best explained by referring to Umberto Eco's term *opera aperta*.[3] Only the reading of the *Periphyseon* as an "open work" can provide us with a legitimate basis for an analysis of its disparate ideas.

In order to move beyond the *Periphyseon*'s isolation and assess its position in the history of Christian thought, I shall next try to integrate the individual results of my analysis with an evaluation of the work as a structured whole by analyzing how Eriugena proceeds in his central discussion of *natura*. To underscore further my claim that the *Periphyseon*'s elaboration of ideas is rooted in the broader intellectual outlook of its author, I shall turn to an earlier stage of Eriugena's thought, when he wrote the *De divina predestinatione*.[4] By linking his mature writing to this early work, the case can be made that the *Periphyseon*, far from being a chance product, warrants analysis as a treatise of structural theological reflection. It represents the author's constant attempt to integrate the universe of nature with the presence of the divine through the mediation of human reason. By revealing how this Eriugenian outlook was essentially present before he composed his masterpiece, the *Periphyseon*'s rightful place in the history of Christian thought will be validated and clarified.

The nature of the *Periphyseon*'s theological enterprise will be the subject of some concluding remarks. These are meant to highlight Eriugena's anthropology as a cornerstone of his contribution to the theological tradition. To characterize the collective picture deriving from both works, I have broadly labeled Eriugena's contribution to the theological tradition as a Carolingian one. While refraining from any doctrinal qualifications that suppress Eriugena's creative originality, I want to make it clear that in order to fit Eriugena in the tradition one need not overstep the boundaries of his Carolingian background. In the context of this volume, my conclusion concretely implies that I see Eriugena's place ultimately more as western than eastern.

A. The *Periphyseon*'s Compositional Structure in Relation to the Problem of Its Eastern and Western Sources

When read as a work of philosophico-theological speculation, the *Periphyseon* brings up numerous difficulties of interpretation hampering a straightforward analysis of the text. These are largely due, as I have argued above, to conflicting tendencies underlying the literary composition of this work. Two such factors deserve comment here, dealing with the textual genre and the textual method of the *Periphyseon*.

At the outset, we are confronted with the problem of the different genres Eriugena uses to express his thought. Thus in the context of one and the same work we find a philosophical debate on the categories intertwined with a theological discussion of the divine names[5] which changes next into the discourse of historical, and even allegorical, exegesis. The discrepancy between these genres has given rise to divergent interpretations of the work, which broadly waver between one of the following two positions. Whereas Guy Allard has tried to make the case that the whole of the *Periphyseon* can be seen as an intellectual exegesis of the Genesis creation story, considering it essentially as one extended *Hexaemeron* commentary,[6] Etienne Gilson, maintaining that the *Periphyseon* is a philosophical interpretation of Scripture, seems ultimately to characterize the work more as an exercise in issues of reason and faith than as a purely exegetical study.[7] A middle position between Allard's intellectual exegesis and Gilson's exegetical philosophy was taken by I. P. Sheldon-Williams, when he suggested that book I may have been written separately, as an instruction on the theme of dialectics,[8] whereas books II–V loosely hang together as a paraphrase on the Platonic theme of the descent of the soul and its return to God.

It is the theme of descent and ascent of the soul, as Sheldon-Williams identified it, which leads us to a second textual difficulty thwarting an unequivocal reading of the *Periphyseon*. This concerns Eriugena's textual method, which hinges on the explicit application of the Neoplatonic pair of *processio* and *reditus*. The notions of procession and return, which are generally seen as responsible for the dynamics of the work, are notable on two distinct, albeit interrelated, levels of the *Periphyseon*'s text.

On the epistemological level, this Neoplatonic pair functions as a means of progress for Eriugena's rational investigation of nature which operates through the categories of division and analysis. On the ontological level, that of the fourfold division of nature and the division into being and nonbeing, this Neoplatonic pair is responsible for outlining *natura*'s all-inclusive structure, thus providing a platform for interchange and communication between the created universe and its omnipotent creator. Because of the dialectical nature of procession and return, the *Periphyseon*'s epistemological and ontological aspects are effectively interrelated.[9] It is due to this dialectical outlook that the *Periphyseon* gives the impression that there is a continuous shift in the development of its ideas.[10] Due to this dialectical outlook also, the *Periphyseon* withstands any clear distinction between essentials and side-issues, as the momentum of an argument may shift with each differing phase of Eriugena's analysis.[11]

Without ruling on the importance of these textual features, I want to stress that it is the conjunction of both textual genre and textual method which makes the *Periphyseon* stand out among Eriugena's works. Despite similarities in outlook and style, none of his other works display the same convergence of textual characteristics.

To analyze the complexity of the *Periphyseon*'s unique compositional structure, scholars have tended to focus on the influence of Eriugena's sources, notably his pledge of allegiance to the Greek Fathers. When comparing the *Periphyseon* to his earlier works, it is clear beyond a doubt that Eriugena's introduction to the Greek tradition caused a significant shift in his thinking. Prior to it he relied on Augustine as a main inspiration for his theological views, and on Martianus Capella, or Alcuin, or both, for his instruction in the liberal arts. His reading of the Greek Fathers—Gregory of Nyssa, Pseudo-Dionysius, and Maximus the Confessor chief among them—which was intensified by his task of translating them, cannot but have opened up his intellectual horizon. It can thus account for the differences that separate the *Periphyseon* from Eriugena's earlier works.

The problems concerning the *Periphyseon*'s compositional structure seem directly linked to Eriugena's predilection for Greek over Latin authorities, as he acknowledges his indebtedness to the Greeks in both cases. On the issue of textual method, Eriugena mentions that he has derived the dialectical method of procession and return from his reading of the Areopagite, though it became clear to him only upon reading Maximus.[12] To this we can add the important theme of negative theology,[13] even if it bears some likeness to Augustinian views as well.[14] As to the issue of textual genre, it is in his exegesis, both historical and allegorical, that Eriugena resorts most often to Greek authorities, using Basil of Caesarea's *Hexaemeron* extensively in book III and, more importantly, Gregory of Nyssa's allegorical views in books IV and V.[15]

If we view the *Periphyseon* as marking a major stage in Eriugena's intellectual career, his exposure to the Greek patristic tradition goes far to explain the work's original features. In many scholarly analyses, this approach has been taken to clarify Eriugena's often confusing positions by sorting out his direct source-influences. Scholars like Cappuyns, Jeauneau, Sheldon-Williams, and Roques have highlighted the Greek theological background of the *Periphyseon*.[16] Their analyses have yielded a more precise understanding of Eriugena's dependence on his Greek sources, as well as of their subsequent modification in certain specifically Eriugenian doctrines.[17] Typical Eriugenian viewpoints have thus been established in a retroactive manner, by setting them off against his Greek sources.[18]

Yet with so much emphasis put on the *Periphyseon*'s Greek background, the side-effect has been that the theological views elaborated in this work became isolated from their immediate historical and literary context. While I do not discredit the study of source-influence in the *Periphyseon*, the cumulative effect of such approaches has been to remove Eriugena further and further from the scene of western theology. Thus Marcia Colish, in an otherwise excellent article, has characterized Eriugena's Christology as being more Neoplatonic than that of either Pseudo-Dionysius or Maximus the Confessor.[19] As a result of the tendency to solve the *Periphyseon*'s complexity by resorting to its Greek sources, the work has become more and more evaluated as a Greek interruption in what is consequently characterized as an ongoing Latin tradition from Augustine, Boethius, to Anselm.[20] Fewer, but equally valuable, attempts have evaluated Eriugena's dependence on Latin sources. Whereas most of these dwell on his dependence on Augustine (such as studies by Russell, J. J. O'Meara, Stock), others have focused on his relation to Boethius (d'Onofrio) and Bede (Stock).[21]

While the study of source influence can help to determine where the *Periphyseon* fits in Eriugena's intellectual career, it is insufficient to solve the textual problems I have mentioned. Although proper credit should be given to undeniable source-influences, the *Periphyseon* as a whole seems to combine, if not fuse, western and eastern theological ideas.[22] Seeing the *Periphyseon* as a fusion of eastern and western ideas thus brings us back to our initial question, namely, how to view its position in the theological tradition. Transcending the question of whether or not at some time before composing the *Periphyseon* Eriugena had completed the translation of his Greek sources, this problem appears to touch on the level to which Eriugena actually absorbed his information. It thus requires an inquiry into the nature of the *Periphyseon* as a creative composition in which ostensibly Greek features such as procession and return, negative theology, and allegorical exegesis are displayed in an integrated fashion.[23] The creative intensity with which Eriugena absorbed his Greek sources, rather than their mere presence, makes the *Periphyseon* stand out in the theological tradition of the western Middle Ages.

To explain the *Periphyseon*'s position in regard to its historical setting, studies by J. Contreni, J. Marenbon, and J. J. O'Meara have focused on the concrete contacts Eriugena had with his Carolingian contemporaries and have brought out his particular affinity with, or similarity to, their intellectual positions.[24] Schrimpf and Marenbon have carried this approach beyond the straightforwardly historical and have drawn systematic conclusions. They have attempted to define the boundaries of the Carolingian character of the *Periphyseon*'s views, such as the employment of the *categoriae decem*, the use of universals, the issue of negative theology and ontology,[25] the strict adherence to the method of the liberal arts, and the systematic verifiability of the division of nature.[26] By putting Eriugena back in his contemporaneous Carolingian setting, these studies are invaluable when one tries to assess the position of the *Periphyseon* in the history of Christian thought.

In light of my question of the *Periphyseon*'s status as a contribution to the theological tradition, however, my approach here differs from Marenbon and Schrimpf. Since I am more concerned with a cross section of the work's line of argument than with samples of its contents, I will apply what may seem to be an indirect or circuitous method by concentrating on the pattern according to which Eriugena develops his intellectual ideas rather than these ideas as such. Establishing an Eriugenian thought-pattern could help us determine whether or not the *Periphyseon* should indeed be perceived as anomalous or whether its place can perhaps be seen as more integrated.

For this purpose a comparison between the text of the *De divina praedestinatione*, on the one hand, and that of the *Periphyseon*, on the other, as the two works directly preceding and succeeding his activities as a translator is particularly revealing. Though there are great differences between these works, as the one is an occasional treatise which Eriugena was commissioned to write whereas the other contains his most thought-out and penetrating reflections, they share some similarities as well. One is their unmistakable theological interest, be it in the matter of "immediate" divine intervention, as in the *On Divine Predestination*,[27] or in that of a hierarchical cosmos permeated by the ineffability of the divine, as in the *Periphyseon*'s idea of *natura*. This warrants a comparison between them, while at the same time it makes a case for the doctrinal importance of Eriugena's early treatise beyond that of its usual classification as belonging merely to his period as a controversialist.[28] Another similarity is their explicit application of dialectical method.[29] In the *On Divine Predestination* this use of dialectics receives a clear expression in its introduction and its first chapter, where the interrelation between religion and philosophy as well as the fourfold method of division, definition, demonstration, and analysis/return are amply examined. Furthermore, chapter 18 condemns the errors of those who out of ignorance of the liberal arts, and interestingly enough also of Greek, misunderstand the Fathers.[30] The *Periphyseon* certainly leaves no doubt as to its interest in rational investigation and employs the dialectical pair of division and analysis as its prime method.

The purpose of my comparison will be to see whether or not on the basis of a reading of the *On Divine Predestination* it is possible to confirm some essential features of Eriugena's theology in the *Periphyseon*. If so, the next question to be answered will be to see if such features can be evaluated as revealing what might be called a coherent pattern throughout, i.e., underlying his reception of various sources and predisposing his response to them, or if his theological opinions in the *Periphyseon* are indeed so dominantly shaped by his encounter with the Greeks as his reverence for their superiority in its text indicates.

B. From the *Periphyseon* to the *De divina praedestinatione:* The Power of Human Reason

1. The Periphyseon

As I stated above, conflicting tendencies are found underlying the *Periphyseon*, notably the issues of textual genre and textual method. In order to establish the *Periphyseon*'s essential thought-pattern, I shall attempt to clarify these conflicting tendencies by analyzing them as building blocks which indicate to us the dynamic character of the *Periphyseon*'s text. By looking first at the textual method and then at the textual genre of this work, we can trace the ultimate congruence of certain Eriugenian features without attempting either to deny or to confirm their obvious inconsistencies.

Clearly a dialectical method, namely that of division and analysis or procession and return, provides the organizational principles for the *Periphyseon*'s ongoing argument. According to our previous analysis, the fundamental importance of these dialectical principles consists in the fact that they are not only central to Eriugena's epistemology, as brought out by his use of division and analysis, but also to his ontology, to the extent that nature's development adheres to the structure of procession and return. Yet it is precisely the indiscriminate overlap of the epistemological and the ontological status of procession and return that makes them a dynamic force in the unfolding of the *Periphyseon*'s argument. On closer inspection, the foundational point of both, i.e., Eriugena's ontological as well as his epistemological interests, is the criterion of human rationality. After all, the division into being and nonbeing, pivoting on what the human mind can and cannot grasp, is found preceding the famous division of the four forms or species of nature. In evaluating the dialectical method of Eriugena's *Periphyseon*, therefore, it seems his epistemological quest ultimately gains priority over the ontological representation of the universe, as it is only relative to the mind's grasp of all things that being and nonbeing can be used as valid predicates.[31]

With the *Periphyseon*'s argument urged onwards by the propelling power of Eriugena's dialectical method, the issue of textual genre soon emerges as a second point breaking up the *Periphyseon*'s internal coherence. The conflict of genres is, if not most apparent, then certainly most striking between books I–III on the one hand and books IV and V on the other. Whereas book I can be seen as a general introduction, focusing on the first species of nature, i.e., God as cause, book II establishes a first connection between nature's fourfold division and the exegesis of Genesis, linking the subject matter of primordial causes to the interpretation of Genesis 1:1.[32] This basic connection is further elaborated in book III where Eriugena employs Basil's literal exegesis in what amounts to a running commentary on the remainder of Genesis 1. He describes how the third species of spatio-temporal creation is brought into being by the primordial causes.[33] Books IV and V stand quite apart from the earlier three books, the most notable difference being that Eriugena commits himself to allegorical, rather than literal or historical, exegesis.

In explaining the *Periphyseon*'s mysterious switch from literal to allegorical exegesis, it is significant to note that the issue of genre touches directly on Eriugena's method. This becomes clear from the *Periphyseon*'s text, as it is precisely on the transitional point from *processio* to *reditus* that the change from historical to allegorical exegesis is found implemented.[34] Having described the unfolding of God's creation as a descending movement from an omnipotent divine cause to individual creatures in the first three books, the beginning of book IV shows Eriugena embarking on what might well be called a counterproject. In this counterproject the plight of human nature, that is, the story of its creation ending with the tragedy of its exile from paradise, functions as a narrative metaphor for nature's ascending return to God. Thus, after the macrocosmic perspective presented in the first three books dealing with the all-embracing scope of an infinite nature, it is on the microcosmic level of human nature that the *Periphyseon*'s return process is first set in motion. Eriugena's allegorical discourse reaches a climax at the beginning of book V, where the story of Adam's expulsion, instead of marking creation's tragic failure, provides Eriugena with a concrete take-off point to implement the return of all creation to its original place in paradise.[35]

Given the prominence of the mind as the only part of human nature which Eriugena, in keeping with Gregory's exegesis, considers to be truly in the image of God,[36] it can be inferred that human rationality will play a central role as Eriugena shifts from procession to return. In the course of books IV and V, therefore, it is not just the microcosmic scale of human nature but the microscopic precision of the human mind that gives access to the universe at large. It seems as if the scale of infinite nature, rather than dominating or outweighing human nature, is gradually reduced towards the single goal of human understanding.

In light of a consideration of the *Periphyseon*'s conflicting tendencies as constructive building blocks of an Eriugenian thought pattern, it is the common factor in both the work's textual method and its textual genre that is of most interest. At the intersection of the *Periphyseon*'s epistemology and its ontology, on the one hand, and of its dialectical philosophy and its exegesis on the other, lies the factor of human rationality. What is remarkable about this is, first of all, this simple fact as such. Despite being a small facet of

the macrocosmic world and overpowered by the structure of the
whole, throughout the *Periphyseon* human nature will maintain
a rational grasp of things. By doing so, human reason obviously
defies the limitations of its own powers to the point of transcending them.

   Even more remarkable, however, is the fact that human rationality, by Eriugena's own admission imperfect, is yet able to function as a driving force of increasing importance. At the very
point where procession is funneled into return, macrocosmic proportions shrink to the microcosmic level, as human nature led
by reason becomes the exclusive vehicle for the return of the
complete universe. In this process Eriugena relies heavily on his
Greek sources, borrowing Maximus's fivefold pattern of return
which begins with the unification of human nature, and basing
himself on Gregory's point that the true image of God resides
only in the human mind.[37] Yet it is his own achievement to stretch
their respective points so as to make the microcosmic dynamics of
human nature the nuclear foundation of a macrocosmic apotheosis. This is markedly clear at the beginning of book IV where the
creation of human nature marks the starting point for the movement of return.[38] Despite the onset of sin by which the untainted
vitality of human nature threatens to be destroyed, despite Adam's
ordeal in paradise and his subsequent expulsion, the attainment
of the return, once the process is set in motion, is never seriously
in danger. As long as the universe's movement of procession and
return is safely linked to human nature (fittingly called by the
Maximian term "the crucible of the universe"),[39] its dialectical
unfolding is not only safeguarded, but its successful ending is
within reach.

   A tentative explanation as to how the very creation of human
nature commands the success of its own development by guaranteeing the rational efficacy of the return is found in book IV, chapters 7–9.[40] In my view, what is striking in Eriugena's reasoning in
these chapters is not just the famous statement "notio quaedam
intellectualis in mente divina aeternaliter facta," by which human
nature is collectively defined as a perfect notion in the divine
mind.[41] It is also not the point that man, who contains the notions
of created things in his own mind just as the Divine Mind contains
the primordial causes, can therefore also be defined in terms of his
own self-knowledge[42] which he could have perfected in his created

state had he merely completed the life he was given without sin.[43] Though important, these points flow forth naturally from Eriugena's Christian-Neoplatonic premises, where the ideal or rational world is naturally found to condition reality as it represents the archetypal human state before sin. What is striking, however, is how Eriugena confronts these two definitions of man—that is, his definition as an eternal cause on the one hand and that as his pure self-knowledge on the other—with the undeniable reality of sin's damaging impact on human rationality.[44] When facing the dilemma that man has not realized his definition as an ideal cause, because of a life spent among the concrete effects of creation and therefore is not able in this life ever to have a perfect knowledge of either his creator or himself, Eriugena counters by insisting that the *appetitus beatitudinis* still remains: "Nevertheless the yearning for the lost beatitude is understood to have remained in human nature even after the fall, which would by no means have happened, if it had ignored itself and its God completely."[45]

The turn of phrase by which the reality of imperfect human knowledge or rationality comes to express an anthropological potential rather than a flaw or defect is a typical Eriugenian one. It gives the *Periphyseon*'s dynamics of the human mind its particular flavor, since it is only a sinful mind, seemingly imperfect and paralyzed by ignorance, which can lie at the heart of Eriugena's near-perfect metaphysical universe. Only a sinful mind, in its urgent longing for pristine purity, can generate the energy needed to carry out what borders on a hybridic return of the universe to its creator.

2. *The* De divina praedestinatione

In turning to the *De divina praedestinatione*, we face a text which, at least from the outside, displays difficulties similar to those commented on in the *Periphyseon*. Again we have the problem of textual genre, as Eriugena promulgates the views of Augustine yet at the same time cares to develop his own, somewhat divergent, positions. The issue of textual method arises when Eriugena presents the liberal arts and the logical quadrivium of division, definition, demonstration, and analysis as crucial to the unfolding of his more theological arguments on predestination.[46]

In studying the issue of genre, it is clear that Eriugena is less skillful here in elaborating his arguments in a systematic fashion, although he definitely develops his own style in linking Augustine's quotes to his own subtle positions. The exegetical interpretation of Scripture, the analysis of Augustine, the increasing use of the device of *enthymema* or *a contrario* in distinguishing between what Augustine literally states and what he actually means[47]—all ultimately tie in with Eriugena's own view of one divine ordinance laid down by one divine substance.[48] This divine ordinance is called predestination for the saints and prescience for the damned.

On the issue of method, the *De divina praedestinatione* shows more attention for the rhetorical use of arguments than for their dialectical structure. Instead of the Neoplatonic pair of procession and return, Eriugena makes increasing use of the *genus locutionum*. The *enthymema/kat 'antiphrasin/a contrario*–argument is clearly favored,[49] as he employs it effectively to interpret texts to his own liking. Whether this results in the elimination of Gottschalk's arguments or in the appropriation of Augustine's texts, the presumption underlying this free use of rhetorical method is that it is a perfectly legitimate strategy for him to complete the task he has been asked to fulfill.

What appears to be totally lacking in the *On Divine Predestination,* however, thus setting this work apart from the *Periphyseon,* is any overlap and perhaps even connection between the rhetorical method employed by the author and the metaphysical structure of the universe as such,[50] which is such a characteristic feature of the procession and return structure in the *Periphyseon.* The epistemological strategies Eriugena employs in this early work are bereft of ontological impact, to the extent that the structure of the universe appears to be neither reflected in nor moulded by the author's descriptions. It is this absence of the dynamic feature, so strikingly dominant in the *Periphyseon,* which may well lie behind its reputation as a mere occasional treatise without special merits of its own.

Consequently, much attention has been given to the static aspects of Eriugena's view of predestination. This is confirmed by the historical accounts of J. Devisse and J. J. O'Meara, according to which Eriugena irritated his contemporaries precisely by taking his point of departure in what is so clearly a static principle, that of divine immutability.[51] At first sight, this seems accurately to reflect the work's main line of argument, for it is because of their underlying divine identity that Eriugena proposes that *praedestinatio* and *praescientia* should be seen as mere alternate terms.[52]

Be that as it may, I cannot refrain from counterbalancing this static interpretation of the *De divina praedestinatione* by pointing to some similarities with the *Periphyseon*. In line with my overall intention, i.e., to show how a coherent interest links Eriugena's early to his mature work, I suggest that the deeper core of Eriugena's theology, fully elaborated in the *Periphyseon,* is in essence already visible in his predestination treatise.[53] This continuing interest pertains to a dynamic, rather than a static, aspect of Eriugena's views in his early work. And, though Eriugena's arguments are less organized, they also point to theological anthropology functioning as the dynamic substructure of his thought. In the treatise on predestination this does not result in the overlap of epistemology and ontology, but rather in the interchangeability of *philosophia* and *religio,* which is the major thesis of chapter 1. To illustrate the central function of anthropology in the *On Divine Predestination* and to point out how this theme is thus a continuing concern for Eriugena, I shall give two examples.

The first is taken from chapter 4, where Eriugena emphasizes that there can only be one true predestination. Having launched a ferocious attack on Gottschalk's views in the previous chapters, this is the first time he actually displays his own views in the matter, having previously used Augustine's as both rhetorical weapon and shield. Discussing what it is exactly that man lost when he sinned, Eriugena says that man could not have lost the beatific life itself, for he did not yet possess this. Also, on the occasion of his fall he could not have lost his free will, for free will is innate to the human substance and remains so even after sin. Still, it is clear that in consequence of the fall, man must have lost something. Given that Eriugena sees the *appetitus beatitudinis* [sic!] as remaining after the fall, it can rightly be inferred that man must originally have aspired to a state of beatitude. Having systematically eliminated all that man did not lose, Eriugena then reaches his final conclusion. What man actually lost was not his free will, but rather its strength and power (*vigor et potestas liberi arbitrii*). In an additional clause which seems designed to salvage the integrity of free will he states that the strength of free will was never *ex substantia,* but always *ex creatoris gratia.* Whatever the disastrous effects of man's loss in paradise, Eriugena makes it clear that it does not deprive human nature of free will itself.[54]

Central to this passage is the implicit connection of the human striving for beatitude through free will on the one hand and the damaging impact of sin on the other. Eriugena explains that the first human could never have been sinful had he merely wanted to choose misery. It thus seems as if the longing for beatitude as the hallmark of human nature is intrinsically bound up with the reality of human sin. Only a sinful mind can develop a clear perspective of its goal: the attaining of divine beatitude, or what the *Periphyseon* will call *reditus*. In the same way, the reality of sin does not appear to interrupt the quest for this beatitude but rather reinforces it. With the junctions of man's intellectual journey openly indicated, its final destination becomes only more clear. Sin and beatitude, like religion and philosophy, thus appear to draw upon the flexible strength of the same human mind.

A second example is found in chapter 8 of the *On Divine Predestination*. In this chapter we find Eriugena discussing the nature of the *liberum arbitrium,* which is seen as distinct from human nature and the human will. The point I want to draw attention to here is the indissoluble connection between the freedom and rationality of the will and the aspect of its mutability. Eriugena defines the *liberum arbitrium voluntatis* differently from Augustine as a *liberae voluntatis motus*, thus separating it out from the will's rational substance. He views the *liberum arbitrium* in essence as a *donum* of God, yet in an explicit qualification he adds that God has subjected this freedom of choice to our human *potentia*. This means that in addition to God as the causal mover moving us to himself, we have the "power" to decide for ourselves whether or not we want to move our wills to God.

Eriugena's intention here in distinguishing between the motion (*liberum arbitrium*) of the will and the will itself (a rational substance) is clear. It is to the motion of the will that he will subsequently attribute the sins and punishments of those who will eventually be condemned without compromising the will as such.[55] Yet by qualifying the motion of the free and rational will as subjugated to human "power," it seems to me he latently postulates the idea of restoration. For instead of choosing evil, the human *potentia* may choose the good, thus contributing to a rebuilding of the original *vigor et potestas* which humanity's free will once possessed.[56] The mutability of the will, therefore, as much as Eriugena invokes it here as a liability to explain evil actions, has a potential positive counterpart, as the rational will is invited to engage in an attempt to turn and return to God in a movement steered by human *potentia*.

Let me now return to my questions in the introduction concerning the *Periphyseon*'s contribution to the theological tradition. Based on my observations about the crucial function of the human mind in Eriugena's thinking, especially his remarkable twist of turning a distinct deficiency (human reason as incapacitated because of sin) into a promising potential, I want to draw the following conclusion. Rather than having the interpretation of the *Periphyseon* get trapped in a stalemate between western (i.e., Augustinian) as opposed to eastern (i.e., Neoplatonic, Dionysian) theology, whereby one runs the risk of neglecting the distinctiveness of its contribution altogether, I urge that a systematic/historical evaluation of specific Eriugenian themes be considered as a valid, alternative way to make progress in the matter of evaluating the *Periphyseon*'s position in the history of Christian thought. My comparison between the *On Divine Predestination* and the *Periphyseon* on the point of Eriugena's anthropological twist is meant as a first and incomplete example.

Though more work needs to be done, my preliminary findings have led me to believe that Eriugena's contribution fits in best with the tradition of "western" theology, be it a broadened one. It is my opinion that Eriugena is a theological thinker deeply rooted in a western tradition that apart from the Augustinian legacy had remained open to numerous other developments. It is largely because of the rapid development of the liberal arts that I have labeled this western tradition in Eriugena's days a Carolingian one. Though it is clear that he was heavily attracted to eastern ideals and substantially influenced by them, to my mind the anthropological optimism at the core of his ideas—a feature which I hope to have shown can be seen as endemic to his thought even before the *Periphyseon*—underlines his western outlook in which the Augustinian awareness of the reality of sin is counterbalanced by a confident assessment of human powers through the liberal arts. It is with an eye on the breadth of the tradition of the early medieval West that still needs to be explored that I have performed the above analysis.

NOTES

I would like to thank my former colleague, Dr. Pamela Bright of Concordia University, Montreal, for her kind assistance in rendering this essay in English.

1. The text of *Periphyseon* (P) I–III will be quoted in the edition of I. P. Sheldon-Williams. See *Iohannis Scotti Eriugenae Periphyseon (De Divisione Naturae)*, ed. I. P. Sheldon-Williams and L. Bieler (Dublin: Institute for Advanced Studies, 1968, 1972, 1981). Books IV and V will be quoted in the edition of H. J. Floss in J. P. Migne, Patrologia Latina (Paris, 1853), vol. 122.

2. In older surveys Eriugena is often excluded. See, e.g., David Knowles, *The Evolution of Medieval Thought* (New York: Random House, 1962), 77, where he is acknowledged as "a voice in the wilderness" but deigned unworthy of any further attention. See also Gordon Leff, *Medieval Thought (St. Augustine to Ockham)* (1958; repr. Atlantic Heights, N.J.: Humanities Press, 1983), 62–73. On p. 63 Leff states: "Where his fellows hardly looked beyond the elementary questions of theology, contained in the writings of the Fathers, and kept within the bounds of the *trivium,* John constructed an entire system largely under the influence of Greek thought." In recent surveys Eriugena receives much more attention and an attempt is made to place him in the intellectual tradition of the West. See, e.g., Michael Haren, *Medieval Thought: The Western Intellectual Tradition from Antiquity to the 13th Century* (London: Macmillan, 1985), 72–82; John Marenbon, *Early Medieval Philosophy (480–1150): An Introduction* (1983; rev. ed., London: Routledge, 1988), 53–70. Still, under the subheading *John Scottus and the Greeks* Marenbon applies the term "anomalous" to the *Periphyseon* (59).

3. See Umberto Eco, *The Open Work,* trans. Anna Cancogni (Cambridge: Harvard University Press, 1989), 1–23. On p. 21 Eco describes "openness" in three ways: (1) works characterized by the invitation to *make the work* together with the author, (2) works which, though organically completed, are "open" to a continuous generation of internal relations which the addressee must uncover and select in the act of perceiving the totality of incoming stimuli, and (3) every work of art is effectively open to a virtually unlimited range of possible readings, each of which causes the work to acquire new vitality in terms of one particular taste, or perspective, or personal performance. While the first definition applies specifically to modern musical compositions, so-called works in movement, it is definition 2 (and perhaps 3) that I want to apply to the *Periphyseon.* I am indebted

to M. B. Pranger of the University of Amsterdam for the application of the term "open work" to the study of medieval theology.

4. See Johannis Scotti, *De divina praedestinatione liber (Praed.)*, ed. G. Madec, CCCM 50 (Turnhout: Brepols, 1978).

5. For an analysis of this interplay, see Willemien Otten, *The Anthropology of Johannes Scottus Eriugena* (Leiden: E. J. Brill, 1991), 48–60.

6. See G. H. Allard, "La structure littéraire de la composition du *De divisione naturae*," in *The Mind of Eriugena*, Papers of a Colloquium, Dublin, 14–18 July 1970, ed. J. J. O'Meara and L. Bieler (Dublin: Irish University Press, 1973), 147–157. On p. 147 Allard states: "Tout se passe en effet comme si l'auteur du *De divisione* avait voulu élaborer un large commentaire des trois premiers chapitres de la Génèse et instaurer, à l'exemple de ses prédécesseurs, son propre *Hexameron*."

7. Gilson calls the *Periphyseon* "une exégèse philosophique de l'Ecriture sainte." See E. Gilson, *La philosophie au moyen âge: Des origines patristiques à la fin du XIVe siècle*, 2d ed. (Paris: Payot, 1986), 204. Whereas I previously saw Gilson as advocating a position similar to Allard's, upon rereading his remarks, I view him as ultimately dealing with Eriugena in the scholastic framework of reason vis-à-vis faith. See Gilson, *La philosophie*, 202–204; Otten, *Anthropology*, 100, n. 48.

8. See P I, introduction, p. 5. Sheldon-Williams seems to think that an essay in dialectic dealing with the four forms of nature served as the initial stage of the *Periphyseon*'s composition. With regard to this volume's theme, it is important to note Sheldon-Williams's comment that in this original essay, preserved in book I, Eriugena did not use Greek sources.

9. I have previously analyzed the conjunction of different lines of development in the *Periphyseon* in W. Otten, "The Role of Man in the Eriugenian Universe: Dependence or Autonomy," in *Giovanni Scoto nel suo tempo: L'organizzazione del sapere in età carolingia*, ed. C. Leonardi and E. Menestò (Spoleto: Centro italiano di studi sull'alto medioevo, 1989), 595–609. Instead of the conjunction of the epistemological and the ontological levels, I focus there on the interplay of the logical and the historical lines of development in the *Periphyseon* (596–599).

10. Eriugena's continuous shifts of emphasis in his argument are due to the fact that his rational investigation of nature is in the form of a "dialectical disputation." For this, see D. O'Meara, "L'investigation et les investigateurs dans le *De divisione naturae* de Jean Scot Erigène," in *Jean Scot Erigène et l'histoire de la philosophie*, ed. R. Roques (Paris: Editions du C.N.R.S., 1977), 232–233. See also Guy H. Allard, "Quelques remarques sur la *disputationis series* du *De divisione naturae*, in *Jean Scot Erigène*, 211–224. Allard views the *Periphyseon*'s dialectical method exclusively as Eriugena's implementation of the arts of the

trivium. Allard and D. O'Meara do not comment on the ontological ramifications of Eriugena's use of dialectic.

11. A case in point is Eriugena's discussion of the categories in book I. Scholars hold widely different views on this issue. According to Marenbon, the categories are Carolingian school material, the exposition of which gives Eriugena a chance to develop a "negative ontology." According to Allard they are propaedeutic to book's I central question of the divine nature. According to Otten the categories, like the divine names, form part of Eriugena's discussion of negative theology allowing him to demonstrate the uncaused nature of God. See Marenbon, *From the Circle of Alcuin to the School of Auxerre: Logic, Theology and Philosophy in the Early Middle Ages* (Cambridge: Cambridge University Press, 1981), 67–87; Allard, "Quelques remarques," 219; Otten, *Anthropology,* 48–60.

12. See his preface to the translation of Maximus, in which he explains that Maximus has revealed some of the difficulties he had in reading Dionysius: "Exempli gratia, . . . qualis sit processio . . . Et iterum, ejusdem, divinae videlicet, bonitatis qualis sit reversio" (see PL 122:1195B–1196A).

13. See Eriugena's preface to his *Versio Dionysii* (PL 122:1036A), where he states about mystical theology: "Unde et in duas maximas logicae disciplinae dividitur partes, cataphaticam plane et apophaticam, id est in esse et non esse." See further again the preface to Maximus: "Quid κατα φατικὴν et ἀποφατικὴν dicam θεολογίαν, in quibus maxime praedicti beati Dionysii Areopagitae profundissima divinissimaque admiranda est disputatio" (PL 122:1196A).

14. Cf. Augustine's *De ordine* II, 16, 44: "summo illo deo, qui scitur melius nesciendo." Eriugena quotes this text in P I 510B (without recognizing Augustine as his source); II 597D (where he connects it with Dionysius's statement: "cuius ignorantia vera est sapientia"); III 687A (without acknowledgment); IV 771C (again connected with Dionysius's statement, without the names of either author). It seems Eriugena conflates Augustine's and Dionysius's statements into one concept of negative theology. See also *Praed.* XV, 9.

15. Eriugena mentions Basil a total of 22 times, 17 of which occur in book III. Of these 22 instances, Basil is twice brought up as brother to Gregory, the other times Eriugena makes reference to his *Hexaemeron*. See Goulven Madec, *Jean Scot et ses auteurs: Annotations érigéniennes* (Paris: Etudes augustiniennes, 1988), 31–32. Gregory of Nyssa is mentioned passim throughout the *Periphyseon*, though Eriugena confuses him with Gregory of Nazianzus. A more precise indication of his influence on Eriugena has been given by Jeauneau who mentions that Eriugena quotes roughly 25 percent of the text of his *De hominis*

opificio, which he had translated as *Sermo de imagine*, in P IV. For Eriugena's full translation of this work, see Maïeul Cappuyns, "Le *De imagine* de Grégoire de Nysse traduit par Jean Scot Erigène," *Recherches de théologie ancienne et médiévale* 32 (1965): 205–262.

16. See Maïeul Cappuyns, *Jean Scot Erigène: Sa vie, son oeuvre, sa pensée* (1933; reprint, Bruxelles: Culture et Civilisation, 1969), 128–232; E. Jeauneau, "Pseudo-Dionysius, Gregory of Nyssa, and Maximus the Confessor in the Works of John Scottus Eriugena," in *Carolingian Essays: Andrew W. Mellon Lectures in Early Christian Studies*, ed. Uta-Renate Blumenthal (Washington, D.C.: Catholic University of America Press, 1983), 137–149, reprint in Jeauneau, Etudes érigéniennes (Paris: Etudes augustiniennes, 1987), 175–187; idem, "Jean Scot Erigène et les *Ambigua ad Iohannem* de Maxime le Confesseur," in *Maximus Confessor*, ed. F. Heinzer and C. von Schönborn (Fribourg 1982), 343–364, reprint in Jeauneau, *Etudes érigéniennes*, 189–210; I. P. Sheldon-Williams, "The Greek Christian Platonist Tradition from the Cappadocians to Maximus and Eriugena," in *Cambridge History of Later Greek and Early Medieval Philosophy*, ed. A. H. Armstrong (Cambridge: Cambridge University Press, 1967), 421–533; idem, "Eriugena's Greek Sources," in *The Mind of Eriugena*, 1–14; René Roques, "Traduction ou interprétation? Brèves remarques sur Jean Scot traducteur de Denys," in *The Mind of Eriugena*, 59–76, reprint in R. Roques, *Libres sentiers vers l'érigénisme* (Roma: Edizione dell'Ateneo, 1975), 99–130. For Dionysius's influence on Eriugena, see also the chapters "Tératologie et théologie chez Jean Scot Erigène" and "*Valde artificialiter:* Le sens d'un contresens," in Roques, *Libres sentiers*, 14–43, 45–98.

17. For a comparison between Pseudo-Dionysius and Eriugena, see Thomas M. Tomasic, "The Logical Function of Metaphor and Oppositional Coincidence in the Pseudo-Dionysius and Johannes Scottus Eriugena," *Journal of Religion* 68 (1988): 364–367.

18. A particularly fine example is Jeauneau's analysis of Eriugena's handling of Gregory of Nyssa's division of the sexes. See Jeauneau, "La division des sexes chez Grégoire de Nysse et chez Jean Scot Erigène," in *Eriugena: Studien zu seinen Quellen*, ed. W. Beierwaltes (Heidelberg: Carl Winter, 1980), 33–54, reprint in Edouard Jeauneau, *Etudes érigéniennes*, 341–364.

19. See Marcia L. Colish, "John the Scot's Christology and Soteriology in Relation to His Greek Sources," *The Downside Review* 100 (1982): 138–150; the quotation is found on p. 148. For reactions to this statement, see Bernard McGinn, "Eriugena mysticus," in *Giovanni Scoto nel suo tempo*, 241, n. 11; and Donald F. Duclow, "Dialectic and Christology in Eriugena's *Periphyseon*," *Dionysius* 4 (1980): 99.

20. See above, n. 2.

21. On Augustine, see J. J. O'Meara, "Eriugena's Use of Augustine in His Teaching of the Return of the Soul and the Vision of God," in *Jean Scot Erigène et l'histoire de la philosophie*, 191–200; idem, *"Magnorum Virorum Quendam Consensum Velimus Machinari* (804D): Eriugena's Use of Augustine's *De Genesi ad litteram* in the *Periphyseon*," in *Eriugena: Studien zu seinen Quellen*, 105–116; idem, "Eriugena's Use of Augustine," *Augustinian Studies* 11 (1980): 21–34. See further R. Russell, "Some Augustinian Influences in Eriugena's *De divisione naturae*," in *The Mind of Eriugena*, 31–40; Brian Stock, "Observations on the Use of Augustine by Johannes Scottus Eriugena," *Harvard Theological Review* 60 (1967): 213–220; idem, *"Intelligo me esse:* Eriugena's 'Cogito'," in *Jean Scot Erigène et l'histoire de la philosophie*, 327–336. On Augustine and Bede, see Stock, "In Search of Eriugena's Augustine," in *Eriugena: Studien zu seinen Quellen*, 85–104. On Boethius, see Giulio d'Onofrio, "Giovanni Scoto e Boezio: Trace degli 'Opuscula sacra' e della 'Consolatio' nell'opera eriugeniana," *Studi medievali* 3, 21 (1980): 707–752; idem, "A proposito del 'magnificus Boethius': un'indagine sulla presenza degli 'Opuscula sacra' e della 'Consolatio' nell'opera eriugeniana," in *Eriugena: Studien zu seinen Quellen*, 189–200.

22. I have argued this position in a paper presented at the Ninth International Conference of Patristics, 19–22 August 1992. Starting from the traditional premise that the *Periphyseon* marks a new stage in Eriugena's career because of the influence of the Greeks, I argue there that one should not overemphasize the Greek influence but analyze *both* Eriugena's Greek and his Latin influences within the framework of the *Periphyseon*. The text of this paper will be forthcoming in *Studia Patristica*, vols. 24–28, 28:217–224.

23. Though Eriugena usually sees allegorical exegesis as a Greek phenomenon, an exception to this rule is formed by Ambrose, who is ranked more as a Greek theologian, on a par with Origen, than a Latin one. For Eriugena's specific references to Ambrose, see G. Madec, "Jean Scot et les Pères latins: Hilaire, Ambroise, Jérôme et Grégoire le Grand," in *Jean Scot et ses auteurs: Annotations érigéniennes* (Paris: Etudes augustiniennes, 1988), 56–62.

24. See John J. Contreni, "The Irish 'colony' at Laon during the time of John Scottus," in *Jean Scot Erigène et l'histoire de la philosophie*, 59–68; John Marenbon, *From the Circle of Alcuin;* J. J. O'Meara, *Eriugena* (Oxford: Clarendon Press, 1988), 1–15, 198–212; idem, "Eriugena's Immediate Influence," in *Eriugena Redivivus*, ed. W. Beierwaltes (Heidelberg: Carl Winter, 1986), 13–25. In his earlier work, Jeauneau has also focused on Eriugena's Carolingian contacts, see, e.g., his 1972 article "Les écoles de Laon et d'Auxerre au IXe siècle," reprint in Edouard Jeauneau, *Etudes érigéniennes*, 55–84.

25. See Marenbon, *From the Circle of Alcuin,* 12–29, 67–87.

26. See Gangolf Schrimpf, *Das Werk des Johannes Scottus Eriugena im Rahmen des Wissenschaftsverständnisses seiner Zeit: Eine Hinführung zu Periphyseon* (Münster: Aschendorff, 1982), 132–148.

27. In fact, the point of Eriugena's treatise on predestination is to show that divine predestination ought not to be seen as direct intervention, as it cannot be separated from creation. Cf. *Praed.* III, 1: "Non enim deo aliud est velle, aliud praedestinare, quoniam omne quod fecit praedestinando voluit et volendo praedestinavit. Multimodas etiam voces quibus deum suum rationalis anima significare appetit unum atque idem innuere, hoc est ipsam ineffabilem creatoris essentiam, quamvis nominum quaedam relative dicantur."

28. Both Cappuyns and J. J. O'Meara situate Eriugena's views on predestination in the context of the controversy surrounding the historical debate rather than analyzing it from a more systematic theological perspective. See Cappuyns, *Jean Scot Erigène,* 102–127, and J. J. O'Meara, *Eriugena,* 32–50.

29. While Eriugena's dialectical method in the *Periphyseon* has been extensively analyzed, the *De divina praedestinatione* has overall received less attention. A good analysis of Eriugena's method and its consequences in this early work is found in Schrimpf, *Das Werk des Johannes Scottus Eriugena,* 84–131. I have not been able to consult G. d'Onofrio, *Fons scientiae: La dialettica nell'Occidente tardo-antico* (Naples, 1986), 277–320, on Eriugena's use of logic in the *De divina praedestinatione.*

30. See *Praed.* XVIII, 1: "Errorem itaque saevissimum eorum qui venerabilium patrum maximeque sancti Augustini sententias confuse ac per hoc mortifere ad suum pravissimum sensum redigunt, ex utilium disciplinarum ignorantia, quas ipsa sapientia suas comites investigatricesque fieri voluit, crediderim sumpsisse primordia, insuper etiam graecarum litterarum inscitia, in quibus praedestinationis interpretatio nullam ambiguitatis caliginem gignit."

31. Of the two divisions of nature found in the prologue to the *Periphyseon,* Eriugena ranks the first (that into *things that are,* i.e., which succumb to the human mind or the senses, and *things that are not,* i.e., which transcend the human mind or senses) as superior to the second, see P I 441A–442A. For an analysis of these two divisions as well as their interrelatedness, see W. Otten, *Anthropology,* 7–39.

32. See P II 546B–C: "Mihi autem multorum sensus consideranti nil probabilius nil verisimilius occurrit quam ut in praedictis sanctae scripturae verbis (scil. In principio fecit deus caelum et terram), significatione videlicet caeli et terrae, primordiales totius creaturae causas quas pater in unigenito suo filio qui principii appellatione nominatur ante omnia quae condita sunt creaverat intelligamus. . . ."

33. This commentary starts in P III 690B. In P III 693C the Master and his Student embark on a discussion of the second and following days of creation. At this point the Master states his explicit preference for historical exegesis: "Transeamus igitur ad secundi diei considerationem. Ac prius dicendum quod de allegoricis intellectibus moralium interpretationum nulla nunc nobis intentio est, sed de sola rerum factarum creatione secundum historiam pauca disserere deo duce conamur." See also P III 705A–706C, passim.

34. After a brief summary of the preceding three books, Eriugena begins his exegesis of the sixth and last day in P IV 743C, stating that this marks the beginning of the return. All elements of the sixth day are explained with regard to human nature, which thus becomes a kind of microcosm. See below, n. 38. The fullest statement of this can be found in P IV 755B: "Constat enim inter sapientes in homine universam creaturam contineri." One should note, however, that while Eriugena's method in the early parts of book IV can loosely be called "spiritual" or "allegorical," it is only after P IV 815C that Eriugena develops a more technical allegory, in which he equates paradise with human nature. On Eriugena's exegesis of paradise, see R. R. Grimm, *Paradisus Coelestis, Paradisus Terrestris: Zur Auslegungsgeschichte des Paradieses im Abendland bis um 1200* (München: Wilhelm Fink, 1977), 111–120.

35. The culmination of Eriugena's allegorical exegesis can be found in the beginning of book V, where he interprets the words with which God announces Adam's expulsion from paradise as nothing other than a divine promise for his return, see P V 859C–860B. Thus, though the return process sets in in book IV, book V marks what could be called the "return proper" of the *Periphyseon*.

36. See P IV 790C–D: "Ac per hoc quadam ratione per humanae naturae consequentiam totus homo ad imaginem Dei factus non incongrue dicitur, quamvis proprie et principaliter in solo animo imago subsistere intelligatur."

37. Eriugena uses Maximus's scheme of division and unification twice, see P II 529C–536A and P V 893B–C.

38. See P IV 743C: "Quartus hic, ab operibus sextae propheticae contemplationis de conditione universitatis inchoans, reditum omnium in eam naturam, quae nec creat nec creatur, consideraturus, finem constituat." In 744C Eriugena starts explaining Gen. 1:24–26.

39. For Maximus's definition of man as *officina omnium*, see P II 530D: "Nulla enim creatura est a summo usque deorsum quae in homine non reperiatur, ideoque officina omnium iure nominatur." It is interesting to note that the term itself is used only once in the final two books of the *Periphyseon*, namely, P V 893C.

40. See P IV 768B–778A. For an analysis of these chapters, see Jorge J. E. Gracia, "Ontological Characterization of the Relation Between Man and Created Nature in Eriugena," *Journal of the History of Philosophy* 16 (1978): 155–166; Dermot Moran, "*Officina omnium* or *Notio quaedam intellectualis in mente divina aeternaliter facta:* The Problem of the Definition of Man in the Philosophy of John Scottus Eriugena," in *L'homme et son univers au moyen âge,* ed. C. Wenin, 2 vols. (Louvain-la-Neuve, 1986), 1:195–204; C. Steel, "La création de l'univers dans l'homme selon Jean Scot Erigène," in *L'homme et son univers,* 1:205–210.

41. Cf. P IV 768B. See also the Student's preceding remark which amounts to his rationale for this definition: "Imo vero intelligo, non aliam esse substantiam totius hominis, nisi suam notionem in mente artificis, qui omnia, priusquam fierent, in seipso cognovit; ipsamque cognitionem substantiam esse veram, ac solam eorum, quae cognita sunt, quoniam in ipsa perfectissime facta et aeternaliter et immutabiliter subsistunt."

42. See P IV 770A: "Itaque si notio illa interior, quae menti inest humanae, rerum quarum notio est, substantia constituitur, consequens, ut et ipsa notio, qua seipsum homo cognoscit, sua substantia credatur."

43. See P IV 777A–B: Mag. "Quare ergo unusquisque mox, ut per generationem in hunc mundum provenerit, non seipsum cognoscit? Disc. Poenam praevaricationis naturae in hoc manifestari non temere dixerim. Nam si homo non peccaret, in tam profundam sui ignorantiam profecto non caderet."

44. In P IV 770C the Student asks the Master how these two definitions can be reconciled: "Numquid paulo superius ad purum deduximus hominis definitionem, dicentes, homo est notio quaedam intellectualis, in mente divina aeternaliter facta? Et si ita est, quomodo illa notio, qua homo seipsum cognoscit, substantia sua sit, si praedicta definitio non temere statuta est?" While the Master first explains these two definitions as representing a double perspective on human nature, i.e., from the angle of the causes and that of the effects, in P IV 777A–D he explains the difference between human nature as cause vs. effect by adducing the factor of human sin. For a fuller analysis of these chapters, see also Otten, *Anthropology,* 172–189.

45. P IV 777D. The full quotation (P IV 777C–D) runs as follows: "Mag. Inerat ergo humanae naturae potentia perfectissimam sui cognotionem habendi, si non peccaret. Disc. Nil verisimilius. Casus quippe illius maximus et miserrimus erat, scientiam et sapientiam sibi insitam deserere, et in profundam ignorantiam suimet et Creatoris sui labi, quamvis appetitus beatitudinis, quam perdiderat, etiam post

casum in ea remansisse intelligatur, qui in ea nullo modo remaneret, si seipsum et Deum suum omnino ignoraret."

46. See *Praed.* I, XVIII.

47. See, e.g., *Praed.* XI, 4–6 where Eriugena uses the same quotes from Augustine as Gottschalk did to contradict Gottschalk's view of double predestination. Eriugena points out that one needs to take account of the *genus locutionum* of Augustine's discourse.

48. See above, n. 27.

49. See esp. *Praed.* X, 1: "Restat considerare locum qui, ut praediximus, a dialecticis et rhetoricis entimema vocatur, a grammaticis vero κατ'ἀντιφρασιν, et est omnium argumentorum signorumque verbalium nobilissimus." On Eriugena's use of enthymema, see J. J. O'Meara, *Eriugena*, 42–46.

50. An interesting way of connecting Eriugena's methodology to his ontology or cosmology in this early work is put forth by Marta Cristiani, who sees the notion of *lex* as central to Eriugena's argument in the *On Divine Predestination.* See M. Cristiani, "La notion de loi dans le *De Praedestinatione* de Jean Scot," in *Jean Scot Erigène et l'histoire de la philosophie*, 284–288.

51. See Jean Devisse, *Hincmar: Archevêque de Reims 845–882* (Genève: Librairie Droz, 1975), 1:126, 133, 150 n. 177. According to Devisse, Eriugena emphasizes the immutability of God, a point which he has in common with his opponent Gottschalk but in which he differs from Hincmar. On p. 126 he states: "Pour Augustin et pour Gottschalk qui le suit sur ce point clairement et fidèlement, pour Jean Scot Erigène par d'autres approches, les réalités les plus vraies se situent au plan de Dieu, non à celui de l'homme. . . . Dieu seul a une totale réalité d'existence puisqu'il est immuable." See also J. J. O'Meara, *Eriugena*, 47, where it is mentioned that Eriugena thought in terms of God, not of man, which was uncommon in the ninth century.

52. See *Praed.* II, 2: "Recte ergo dicitur omnis praedestinatio praescientia, non omnis praescientia praedestinatio, ut intelligamus quod est praescire, hoc est praedestinare, et quod est praedestinare, hoc est praescire; unius enim eiusdemque substantiae sunt, divinae videlicet, et naturae."

53. John Marenbon deserves credit for his attempt to connect Eriugena's earlier to his later work. His point is quite different from mine in that he wants to prove that in book V of the *Periphyseon* Eriugena, apparently under the influence of the criticisms that were made by his opponents, comes to modify the positions he had advocated in the *On Divine Predestination.* Thus Marenbon's point is to show that Eriugena was involved in a dialogue with his contemporar-

ies. See Marenbon, "John Scottus and Carolingian Theology," in *Charles the Bald: Court and Kingdom,* ed. Margaret T. Gibson and Janet L. Nelson (1981; rev. ed., Aldershot: Variorum, 1990), 303–304, 314–323.

54. My paragraph here is essentially a summary of *Praed.* IV, 6.

55. See *Praed.* VIII, 9: "Hoc ergo, nisi fallor, prolixae ratiocinationis ambitu confectum est causas omnium recte factorum quibus ad coronam iustae beatitudinis pervenitur in libero humanae voluntatis arbitrio, praeparante ipsum ipsique cooperante gratuito divinae gratiae multipliceque dono, constitutas esse; malefactorum vero, quibus in contumeliam iustae miseriae ruitur, in perverso motu liberi arbitrii suadente diabolo principalem radicem esse fixam."

56. See *Praed.* VIII, 6–8. Unlike Marenbon, who points out the differences between these two chapters, but in apparent accordance with J. J. O'Meara, I want to emphasize their connection here, thus tracing a certain consistency in the development of Eriugena's argument. See esp. *Praed.* VIII, 7: "Qui motus merito vocatur liberum arbitrium nostrae voluntatis, quoniam potestati nostrae subiectus est. Possemus quippe pro nostro iudicio recto cursu eum dirigere, possemus cohibere. Unde igitur haberemus talem motum et talem potentiam, nisi a deo qui nobis largitus est hoc proprium quod esset et nostrae naturae non minimum bonum et creatoris laudibile donum." Cf. Marenbon, "John Scottus and Carolingian Theology," 309, n. 33; J. J. O'Meara, *Eriugena,* 41.

Dialectical Use of Authority in the *Periphyseon*

J. C. MARLER

IN THE ANCIENT AND MEDIAEVAL PERIODS, especially after the formation of schools, much concern is evident among philosophers and theologians, and their scholiasts and commentators, to anchor their writings in the authoritative weight of doxographic traditions. And, to the student of these periods, the concept of *auctoritas* most often seems inseparable from an accumulation of teachers and texts which, in developing over time, forms the genius of a tradition.

Traditions, however, are fragile; and their participants must sometimes resort to fictions and myths as a way of mending the breaks in time upon which a succession of teachers and texts, and the authority it conveys, may have faltered and failed. Of such devices in mythology as may conjure a tradition, an instance can be found in the "golden chain" (*ἡ χρυσή σειρά*), the dynastic allegory in reference to which the Athenian heirs to the school endowed by Plutarch the Great (*ὁ μέγας*, d. c. 431) could ornament themselves with the titular conceit of "successors" (*οἱ διάδοχοι*) not only to the founding scholarch but also to the "divinely inspired" (*ἔνθεος*) philosophy of Plato.[1]

A more noteworthy example of fabricated authority is furnished by Pseudo-Dionysius the Areopagite (fl. 500) who, with his invention of Hierotheus the Thesmothete, makes the Plutarchean *διάδοχοι*, especially Proclus (c. 410–485), to have been, symbolically and collectively, the protevangelist of Athens.[2] Proclus, his tutor, and his auditors, as is well known, bore a considerable animus toward the Christian empire and, as symbolized in the *corpus dionysiacum*, their import to Christianity, and to its *magisterium*, was best expressed by Ronald F. Hathaway: "the *Corpus* had a comprehensive and irreversible effect on the Christian traditions which it mimics; in vicariously promoting a ghostly Neoplatonist Succession the works of Ps.-Dionysius, especially the *Letters, re-found the Church's Apostolic Succession* upon a total literary innovation."[3] By means of the innovation, which many were to accept as history, Pseudo-Dionysius could insinuate the very words, as well as the doctrines, of the Plutarchean διάδοχοι with the semblance of Christian authority and, in so doing, would reconstruct their philosophy as an ingredient of civil religion. Even if the *corpus dionysiacum* did not succeed, as its author is likely to have wished, in removing the grounds for dispute between opposing points of view, its ease of passage to Christian wisdom seems proof enough that, in the logic of history, fallacies are axiomatic, and, in the whole catalogue of fallacies by which history is afflicted, none is more effective than *argumentum ad verecundiam*.[4]

In the logic, not of pragmatic history, but of the sciences, the relation between authority and truth is accidental, and arguments from authority are no measure of valid reasoning. But it was John the Scot, the major translator of Pseudo-Dionysius, who, for the early Middle Ages in Atlantic Europe, made most explicit the need of truth in the reasoning of all authorities. And though, by his account, the authoritative and the true differ from each other as contingency from eternity, Eriugena esteems the authority which is conversant with truth and which, as the conservator of any truth, is the bond in history of truths and traditions.

In *Periphyseon* book II, Eriugena reflects upon the controverted *Filioque* by which the Carolingian bishops were opponents of the Oriental patriarchs, dividing the Church and its creed. He does not mention the document, known in modern scholarship as the *Libri Carolini* (= *LC*), the original of which is preserved in MS lat. 7207 at the Biblioteca Vaticana, but it provides the best evidence, in the generation before Eriugena, of Carolingian hostility toward theological learning among the Greeks.[5]

The *LC* were composed in the name of Charlemagne (742–814) by Theodulf of Orleans (d. c. 820) to refute the acts of the Second Nicene Council (787) which the Empress Irene (c. 752–803), in her capacity as regent on behalf of Constantine VI (*Flavius*, 771–c. 797), had summoned for the express purpose of reinstating, throughout the Church, the veneration of images. As can be seen from the manuscript at the Bibliothèque de l'Arsenal (MS 663, fol. 3v), in which the *LC* are dated, Theodulf was at work on the text no later than three years after the council, under the guidance of

Tarasius (c. 745–806), the patriarch of Constantinople, had submitted its proceedings to Pope Hadrian I (pope 772–795).[6] Since it was by this pope that the Carolingian bishops were informed of the *acta concilii*, it was to him, in reply, that Charlemagne sent the *capitula* of the *LC* and, later, the text in its entirety.

The *LC* are an iconoclastic polemic which Ann Freeman, their principal modern expositor, has called "the most ambitious of its age" and the "*Summa* of Carolingian thought."[7] But, in her opening study published in 1957 of Bib. Vat. MS lat. 7207, she remarked that the theological outlook of the *LC* is "parochial" and shows the "Western inability to deal with the subtleties of Eastern argument."[8] For the author of the *LC*, and his Carolingian editors and correctors, Latinity is the criterion of faith, and on that basis, ignorance of Christian religious teachings in the Greek language—like those of Gregory of Nyssa (332–c. 398), to whom a chapter is devoted—seems a virtue to be boasted.[9]

At the beginning of book III, the faith of Charlemagne is summarized by the creed which appears in the Vatican manuscript (fol. 117v–119v) as an interpolation cited on the authority of Jerome (c. 340–420). Since it does not predicate the *Filioque,* or any equivalent formula in respect of the Holy Spirit, its use against Tarasius, for whom the Spirit proceeds from the Father through (δι', *per*) the Son, must be problematic.[10] When the procession of the Holy Spirit is discussed in *LC* III.3, no reference is made to the creed at all. The armaments of scripture, and not any *confessio fidei catholicae*, are deployed against Tarasius to prove that *ex Patre procedentem*, as the creed of Charlemagne plainly asserts, really means *ex Patre et Filio procedentem.*[11] Even so, it turned out well that neither the pope nor the patriarchs would conform themselves to all that Charlemagne and his theological entourage saw fit to recommend. After the end of the Carolingian epoch, the *LC* were to vanish from history until their recovery and subsequent publication in 1549 by Jean II du Tillet (c. 1510–1570), the future bishop of St. Brieuc and, later, of Meaux, from the manuscript at Paris (Arsenal, MS lat. 663) which, in the middle of the ninth century, had been transcribed for Hincmar (806–882), the archbishop of Rheims. And it was Cesare Baronio (1538–1607), the cardinal-prefect of the Biblioteca Vaticana, who in 1596 published his finding of a Latin confession, the same as expounded in the *LC,* among the papers of Pope Zosimus (pope 417–418) in the *libellus* which

Pelagius (c. 354–430) had addressed to Pope Innocent I (pope 401–417).[12] The faith of Charlemagne, as scholarship now could prove, was not altogether dependent upon Jerome.

Although the hagiographic conflation of St. Dionysius the Areopagite (d. c. 95) with St. Denis of France (d. c. 272), brought about by Hilduin (d. 840) after finding in Pseudo-Dionysius a theologian who could be Gallican as well as Greek, was an opening of sorts to Christendom in the East, the Eriugenian synthesis of Greek and Latin traditions stands by itself as an ecumenical theology.[13] Eriugena, in his *Periphyseon*, looked beyond the division of Christian authority between Greeks and Latins to seek the only tradition, and its underlying principles, which all must have in common. In doing so, he undertook a theory of *auctoritas* which, among the philosophical achievements of the early Middle Ages, deserves the acknowledgment of modern scholarship.

In *Periphyseon* II, Eriugena defers to the authority of Maximus the Confessor (c. 580–662) to find support for his own analysis of the structure of all authorities, distinguishing them by divine origins and historical results: "Sancti . . . qui multa diuinorum mysteriorum ex his qui pedisequi et ministri fuerunt uerbi et inde immediate eorum quae sunt eruditi scientiam per successionem per eos qui ante se erant in se ipsos distributa accipiunt. . . ."[14]

Eriugena interprets this text, which he had translated from the *Ambigua,* to mean that authority in perfect doctrine (*perfecta doctrina*) has proceeded in history from the Word made flesh to the disciples and apostles and that, from them, its movement through successors (*per . . . successores*) has settled into the tradition in which Maximus himself participates. Furthermore, Eriugena defends the purity of this tradition by assuming each of its moments to have descended immediately (*immediate*) from its precedents so as to generate a continuum (*nulla alia auctoritate interposita*).[15] Including, as it does, the scriptures and the creed, it is the temporal extension of the Catholic faith.

Apart from the Catholic faith, in which Eriugena finds the *expositores diuinarum scripturarum* upon whom he defines his orthodoxy, the *Periphyseon* draws upon the *eruditi saecularium litterarum,* that is, from the philosophers and natural scientists of pre-Christian antiquity, both Greek and Roman. And, among these worldly *eruditi,* Eriugena numbers the poet Virgil.[16]

Biblical, apostolic, and patristic authority is founded upon the revelation of God to man and is signified throughout the *Periphyseon* with the epithet *sanctus*. In contrast, and in distinction from the saintly, philosophical traditions are determined by the guidance of "right reason" (*recta ratio, uera ratio*).[17] Between these traditions, the differences are not strictly historical but also refer to matters of principle.

Among the saints and their expositors, the nature of *auctoritas* is, for Eriugena, illustrated most clearly by Pseudo-Dionysius in reference to the scriptures from which we obtain the positive knowledge of God. But, as also pertaining to a knowledge of God, Pseudo-Dionysius shows the path of reason to be that of systematic negativity.[18] Reason, therefore, cannot be so authoritative as the positive content of scripture; Eriugena, quite simply, does not employ *auctoritas* as a term by which to identify *uera ratio*.

Constituted as it is in the tradition of faith descended from the scriptures, authority is not to be contradicted.[19] But, since reason, like authority, also has claims to divine origination, Eriugena denies that *uera auctoritas* can be in conflict with *recta ratio*.[20] He is careful, then, to emphasize that rational investigation of the natures of things (*sensibilium rerum notitia ad intelligibilium intelligentiam*) has the sanction of scriptural authority.[21] For Eriugena, it is in the agreement of reason and authority that the whole power of discovering truth remains permanently established.[22]

In right reason Eriugena acknowledges a principle or a power not subject to human opinion but which, as he understands it, discriminates among opinions to compel acceptance or rejection.[23] And reason, as expounded in the *Periphyseon*, is a species of life. It is differentiated by its objects and, as such, allows division into the subspecies of wisdom (*sapientia*) and science (*scientia*). Of these further divisions, wisdom is the primary.[24]

Wisdom, in the *Periphyseon*, is a kind of power (*uirtus*), the ability of the mind (*siue humanus siue angelicus*), to contemplate (*considerare*) its own eternal causes in God, whether viewed as the uncreated cause of every nature or as the primordial causes by which all of nature is divinely exemplified. And wisdom, by this account, is the synonym of theology (*theologia*).[25]

Science, as Eriugena would have it, is also a kind of power, but differing from wisdom by its application to the generable natures

which the divine exemplars have effected and which, in their mutability, are subject to the operations of intellect and sensation. At
this, the level of nature of changing things, Eriugena believes that
reason—taken as *scientia*—is the synonym of physics (*physica*).[26]

Theology, because of the eternity of its objects, is the leading
science. But in the context of Eriugenian wisdom, it seems neither
to be dogmatic nor scriptural. Expressing himself in terms with
which Pseudo-Dionysius could agree, Eriugena restricts theological wisdom to a state of being which should be called "mystical":
"Rationem participant sapientia et scientia, sapientiam uero soli
illi intellectus qui circa deum ultra omnem naturam uisibilium et
inuisibilium et extra se ipsos aeterno et ineffabili motu et circa rerum principia reuoluuntur."[27] Since he maintains that the second
person of the Trinity is the "wisdom which all the wise participate"
(*sapientia quam omnes sapientes participant*), there could be difficulty
for Eriugena in his saying of wisdom that it, like the species in a
genus, participates the higher principle of reason.[28] But, if the
logic of the *Periphyseon* be strictly followed, it will be seen that theology—as a *sapientia*—differs from *auctoritas* to the same extent as
reason, and in the same way.

In man, reasoning (*ratiocinatio*) begins with examples drawn
from nature and leads, eventually, to the highest objects of physics
and theology.[29] For the author of the *Periphyseon*, reasoning is
also devoted to that component of wisdom which, as is consistent
with the tradition of European science after Aristotle, is called
ἡ πρακτική (*actiua*), a knowledge exercised in pursuit of virtue and
for the removal of vice.[30] As Eriugena takes them into consideration, the practical, physical, and theological sciences are regu-
lated, but not defined, by the rational science (ἡ λογική), which
prescribes the laws of inquiry applicable in each. This rational science, or logic, is occupied with reasoning well and is the instrument of other sciences by its furtherance of their distinctive
techniques.[31] The method of dividing nature into genera and species, for example, and that of distinguishing history from the laws
of allegory (*leges allegoriae*) are among its contributions.[32]

In several passages of the *Periphyseon*, Eriugena alludes to those
by whom philosophy is done correctly (*recte, rite*), but he does
not place philosophy, however correct, in a univocal relationship
to other sciences. There are many instances in which, for Eriugena, "philosophy" means "natural philosophy" or physics; and

there are passages in which "philosophy" seems equated with theology.[33]

Like the history of *auctoritas*, philosophy constitutes a tradition of its own, the founder of which Eriugena identifies as Pythagoras.[34] But the fact that philosophy originated among the *pagani* gives Eriugena no reason to define it as a tradition from which the Christian *patres* should be excluded.[35] He names Basil, Gregory Nazianzen, Gregory of Nyssa, Augustine, and Pseudo-Dionysius as among the heirs in philosophy of Plato and Pliny Secundus;[36] and, by this means, he combines *uera ratio* and *auctoritas* in the same succession of persons.

It is certain, for Eriugena, that a difference has been made to philosophy by the Christian revelation, a historical fact which he notes in reference to questions about the eternity of matter.[37] Though some problems, especially those which can be decided only by reference to divine law (*haec omnia diuinis legibus . . . attribuenda sunt*), are outside the limits of philosophical conjecture, Eriugena believes that, since there is more to God and nature than human thought may contain, further inquiry is always possible.[38] Whatever, then, is not expressly forbidden by the scriptures to be questioned remains open to investigation.[39] And those by whom right reason is followed, whether saintly or secular, are always in agreement on fundamental matters of principle.[40]

With right reason as his criterion, Eriugena can distinguish the truly wise from those who only appear to be; and, among the authorities who command his admiration, he admits no basic differences.[41] When, for example, Augustine and Gregory of Nyssa seem not to agree upon the origin of the human body, Eriugena finds only that the explanation provided by Gregory is the nearer to being complete.[42] And, when Augustine and Paul seem not to be in accord on questions of angelic knowledge, Eriugena prefers to uphold the truth of both by taking the path which lies midway between them (*recta mediaque via*).[43]

Eriugena is sensitive to the differences separating Latin from Greek, not only in speech but also in faith.[44] But for him the differences are not essential. In context, thus, of the *Filioque* controversy, he argues that a mean can be found between the Latin and the Greek and, upon that middle ground, he expounds, not two creeds, one Latin and the other Greek, but a single creed in two modes. For the author of the *Periphyseon*, it suffices for the substance of faith that both its claimants are committed in speech—whether in Greek or in Latin—to the procession of the Spirit from the Father.[45] Because in the *Periphyseon* true authority and right reason are both in tendency to the same eternal Wisdom, doctrinal conflicts are always thought to be in reach of perfect settlement.[46] And the treatment given by Eriugena to the scriptures is the model showing how, in practical terms, reason is joined to authority.

As Eriugena makes plain, scripture is not always authoritative, at least not in its very letter, for its authority, especially concerning God as an ultimate nature, is determined not by the written letter but, instead, upon its unwritten allegorical content.[47] In the scriptures, the differences between word and allegory are placed—so Eriugena thinks—out of condescension to human weakness, on the principle that infants must have milk before meat.[48] And he applies the same principle to the patristic successors of Christian revelation.[49]

Because, as Eriugena believes, reason is at the discretion of no authority at all, it suffers no opposition of any kind from the literal sense of authoritative texts. The allegorical sense, which belongs to true authority, originates—as an objective datum—within the text itself; for Eriugena it is by no means the invention of any by whom the text is properly expounded. On the assumption of its agreement with right reason, true authority must always embody the principles of its true interpretation.[50]

In defense of his treatment of authority in the scriptures, Eriugena invokes the authority of Pseudo-Dionysius, who in the *De diuinis nominibus* reveals the logic to which oracular descriptions of ultimate principles are everywhere subject. From the premises given by Pseudo-Dionysius, Eriugena states his own conclusion: "Ratio uero in hoc uniuersaliter studet ut suadeat certisque ueritatis inuestigationibus approbet nil de deo proprie posse dici quoniam superat omnem intellectum omnesque sensibiles intelligibilesque significationes qui melius nesciendo scitur, cuius ignorantia uera est sapientia, qui uerius fideliusque negatur in omnibus quam firmatur."[51]

On the basis of scriptural authority, man learns what can be said of God; on the basis of right reason, man learns what should be denied. Since Eriugena takes his theology from Pseudo-Dionysius, however, ἡ ἀπόφασις is superior to ἡ κατάφασις. What agreement there can be between reason and authority is, therefore, determined on the side of reason. Although both, it is certain, are the products of divine wisdom (*diuina sapientia*), they are not equally bound together.[52] Reason, Eriugena argues, is the cause of true authority; and, upon reason, authority has no effect.[53]

Eriugena defines true authority as "nil . . . aliud . . . nisi rationis uirtute reperta ueritas et a sanctis patribus ob posteritatis utilitatem litteris commendata."[54] In relation, therefore, to authority, reason is both necessary and definitive; but, in its relation to right reason, authority is wholly contingent. If, as Eriugena means, true authority is no more than reason conserved in texts, authority— unlike reason—must be in bondage to time: "Rationem priorem esse natura, auctoritatem uero tempore didicimus. Quamuis enim natura simul cum tempore creata sit non tamen ab initio temporis atque naturae coepit esse auctoritas, ratio uero cum natura ac tempore ex principio rerum orta est."[55] Authority, understood as written precedent, is previous to every occasion in which it may be invoked; but reason, as prior by nature *ab initio temporis,* is neither older nor younger than time itself. By its exception to all precedents, and, as a result, by its exemption from transience, reason— and not authority—is the companion of eternity.[56]

Like the patristic writings, the letter of the scriptures is a product of time and, by its own account, was antedated by the patriarchs. It was not, therefore, on the basis of any scriptural authority that the faith of Abraham could have been inspired but, as seems evident to Eriugena, it was formed in the science of astronomy.[57] And if Eriugena means that Abraham should be taken as the model of faith, then it follows—according to the model—that faith must not be more consistent with the scriptures than with reason or with nature and, further, that no *auctoritas* precedes *scientia.*

On the basis of the division of theology by Pseudo-Dionysius into ἡ καταφατική and ἡ ἀποφατική, Eriugena treats the authority of the scriptures, and other authorities also, with a theory of textual hermeneutics in which the positive content of written words must yield to reason and, therefore, to negativity. For him, authority in the scriptures, like that in the Christian *patres,* often makes concessions to ignorance, but no one in pursuit of truth is likely to have any need of such literary concessions.[58] Neither the scriptures nor the *patres,* however, should be contradicted. For Eriugena the means of pursuing the truth are those—in fact—by which authority is explained away, that is, the laws of allegory.[59]

Authority, as Eriugena sees it, is not distinct from authorship, and, as noted before, authorities are found cited in the *Periphyseon* for the purpose of discerning among them a *recta mediaque via* toward the goal of a consensus among philosophers which adheres to right reason: "Vera enim auctoritas rectae rationi non obsistit neque recta ratio uerae auctoritati."[60] Like Pseudo-Dionysius, Eriugena intends to remove the grounds for dispute among factions, especially between Greek and Latin Christendom, and also between the masters of profane letters and the expositors of Christian scripture. To the extent that Eriugena aims at inquiry, his own citation of authorities cannot be for the sake of choosing sides.[61]

The use which Eriugena makes of authorities, including Pseudo-Dionysius upon whose authority he defines his use of authorities, bears some comparison to what Aristotle treated as dialectic (ἡ διαλεκτική). In the *Topics*, Aristotle understands dialectical reasoning to be that which proceeds from "generally accepted opinions" (ἔνδοξα), that is, from beliefs which are commended either by all or by most of the wise, or, at the very least, by the most notable and illustrious among them.[62] Dialectic, accordingly, is not demonstrative. It is, instead, a way of recapitulating the history of each science with a view to first principles:

> . . . being able to draw up the difficulties in the face of opposite views, we will observe in every one of them more easily the true and the false. This holds moreover in regard to the first principles in each science. For it is impossible to say anything about these on the basis of the proper principles of the science in question, since the principles in every case come first; and it is through the "commonly received notion" about each that we have to proceed in dealing with them. This is the proper or most appropriate function of dialectic. For dialectic, being an ability of scrutinizing, holds the path toward the principles of all scientific treatment.[63]

Unlike demonstrative reasoning, dialectic is introductory to science. But, for Aristotle, the dialectical preparations for any science are no less an ingredient of the sciences than the demonstrative syllogisms in which each of the sciences is proven.[64] What Aristotle meant by dialectic approximates what is taught in the present day and age as the history of science or, better still, as the history of philosophy.

Plato and Aristotle are both inclined to devalue authority against the truth which should be loved far more than Homer or even more than friends.[65] But, as Aristotle has it in the *Metaphysics,* because "the same thing may be known in many ways" (πολλαχῶς γάρ ἐπισταμένων τὸ αὐτό), dialectical reference to authority is always consistent with the aims of science.[66] Furthermore, because the sciences are found in the human, the being whose nature it is to have a history, it is upon history that the sciences must be built: "neither is anyone able to grasp the truth firmly enough nor does everyone fail to reach it, but each says something about the natures of things; and, though each by himself adds little or nothing to the truth, by the collection of it all, a great amount is produced."[67]

There is, so it appears to Aristotle, none among the men of science in whom the sciences are perfected, and, as a result, none in whom unconditional claims to authoritative knowledge may be endorsed or supported. But it is not only for attainments of truth that, for Aristotle, the history of any science deserves complete scrutiny: "It is just to give thanks not only to those whose opinions we share but also to those having expressed anything more superficial; for they also have added something—the habit of thought exercised before us."[68] Within the framework of dialectic, as Aristotle has portrayed it, every reference to authority is tested by truth, and, under the test of truth, there should be no objection to the wise employment of authorities.

With authority proceeding from reason, and not reason from authority, Eriugena conforms to what Aristotle required in a dialectical treatment of philosophical issues. In doing so, he adds a historical dimension to his own idea of dialectic, as he understood it in *Periphyseon* I, to distinguish what must be said properly from what can be said metaphorically in all the predicables of nature, the Aristotelian categories of natural things.[69]

Everything, however, that Eriugena means by *auctoritas* is even more than what can be found in authoritative texts. For him, it also connotes repression. Thus, in *Periphyseon* I, Nutritor counsels Alumnus that he should be intimidated by no authority from the exercise of a rational nature: "Nulla itaque auctoritas te terreat ab his quae rectae contemplationis rationabilis suasio edocet."[70] And, in another context, Alumnus describes to Nutritor the very type of authority by which reason is answered, not with reason, but with fear: "Edissere quaesso quodcunque de hac questione soluenda uidetur tibi uerisimilia neminemque uerearis quoquo modo ferat,

siue non intelligat quod dicas luce ueritatis repercussus, siue sper-
nat ueneno inuidiae corruptus, siue ueterum opinionum zelo
contentiosus."[71]

From these instances, it would appear that the author of the
Periphyseon had been chastened already at the hand of some authority and that, as a result, he was determined to conceal his own
voice behind a literary facade of voices in dialogue. By his earlier
work against Gottschalk on predestination, Eriugena had become
an object of controversy; and, before completing the *Periphyseon*,
he was to see his theses repudiated by the councils of Valence and
Langres. Though it would not be until 1210 that the Council of
Paris would condemn the *Periphyseon* itself, he must have anticipated such objections as could, and would, be made against it.[72]

Eriugena urges that the path of reason should be followed most
cautiously and most circumspectly (*cautissime ac uigilantissime*). So
that none in authority should be offended by the alliance of reason
with speech, the wise for whom right reason is the leading principle of discourse, and upon whom no authority has devolved,
must enclose their discussions among themselves.[73]

Similarly to Pseudo-Dionysius, Eriugena distinguishes the ignorant and uninstructed from those in pursuit of truth. Except under the guise of metaphor and allegory, he forbids the whole of
truth to be conveyed to any who yet remain in the childhood of
learning.[74]

For Eriugena, it is the Word made flesh, eternally the principle
of wisdom in nature, who is the mediator of reason and allegorical
discourse and who constitutes the aim of the wise and unwise
alike.[75] But the alliance between power and untruth to which the
Periphyseon makes glancing reference shows, as far as Eriugena can
judge, that Christendom has not kept pace with the perfections of
its founder.

In *Periphyseon* III, the Christ of transfiguration wears the ves-
ture not only of oracular letters but also of *sensibilia*. And Eriugena
typifies the meaning of *sensibilia*, as the wisdom having no need of
scripture, in the figure of Abraham.[76] Like the scriptures, sensible
things are the temporal products of their timeless reasons. The
sensibilia provoke knowledge, and, for the author of the *Periphyseon*, all knowledge tends toward divinity: "Vt enim per sensum
peruenitur ad intellectum ita per creaturam reditur ad deum."[77]

The senses, both the exterior powers of corporeal sensation and
the interior capacity of judging the *sensibilia*, are the site from

which human understanding returns to the ultimate cause it shares in common with all natures, both known and sensed.[78] The impermanence of sensible things proves them, like the letter of the scriptures, not to be the haven in which reason can come to rest; but, as theophanies by which the soul can be initiated to higher mysteries, they are no less indispensable.[79] Accordingly, when Eriugena begs for the rights of inquiry, his plea takes the form of an understated protest: "Et si duo uestimenta Christi sunt tempore transformationis ipsius candida sicut nix, diuinorum uidelicet eloquiorum littera et uisibilium rerum species sensibilis, cur iubemur unum uestimentum diligenter tangere, ut eum cuius uestimentum est mereamur inuenire, alterum uero, id est creaturam uisibilem, prohibemur inquirere, et quomodo et quibus rationibus contextum sit non satis uideo."[80] In this context, the operative phrase is *cur . . . prohibemur inquirere*. Perhaps considering that inquiry is forbidden by the protagonists of scripture, Eriugena takes his stand by inquiring upon the scriptures. And if, as he notes, it was permissible for Israel to plunder the idolatrous goods of Egypt, he should not be held at fault for any use of philosophical reasoning.[81]

In the minds of those who piously seek (*quaerentium*) and love their creator, it is the truth itself (*ueritas ipsa*) which, with its own intelligible voice, speaks in defense of truth.[82] The one by whom the truth is, in truth, pursued should not be concerned to advance his own authority but, instead, to advance the truth at the expense of his untrue beliefs. Thus, in the role of Nutritor, Eriugena retracts a number of his former beliefs and, while doing so, deplores what he takes to be the greatest evil: "Nulla enim peior mors est quam ueritatis ignorantia, nulla uorago profundior quam falsa pro ueris approbare, quod proprium est erroris."[83]

Subject, as they are, to limitations of time and place, no authorities are universal and all must fall short of the truth upon which, for the author of the *Periphyseon*, no limits can be imposed. Since it was for the good of a rational nature that the world (*mundus*) was created and since, in nature, *sensibilia* are the ground from which reason makes its progress, all men are able to participate truth under the guidance of reason, and, as far as possible, without the aid of any authority.[84]

To Eriugena, Pseudo-Dionysius is the *summus theologus* and it is upon his authority, more than any other, that the author of the *Periphyseon* criticizes human authority.[85] In the tradition of Pseudo-

108 J. C. Marler

Dionysius, Eriugena bends authority to reason in a way that renews the influence of Plato in Latin Christianity. And if, to Eriugena, Pseudo-Dionysius is the *summus theologus*, then it is also fitting that Plato should be *philosophorum summus*.[86] The author of the *Timaeus* had evidently left his mark upon the mind of Eriugena. Like the Chaldean patriarch gazing at stars, Plato, in the conduct of science, seemed to have found God.[87] With telling discretion, Eriugena alludes to the principal figure of his philosophical loyalties: "De Platone sileo, ne uidear sectam illius sequi. . . ."[88] But, rather than maintaining any diplomatic silence about the *summus* of philosophers, Eriugena goes on to commend his authority.[89]

Assuming from Pseudo-Dionysius the mantle of Platonic rationalism, Eriugena takes the side of such liberality in discourse as he thinks may transcend controversies, including the schism in Christendom between East and West. His use of authorities is consistent with Aristotelian principles of dialectical citation. In the apology at the end of book V which closes the *Periphyseon*, he makes it plain that until the Light has finally converted all darkness into light no man should be robbed of his own point of view.[90]

NOTES

I am grateful to the Institute for the Advanced Study of Religion of the Divinity School of the University of Chicago, the Center for Medieval Studies of the University of Notre Dame, and the Department of Theology of Loyola University of Chicago for the subventions which made it possible for me to present this study to the Eighth International Colloquium of the Society for the Promotion of Eriugenian Studies. Some of the material in this study was adapted from my dissertation, "The Logic of Ultimacy: Negativity and Unknowing in Pseudo-Dionysius the Areopagite and in Johannes Scottus Eriugena" (University of Toronto, 1988).

1. John Glucker, *Antiochus and the Late Academy* (Göttingen, 1978), 306–31. On Plutarch, cf. "τοῦ μεγάλου Πλουτάρχου," in Damascius Diadochus, *Damascii vitae Isidori reliquae*, ed. Clemens Zintzen (Hildesheim, 1967), 285, line 9. Proclus Diadochus, *Théologie platonicienne*, ed. H. D. Saffrey and L. G. Westerink (Paris, 1968), vol. 1 (I.2), 8, line 22.

2. On Hierotheus, for a different point of view, cf. I. P. Sheldon-Williams, "The Ps.-Dionysius and the Holy Hierotheus," *Studia Patristica* 8.2 in *Texte und Untersuchungen* 93 (1966): 108–45.

3. Ronald F. Hathaway, *Hierarchy and the Definition of Order in the Letters of Pseudo-Dionysius* (The Hague, 1969), 27. On the Christian empire, or Dominate (*dominatus*), see P. R. Coleman-Norton, *Roman State and Christian Church*, 3 vols. (London, 1966), 1:li–liii.

4. *Argumentum ad verecundiam*, the appeal to shame and, thus, *ad auctoritatem*, is an instance of *ignoratio elenchi*. On *ignoratio elenchi*, see Aristotle, *De sophistici elenchi* 5.167a21–168a33.

5. In scholarship, the *Libri Carolini* (*LC*) are also known as *Caroli magni capitulare de imaginibus*. In manuscript (Arsenal, MS 663, fol. 1r), it is called the OPUS ILLUSTRISIMI ET EXCELLENTIS-SIMI SEU SPECTABILIS VIRI CAROLI, NUTU DEI REGIS FRANCORUM, GALLIAS, GERMANIORUM ITALIAMQUE SIVE HARUM FINITAS PROVINTIAS DOMINO OPITULANTE RE-GENTIS, CONTRA SYNODUM, QUE IN PARTIBUS GRAETIAE PRO ADORANDIS IMAGINIBUS STOLIDE SIVE ARROGANTER GESTA EST. The standard—and somewhat defective—edition of this work was edited and published in fascicules from 1912 to 1924 by Hubert Bastgen in MGH, Leg. III, Conc. II, supp. The "working copy" of *LC* is Bib. Vat. MS lat. 7207, one of the most interesting Latin manuscripts, paleographically and codicologically, of the Carolingian epoch. I am grateful to Charles Ermatinger, Director of the Knights of Columbus Vatican Film Collection at St. Louis University, for the privilege of consulting the microfilm copy of this manuscript.

6. Bastgen, 3, line 36.

7. Ann Freeman, "Theodulf of Orleans and the *Libri Carolini*," *Speculum* 32 (1957): 665. This article was succeeded by her work in "Further Studies in the *Libri Carolini*," *Speculum* 40 (1965): 203–89; and in "Further Studies in the *Libri Carolini*," *Speculum* 46 (1971): 597–612.

8. Freeman (1957), 664.

9. *LC* II.17; in Bib. Vat. MS lat. 7207. fol. 83r.

10. To see how Tarasius understood the procession of the Holy Spirit, cf. G. B. Mansi, *Sacrorum Conciliorum Nova et Amplissima Collectio*, 31 vols. (Venice, 1759–93; reprint, Paris and Leipzig, 1901–27), 12:1122d, in the *actio tertia* of Nicaea II. Also, compare the Latin translation made by Anastasius, the papal librarian, of the Nicene-Constantinopolitan creed as proclaimed at Nicaea II. Anastasius made his translation well after the *LC* had been sent to Rome. He reads *qui ex patre filioque procedit* for "τὸ ἐκ τοῦ πατρὸς ἐκπορευόμενον," in Mansi, 13:375d–e and 376d–e.

11. *LC* III.3; in Bib. Vat. MS lat. 7207, fol. 122r–125v.

12. On Jean II du Tiller (du Tillay, Dutiller), cf. Ludwig Schmitz-Kallenberg, *Hierarchia Catholica Medii et Recentoris Aevi* 3 (Regensburg,

1923; reprint Padua, 1960): 140 and 240; Freeman (1957), 668; and the notice by Roman d'Amat in the *Dictionnaire de biographie française,* fasc. 70, ed. Roman d'Amat (Paris, 1969), 916–17. For the Pelagian *libellus,* cf. Cesare Baronio, *Annales Ecclesiastici* 7 (reprint, Paris, 1880): 92–94.

13. Cf. Hilduin, *Passio sanctissimi Dionysii,* PL 106:23–50.

14. "The saints ... who receive many of the divine mysteries handed down from those who were followers and ministers of the Word, and hence, who learned immediately the science of the things that are, by succession unto themselves through those who were before them": Eriugena (= Johannes Scottus), *Periphyseon* (= *De diuisione naturae*), 3 vols., ed. I. P. Sheldon-Williams (Dublin, 1968–81), II.529d–530a. Hereafter, the *Periphyseon* will be referred to as P. Citations from the first three books will be from the edition of Sheldon-Williams. Other citations will be from the edition of H. J. Floss, reprinted in PL 122. Eriugena here translates Maximus the Confessor from the *Ambigua* I.37; for this text in Maximus, "Περὶ διαφόρων ἀποριῶν τῶν ἁγίων Διονυσίου καὶ Γρηγορίου πρὸς Θωμᾶν τόν ἡγιασμένον," see the edition of Franz Oehler, reprinted in PG 91, at 1304d.

15. P II.530a.

16. P I.476c; II.550b; III.712b, 721c.

17. P I.511b; III.641c, 649c.

18. P I.455d–462d; 509b–513a. Pseudo-Dionysius the Areopagite, *De caelesti hierachia* (= *CH*), in PL 3:140c, 144c–d, 145a. *De divinis nominibus* (= *DN*), in PL 3:585b–588c, 596c, 597c, 716c, 724c, 893d, 980c–981b; and *De mystica theologia,* in PL 3:1032d–1033c. All of these texts, in PL 3, were edited by Balthasar Cordier.

19. P I.446a–b.

20. P I.511b–512b.

21. P III.723b–c.

22. P I.499b; III.636a, 636d, 641c.

23. P I.522b; II.603c, 604a, 605d; III.649c, 670c.

24. P III.629a.

25. Ibid.

26. P III.629a–b.

27. "Wisdom and science participate reason; but in fact only those intellects participate wisdom which, beyond every nature, visible and invisible, and beyond themselves, with a motion, eternal and ineffable, revolve about God and about the principles of things" (P III.629c–d).

28. P II.530a.

29. P III.651a; cf. Plato, *Republic* 6.510b–511a.

30. P III.705b.
31. Ibid.
32. P III.628c–d, 705a–c.
33. P II.602b, 604b–c, 608b–c; III.626b, 662b–c, 664c, 695b, 710a, 711b–c, 712b, 713c, 717c–d, 720d, 721a, 723a, 727a, 738c. On the theme of *recte philosophantes* (οἱ ὀρθῶς φιλοσοφοῦντες), cf. Plato, *Phaedo* 67e; and [Plato], *Ep.* 7.326c.
34. P III.722a.
35. P III.664c.
36. P III.735c–736b.
37. P III.664c; P V.888a–892c.
38. P III.669c–670a, 724c.
39. P III.723a–723d.
40. P III.649c, 662b, 695b.
41. P I.508d–509b.
42. P IV 804c–805b.
43. P I.446a–b.
44. P I.483c–484a, 502a–b, 507c–508a; II.567b–c, 601c–d; V.876c–878d.
45. P II.601b–613a.
46. P I.511a–512b.
47. P I.508d–509a.
48. P I.509a–b.
49. P III.708b–709b, 739b–739c; V.986a–987a. From these passages, it is clear that Eriugena understood the *patres* to have dissimulated their beliefs to accommodate the faith of those among their auditors and readers who were simple and uninstructed. The *patres* did not mean all they said nor did they say all they meant. For Eriugena, the difference between saying and meaning is most evident to the one whose faith is schooled in reason.
50. P I.509a–b.
51. "But in fact reason deliberates universally on this [the divine] in order to propose and to prove with certain inquiries about the truth that nothing can be said properly about God, because he is beyond every intellect and all sensible and intelligible meanings, who is better known by unknowing, of whom ignorance is true wisdom, who is more truthfully and faithfully denied in all things than is affirmed" (P I.510b; cf. *CH* 140c; and *DN* 585b–588c, 716c, 724c).
52. P I.510b–511a; IV.757c–758b.
53. P I.513b–c.
54. "... nothing ... other ... than the truth discovered by the power of reason and commended to writing by the holy fathers for the benefit of posterity" (P I.513b–c).

55. "We have learned that reason is prior by nature, but authority in time. For though nature was created together with time, authority did not commence at the beginning of nature and time, but reason came into being with nature and time from the beginning of things" (P I.513b).

56. P I.512b–513b.

57. P III.723d–724a. Although the tradition which says that Abraham was an astrologer probably depends upon Gen. 15:5, it may not be much older than the pseudepigraphical Book of Jubilees (c. 161–140 B.C.); cf. Jubilees 12:16–18 in the translation by O. S. Wintermute from Ge'ez, the precursor of Amharic, in *The Old Testament Pseudepigrapha,* ed. James H. Charlesworth (Garden City, N.J., 1985), 2:35–142. Jubilees has not survived in its Hebrew original, or in Greek translation. Also, see the fragments cited by Alexander Polyhistor of [pseudo-]Eupolemus in Eusebius, *Praeparatio evangelica,* ed. Karl Mras, in *Die griechischen Schriftsteller der ersten drei Jahrhunderte* 43.1–2 (Berlin, 1954–56), 9.17–18.

58. P I.509a, 511b–512b.

59. P I.508d–513c; III.705a–707b, 708b–709b.

60. "For true authority does not stand in the way of right reason, nor right reason in the way of true authority" (P. I.511b).

61. For comparison, see Plato, *Sophist* 64c–d.

62. Aristotle, *Topics* 1.100a30–100b23.

63. Aristotle, *Topics* 1.101a34–b4, trans. in Joseph Owens, *The Doctrine of Being in the Aristotelian Metaphysics* (Toronto, 1978), 205.

64. Aristotle, *Magna moralia* 1.1197a27–30; cf. Owens, 207.

65. Aristotle, *Nicomachean Ethics* 1.1096a14–18. Plato, *Republic* 10.595b–c; *Phaedo* 91b–c; *Charmides* 161c; *Sophist* 246d.

66. Aristotle, *Metaphysics* 3.996b14–18.

67. Aristotle, *Metaphysics* 2.993a31–993b4.

68. Aristotle, *Metaphysics* 2.993b12–15.

69. P I.463a–c.

70. "And so, let no authority deter you from the things which the reasonable counsel of right contemplation instructs you" (P I.511b).

71. "I beseech you to explain whatever seems to you like the truth about the question being treated, and let yourself be afraid of no one, whatever the manner he bears, whether—repelled by the light of truth—he does not understand what you say, or deformed by the poison of envy he despises you, or is combative out of zeal for outdated beliefs" (P III.700b).

72. Eriugena, *De praedestinatione,* in PL 122; John Marenbon, *Early Medieval Philosophy (480–1150): An Introduction* (London, 1983), 58; H. Denifle and E. Chatelain, *Chartularium Universitatis Parisiensis* 1:70;

M. T. d'Alverny, "Un fragment du procès des Amauriciens," *Archives d'histoire doctrinale et littéraire du moyen âge* 18 (1950–51): 325–36; Paolo Lucentini, "L'eresia di Amalrico," in *Eriugena Redivivus,* ed. Werner Beierwaltes (Heidelberg, 1987), 174–191.

73. P I.512b.

74. P I.508d–513c; III.693b, 705a–707b, 708b–709b.

75. P III.723d–724b.

76. Ibid.

77. "For as through sense we come to the intellect, so through the creature we return to God" (P III.723c).

78. P III.723b–c.

79. P III.651a, 689a–b, 723b–724b.

80. "And if there are, white as snow, the two vestments of Christ at the time of his transfiguration, namely, the letter of the divine oracles and the sensible species of visible things, why should we be urged diligently to touch the one garment, that we may be worthy to approach him whose clothing it is, but forbidden to seek out the other, that is, the visible creature, both how and for what reasons it was woven, I do not clearly see" (P III.723d–724a).

81. P III.724a; cf. Joseph De Ghellinck, *Le mouvement théologique du xiie siècle* (Bruges, 1948), 94–95.

82. P III.643d–644a.

83. "For there is no death worse than ignorance of the truth, no deeper chasm than to endorse the false for the true, which is the property of error" (P III.650a).

84. P III.723b–c.

85. P III.644b.

86. P III.728a. Aristotle, however, is not *summus* but *acutissimus;* cf. P I.463a.

87. P III.724b.

88. "About Plato, I am silent, lest I should seem to follow his sect" (P III.732d–733a).

89. P III.735c.

90. P III.627a–c; V.1021b–1022d.

The *Concordia* of Augustine and Dionysius: Toward a Hermeneutic of the Disagreement of Patristic Sources in John the Scot's *Periphyseon*

Giulio d'Onofrio

The definition of *VERA AUCTORITAS* that John the Scot introduces in the first book of *Periphyseon* in the course of a discussion of the relations of reason and authority in theology evidently relates only to doctrinal tradition of human origin (the Fathers of the Church and conciliar decisions) and not to the credibility of Sacred Scripture.[1] "For it seems to me that true authority is nothing else but the truth that has been discovered by the power of reason and set down in writing by the Holy Fathers for the use of posterity."[2]

In this way John the Scot clearly distances himself from the leading idea of the chapter of Augustine's *De ordine* that provides the thematic perspective for these pages.[3] Augustine makes the point there that "authority is in part divine, in part human, but that which is named divine is *true*, steady, and supreme," because "human authority often fails."[4] Eriugena, on the other hand, certainly considers the authority of the Fathers as also *true* (*vera*), especially because it appears as immediately based on a correct application of *ratio* which is superior in nature and dignity to every other way of knowing the truth. The principle that guarantees the genuineness of patristic sources also belongs to reason and not vice versa:

> For authority proceeds from true reason, but reason certainly does not proceed from authority. For every authority which is not upheld by true reason is seen to be weak, whereas true reason is kept firm and immutable by its own powers and does not require to be confirmed by the assent of any authority.[5]

115

There is not, then, a hierarchical relation but, rather, an identification of patristic authority and true reason. Many implicit confirmations of this programmatic idea are found in *Periphyseon*. At least once a patristic citation, from Maximus the Confessor, is introduced by Eriugena with an explicit identification between its teaching and that of true rationality.[6] The Church Fathers, therefore, have their authoritativeness insofar as they are the most trustworthy of the wise men who have practiced rational thought. This is not only because they were prepared and competent on a scientific level (specifically, in the study of the liberal arts that are the exercise and guide of human intelligence), but above all because they based the very rationality of their inquiry on the prior and foundational acceptance of revealed truth. Even the *auctoritas* of Sacred Scripture is rational in origin in that it is the free manifestation of the highest truth known by humans through direct participation in the Divine Mind by way of prophetic inspiration—something which is identical with the Universal Logos that governs creation. Scriptural authority therefore is the one perfect authority as such, "unshakable" (*inconcussa*) because it is superior to every accidental limitation and to every confrontation with other sources of the truth.[7]

This means that the sources of science—reason, patristic authority, scriptural authority—are arranged by Eriugena in a line of progressive continuity in which they all form expressions of the same truth. While created reason, especially after original sin, can only orient itself toward truth with partial results after intermittent and tiring inquiry, Scripture contains truth in a form that is total, immediate, and definitive, even if not conceptualizable as such by human logic. Patristic authority is located between these two extremes. Here rational consciousness, thanks to a special skilled synthesis both in the techniques of demonstration and in an intimate familiarity with the revealed communication of truth, has been able to attain the very highest peaks of wisdom which it was then capable of expressing in an intelligible and accessible way even to those of the faithful who are less speculative. This is why the Fathers, according to the typical Augustinian and early medieval way of thinking, were "true theologians" (*veri theologi*), investigators and illuminators of the divine because they were believers and men of understanding.

The importance that the appeal to patristic authority assumes in Eriugena's work transcends the strictly rhetorical scope of the argument *ex auctoritate* worked out in the antique and late antique schools. According to the teaching of Cicero's *Topics* and Boethius's commentary on this work, such an argument is above all persuasive, designed to corroborate and strengthen, rather than to prescribe rules for the development of a line of inquiry.[8] In obedience to the principle of the unity and finality of truth, the introduction into *Periphyseon* of patristic citations already predetermined as true and acceptable cannot, in fact, follow the doubtful procedures of rhetorical analysis which could argue either for right or for wrong.[9] By recognizing in the words of the authorized interpreters of Scripture who preceded him an incontrovertible result of an already accomplished effort of human rationality in pursuit of truth, John the Scot was in a position to reclaim the usefulness of the principle of *auctoritas* as one of the dialectical *topoi*, that is, the effective principles for necessary demonstration of the truth. This means that the voice of the Fathers of the Church, like the *communes conceptiones animi* (i.e., first principles of thought) from which all true dialectical demonstrations are derived, should be recognized in a universal way and accepted, without discussion, within the interior fund of knowledge common to the human race.

The frequent emergence of striking contradictions among patristic sources, on the other hand, constitutes a serious and unavoidable obstacle to the clear outline of this position. In fact, such differences of teaching would question, if not the orthodoxy of the arguments (which must finally be proved by the teaching of the faith), the formal correctness of rationality itself, which has its primary representatives in the Church Fathers.

This contrast, as is well known, is especially evident between the two great phalanxes of Greek sources on the one hand and Latin on the other. Without doubt, Dionysius the Areopagite leads the first group, followed by his "interpreters": Maximus the Confessor, Gregory of Nyssa, and Gregory Nazianzen (Eriugena often erroneously identifies these); and then by Epiphanius and Origen. On the other side, according to the frequency and authoritativeness with which they are cited, we have Augustine, Gregory the Great, Jerome, Boethius, and (for sources not explicitly named) Marius Victorinus and Claudianus Mamertus.[10] The treatment given to

Ambrose on the one hand and Basil on the other takes an anomalous position, though one coherent with the general outline—each of these is moved to the other camp insofar as their teachings are almost always in agreement with the positions common to the authors of the other language.

The two phalanxes display impressive solidity from the thematic viewpoint. The arguments that display their contrast are always (or almost always) of a theological nature, for the most part about the interpretation of the opening pages of Genesis, that is, the doctrine of creation and the organization of the universe. Simply put, we can say that the position of the Greek Fathers (along with Ambrose) is mostly spiritual, privileging on the ontological level the nature of the causes over that of the effects and seeking to restore the effects to the causes. The Latin Fathers (along with Basil) tend to a historical and "materialistic" reading of the sacred text, avoiding in particular every contact of suprasensible reality with individual entities dispersed in corporeality and sensibility, whether it is the fruit of fall or restoration.

The contrast begins to be exposed in the first two books of *Periphyseon*, though it surfaces again and again, and is especially evident in books III to V during the exegesis of the creation account and the progressive introduction into it of eschatological teaching. Almost at the outset of the work, for example, John the Scot asks how Augustine can argue that the angels can know the primordial causes, while we find in St. Paul a radical denial that creatures can know the divine intellect. It is clear that Eriugena's reading of this New Testament authority was directly influenced by Pseudo-Dionysius, insofar as only the doctrine of theophanies as elaborated by the Greek authorities is able to mediate, at least in a provisional way, between these two positions and to justify the possibility of a vision of God on the part of the angels.[11] Again, in book II, at the end of the discussion of Maximus the Confessor's division of reality, the teaching on the disappearance of sexual differentiation after the resurrection is contested by the Latin Fathers who maintain that the resurrection will take place with all bodily qualities intact.[12]

From here on the contradictions between the sources inevitably multiply through the progressive emergence of the fundamental irreconcilability between the Platonic ontology of the Greeks (monistic and spiritualistic) and the underlying dualism of the Western position which more easily inclines to accept a concrete and autonomous subsistence for corporeal reality in confrontation with spiritual reality. For instance, note the different conceptions of the nature of the human body before original sin—material according to Augustine, spiritual and not subject to the accidental division of sexes according to Gregory of Nyssa.[13] The contrast is even sharper on the question of the spatio-temporal measurability of the condition of humanity placed in the terrestrial Paradise before sin, and hence on the corporeality of Paradise itself. This is accepted by Augustine—and also shared, at least on a possible interpretation of the texts, by Ambrose—while it is radically refuted by the Greeks, especially by Gregory of Nyssa.[14] Augustine interprets in historical-literal terms the words of the divine condemnation of humanity after original sin, while the preference for a spiritual transvaluation of their significance is evident on the part of Maximus Confessor.[15] Again, the dissent is evident on the issue of the temporal change of spiritual substances, accepted by Augustine (for him only God moves without change in space and time), but not by Gregory Nazianzus and Maximus for whom space and time always come into subsistence together and cease together.[16] Over the complete series of issues laid out by Eriugena we must finally superimpose the striking discords among the patristic sources in relation to eschatological teaching, especially regarding the theme that is central in *Periphyseon* and upheld by the authority of the Greeks—the resolution-fusion of corporeal substances into spiritual ones—a position which finds evident resistance among the Latins with the exception of Ambrose.[17]

The phalanxes described are not, however, always compact. Besides the variation shown in the case of Ambrose, other indications demonstrate the possibility of considering the contrasts noted above as resulting from individual positions taken up at one time or another by the interpreters of Scripture, and not as doctrinal manifestos of opposed schools. For example, in book III's discussion of the immortality of the animal soul, Gregory of Nyssa along with Augustine and Basil are in disagreement with the position of Pseudo-Dionysius, later accepted by Eriugena, which is founded on the Neoplatonic idea of the dialectical resolution of opposites within the genus they share. (According to this, the animal soul and the rational soul dialectically recombine within the genus, soul, by participating together in its immortality.)[18]

In the face of the multiplication and the progressive fragmentation of such differences and oppositions of teaching, the problem inevitably arises of how to reconcile the unity of truth with the authoritativeness of the divergent *auctoritates.* It is evident that for John the Scot there was no possibility (or not yet a possibility) of proposing a solution based on the autonomy of critical reason of an Abelardian type, one which would invite a search for an agreement showing the superiority of one testimony over another or commonly introducing a hierarchized reading of their authority. The respectful placing of patristic authority at the foundation of wisdom, a position shared by all Carolingian culture, led him to consider as true *all* the positions taken by his sources, despite their differences and disagreements. On the other hand, if Abelard intentionally underlined the insufficiency of authority in the resolution of a theological problem, it was because he placed the problem itself as posterior to authority. For him theology was the result of solid inquiry on a technical plane done by demonstrative instruments that were still lacking in the sources so that he emphasized the contradictions found in authority with the intention of pointing out the chronological antecedence (not inferiority) of authority with respect to the demonstration. (Just as from Augustine on, the growing Christian philosophy underlined the *dissensio* among the pagan philosophers in order to open up the possibility of selecting and choosing some of their teachings at the very moment when it was overcoming and perfecting them.)[19]

This reconceptualization of patristic authority, resulting from a renewed philological and critical spirit, but also from some loss of the unitary sentiment that characterized the Carolingian ideal of wisdom at its deepest roots, gave Abelard's generation the freedom with which they treated authority's "wax nose" in order to allow the inevitability of the recourse to rational instrumentation to emerge from authority's incompleteness.[20] The famous five rules for the interpretation of sources in the prologue of *Sic et non* allow for the disclosure in the citation of any patristic text of a possible misrepresentation of truth or even an error, without, however, forming a judgment on its universal value as testimony—the question only concerns its form and the conditions of its transmission. This is why it deals with an invitation to verify the authenticity of texts, or rather to recall the inevitably equivocal and polysemous nature of human language, or even to introduce history, or rather mutability, into the evolution of an author's thought, or finally to verify the diverse finalities of his teaching according to particular cases. To crown all this, the fundamental instance of this method is above all clear in the final rule, which permits the establishment of a true hierarchy among the sources to the extent that if, after all this winnowing and verifying, contradiction continues to be sustained, the reader's rationality is explicitly invited to intervene and to express its preference. For Abelard, in fact, just as for Augustine, only the authority of Sacred Scripture is *vera*—and even in this case reason can correct textual ambiguities on the basis of philological revision. Outside of Scripture, nothing is authoritative and obligatory; the writings of the commentators are to be treated with respect, but always with freedom of reading and judging.[21]

It is evidently the opposite for John the Scot, because reason cannot be encouraged to pretend to judge and interpret authority, which too is rational in origin. Even if it is true that John does not hide his preference for the teaching of the Greek Fathers, this tendency never introduces a hierarchy among the sources and does not wind up authorizing that they be examined at will. Rationality is the object of controversy, not the subject; it cannot be employed as the arbiter among the contestants.

Nevertheless, a marked consciousness of the limitation of the faculty of human knowing constantly accompanies the dialogue of the Master and Disciple as an insurmountable mark of the impossibility of guiding the dialectic of human rationality to a definitive comprehension that would exhaust the entire totality proposed at the beginning of *Periphyseon* as the comprehensive object of the work when the concept of *natura* is introduced.[22] For John the Scot the incontrovertibility of truth is at the same time the principle and the criterion of the recognition of both the positive results of inquiry and its inevitable incompleteness—for this reason every difficult passage of inquiry is always characterized at the same time by the irrefutability of the truth acquired and by its provisional and therefore probable character.[23] This is above all true of theological inquiry whose object is the most comprehensive truth and the most distant from the possibility of a proper definition by the human mind. The nearer we get to that object, the more rational debate is led into the range of discussions that aspire only to verisimilitude and not to truth, due to the inattainability of the mystery of the faith.[24] It often happens that what

is received as *probabile* or *verisimile* at the end of a long theological discussion on the basis of arguments that are difficult to understand is only the starting point of a new and more complex
inquiry.[25]

With this position Eriugena attaches himself, in harmony with
the Augustinian approach of the entire early Middle Ages, to a
"probabilistic" consideration of Christian rational theology, emerging from the beginnings of its being put forward as a science.[26]
Symptomatic of this is his aligning himself with the Carolingian
usage of defining as *probabiles* those among the Fathers of the
Church whose texts are cited in support of antiheretical arguments.[27] An example is found in his translation of Maximus's *Ambigua* when he expresses the significance of the Greek adjective
dokimoi (meaning "proved," "authoritative"), which is an attribute
of Christianity's patristic guides, through this same Latin terminology: "probabiles ovium rationabilium pastores."[28] Human authority is probable insofar as, within the Christian speculative
panorama, probability affects everything that human reason is capable of elaborating on its own in its inquiry about the divine.[29] In
this same sense the supreme distinction-contradiction between the
two theological procedures recommended by Pseudo-Dionysius,
the affirmative and the negative, and their necessary complementarity and reciprocity, condition the human mind in its always progressive approach to God. This happens according to the measure
in which, in ever more contradictory fashion, it at the same time
affirms and denies the results of its own investigations.[30]

This conception of theological inquiry sufficiently explains how
John the Scot is able to preserve what is not directly recoverable
among the opposing authorities of patristic wisdom. In a very different way from Abelard's criticism, it also justifies the eclecticism
granted the theologian in confronting the authorities he introduces and comments upon.[31] But Eriugena is ready to go beyond
eclecticism as well. Because contradictions among the Fathers (as
was already the case for Augustine's *dissensiones philosophorum*) are
a consequence of original sin (healed, though not completely, by
baptism and revelation), then their eventual reconciliation can
be of great use as a provisional instrument in moving ahead in
the journey of consciousness toward its true object. This will be
provisional until the completion of all the consequences of redemption will give way to the appearance of the absolute noncon-

tradiction of Truth in itself, which is also the identity of all the diverse perspectives to which human investigation is meanwhile condemned.

This is the meaning of the expression "in this controversy of great men we wish to contrive an agreement" (*machinari consensum*), introduced by John the Scot in a noted place to settle the confrontation between Augustine and Gregory of Nyssa regarding the nature of the human body prior to original sin (it was material for the first and spiritual for the second). Without pretending to adjudicate the quarrel between the Church's great men of wisdom, or to assign right to one and wrong to the other, the theologian is forced to work out the compatibility of their respective views of the problem. For this purpose John the Scot introduced, on this occasion, the idea of an animal and corporeal body that God was able to give to humanity in an artificial and provisional way by foreseeing sin and thereby providing for all its consequences. Joined to the spiritual body that humanity was given by nature, it was superfluous in respect to our original state, but necessary after the fall. He defines such a material body (two lines later) as "added as an external superstructure" (*supermachinatum exteriusque adjectum*). The correspondence between the word used to express the superabundance of the divine intervention in comparison with the natural gift and the word used a moment before for the theologian's artificial composition among his sources is striking.[32] In Eriugenian language *machinor* signifies the elaboration of an ingenious invention to solve a problem, especially for resolving some condition of ontological incompleteness with respect to the divine plan, one which requires a provisional solution while awaiting the *reditus* and the reconciliation of universal perfection.[33] Elsewhere Eriugena explicitly affirms the provisional nature of what results from a *machinatio* of human rationality, as well as its resolution into a direct vision of the truth when the universal and final appearance of divine truth will be found in all things. The same provisionality is true of the artificial agreement among the opinions of the Fathers prior to the final appearance of the absolute identity of all true testimony: "and everything which has been invented by the groundless opinions of mortals shall be proved void, and so be entirely done away with, for it is nothing."[34]

It was therefore possible for John the Scot, before Abelard and in a different way, to work out a series of rules that the interpreter should know how to apply in order to accept, evaluate, justify, and finally to try to reconcile, if only in a partial and provisional way, the divergences in the sources. These are not rules explicitly drawn up in a programmatic prologue, as in the *Sic et non*, but it is not difficult to deduce them from the varied approaches that the author takes in *Periphyseon* relative to the contradictory character of testimonies to the truth.

1. The first and fundamental rule, many times confirmed, consists in the renunciation of the claim to express a judgment on the validity of the diverse testimonies: "It is not for us to adjudicate between the interpretations of the Holy Fathers, but to acknowledge them with piety and veneration." Such a suspension of judgment, as we have noted, does not impose on the theologian an avoidance of a preference for one source that appears to him more acceptable than others for his own comprehension of the sacred text, but it is based on the impossibility of formulating a refutation or a debate about the others: "However it is not forbidden us to select that which seems after rational consideration to accord the better with the divine oracles."[35]

2. The very possibility of such a preference and of the choice that follows it, however, imposes the necessity of introducing also an evaluation, or rather a reasoned measure, of the different degrees of manifestation of the truth ascertained in the various sources. If in fact the theologian is able to choose, it is really because he ascertains that the authorities themselves are adapted to different possibilities of understanding on the part of the various categories of believers to whom their teachings are addressed: "Let each exponent who is concerned with this matter decide for himself which of the two seems to him the more reasonable."[36] The different degrees of understanding on the part of the hearer and reader are thus capable of being satisfied by the diversification of degrees of cognitive depth proposed by the different testimonies.

The Fathers sometimes also speak of being heard by those who are weak in intellect and they adapt themselves to their capability.[37] Basil, for example, as we know, is inclined to approach a dualistic dimension that is not only upheld by the Latin Fathers but is also more acceptable to the common view found among simple people. In fact, he directs his *Homilies* to the whole body of believers, and for this reason he expresses the truth there in a form that is more immediate and easy to share. This is even more significant insofar as he certainly knew how to attain the most universal and unitary intellectual depth of such truth; but, having "foreseen" his hearers' incapacity to take in the profundity of revelation, he has chosen to express himself in a way that was fitting for intelligences that had not yet evolved. (In this "foreseeing," once again, there is an evident correspondence with the Creator's anticipated cure for the consequences of original sin through the mediation of the gift of the *supermachinatum* body to humanity.) The different gradations of the comprehension of truth therefore involve a multiplicity of significations only *ex parte subiecti*, a multiplicity whose accidentality and variability is in no way able to corrupt the authentic substance and self-identity of truth.[38]

This introduces the possibility of at times indicating in the Church Fathers a teaching attitude of an esoteric type, that is, a simplified presentation of faith's teaching for the use of the simple, following a tendency already evident in St. Paul, and one which led to a form of "masquerading" the more spiritual and less accessible doctrines, especially among the Latin Fathers who were more occupied with the catechetical than with the theoretical aspects of their teaching.[39]

3. The very idea of diversity of expression and comprehension of the same truth leads also to the possibility of "devising an agreement" (*consensum machinari*) among the sources, insofar as the diversity of their teaching *ex parte subiecti* can be resolved by means of an ascent from inferior to superior stages of knowledge on the part of the hearer and reader. A doctrine that is valid for the simple is not negated but given more truth, perfected, and therefore liberated from the contradictory character of other approaches, insofar as the theologian's comprehension of it is improved thanks to the application of more perfect cognitive instruments. This definitively confirms the fact that to make a choice among testimonies does not signify an attack on and a renunciation of the validity of all.[40]

Here, then, is the justification of the method of scriptural exegesis put in operation by Eriugena in *Periphyseon:* at first, the exposition of the different testimonies of the Fathers according to their two diverse phalanxes; and afterwards, the assumption of a new interpretive proposal, often innovative with respect to all the patristic witnesses including those of the Greeks.[41] The possibility for considering each of these interpretations as true and trustworthy—among the others and not withstanding their departure from them—is based not only on the famous Eriugenian idea of the inexhaustible multiplicity of the meanings of Sacred Scripture,[42] but also on this hermeneutical rule which interprets the diversity of patristic testimonies as answering to the variation of stages of comprehension of human rationality.

4. The final fundamental rule for the resolution of controversies among authorities consists in the medieval theologian's own engagement in carrying forward the investigation of the Fathers on the basis of the same means which they themselves had already put in practice in their own time—rationality illuminated by faith.[43] The aspiration to proceed beyond the limits laid down by their teaching, apparently bold and presumptuous, rather springs from the most profound respect for their testimony. Precisely because it knows and bases itself upon the preceding interpretations (all already true), John the Scot's own opinion can be introduced as the crown and completion of the exegesis begun with their reasoned exposition, and it itself can be finalized as the recomposition of the apparent differences. Even if an argument has already been amply treated (*explanatum*) by Scripture's holy interpreters and it would seem superfluous and presumptuous to wish to join anything to their authority,[44] there is no reason to avoid a deepening of it, because the recourse (*interrogatio*) to the masters is actually realized by renewing and perfecting rational knowledge of the divine.[45]

This fourth rule is put forward as the most intimate reason of Eriugena's own philosophy. Its scope is not only to clarify, but also to deepen and to lead on to further results the rationality already at work in the patristic precedents.[46]

With respect to Abelard's rules, the Eriugenian program for the treatment of patristic sources and their divergences appears to be founded on a special gnoseological position born from a deepening of the Neoplatonic matrix. While for the Palatine Master reason is capable of defining and judging an objective reality that is knowable in itself because it has been put at the disposition of created intelligences within natural reality, for Eriugena the object of the truth, either of theology or physics, possesses an *ousia,* an interior substantial nature residing in itself, and, as such, it is radically unknowable not only to the human mind but also to angelic knowledge.[47] Therefore, creaturely knowledge is always and necessarily articulated and diversified in its results, because a partial intelligence can only elaborate a contact between the specificity of the subject and the totality of the real on different levels. This leads to the admission, even in the same knowing subject, of the possibility of different levels of comprehension of a single truth, a possibility among which reason is only one of others.

The Neoplatonists had assigned the different levels of knowledge according to a threefold hierarchical articulation that John the Scot used as the support structure of his gnoseology and also of his epistemology. After the five corporeal senses, the first level of the spiritualization of knowing is the internal sense (Greek *dianoia*) which is determined and limited to experience of the corporeal world. Investigation of ultimate and eternal reality is conducted by the universal conceptualizing power of demonstrative and discursive reason (*logos*), while it finally attains completion, although only partial and provisional, still proportional to created possibility, in the intuitive and totalizing vision of intellect (*nous*).[48] In light of this doctrine it is also possible to establish a parallel between the hierarchical distinction of the higher powers of knowing, reason, and intellect, and the dual character of the theological paths sketched by Pseudo-Dionysius, the affirmative and the negative, insofar as they are complementary instruments of investigation, one ordered to rational description, as far as possible, the other to the intuitive removal of every conceptual definition of the divine nature. In fact, the two theologies are accepted by Eriugena as complementary methodologies that accompany, in a problematic fashion, all knowing in the direction of the intuitive vision of the Absolute. Their division is a direct consequence and application of the native incompleteness of human science when it addresses the divine object, as well as of its results that are of necessity more *like* the truth than themselves true.

Reason and affirmative theology on the one hand and intellect and negative theology on the other constitute the two preserves of cognitive investigation also defined, according to Eriugena, by the two major spheres of theological cognition, *scientia* and *sapientia.* The first, obtained from knowledge that is defining and deductive, is mediated, proceeding by way of the division of genus and species and the determination of the differences and properties of each object known. The other, in opposite fashion, is direct and intuitive and pursued by the contemplative soul; it tries to penetrate into the eternal and unchangeable nature of what is true without being able to define it and subject it to the accidental nature of human signifying.[49] The supremacy of what negative theology offers is ordinarily limited by the need to acknowledge and communicate in some way the inaccessible divine nature, and this is the very thing that confirms its complementarity and reciprocal implication with the linguistic expressiveness of affirmative theology.[50] The intellect and its wanderings are inexpressible in themselves, except by way of the manifestation of mediated rationality. Thus the results of negative theology are also tangible only insofar as they support the matching emergence of complementary theological affirmations.[51]

It is also illuminating to suggest a further correspondence that contributes to a greater clarification of the contrast of the different teachings of the Fathers in this intricate panorama of Eriugenian theological science. This is the correspondence between the two theological methods and the two different speculative attitudes of patristic authority in *Periphyseon,* the Latin and the Greek, to the extent that the one is evidently dependent on the line of argument of discursive and deductive rationality and of a theology that affirms its contents through metaphorical reference to natural kinds of knowledge, while the other depends on arguments of nondefining intuitive intelligence and is oriented toward the negation of what can be said and made rational in an anthropomorphic way in speaking about God.

Augustinianism—if we are permitted to use this term to generalize the complete chain of Latin authority in Eriugenian thought—for John the Scot appears to coincide with the attitude of the very ground of discursive and mediating reason in every problematic opening of theological investigation, down to the *De divina praedestinatione.* It reaches its goal above all in the moderate use of dialectic and the other liberal arts to clarify theological concepts and the signification of the terms that express them.[52] The contribution of Greek patristics, especially Dionysius and Maximus, opens on a higher plane insofar as it guides human intelligence in a more decisive way toward the oneness and the homogeneity of the spiritual world that is more directly intuited from the immediacy of noetic knowing. The Greek authors push forward as far as possible toward the suprarational unification of the multiple and the particular, striving to achieve a cure, if only partial, for the cognitive gaps of humanity through the pursuit of noetic intellect and negative theology.

Eriugena explicitly signals his idea that the Latin Fathers witness to a logical-discursive attitude toward theology when, for example, he notes that in the formulation of the dogma of the Trinity they prefer the affirmative formula *filioque* because it is more adequate to the speculative capacity of reason (*rationabiliter*), while the Greeks preferred to conceal this aspect and to omit the liturgical addition, opting for a silence that penetrated deeper into the secret of the mystery.[53] Again, on innumerable other occasions the Oriental theologians preferred to underline the inaccessible depth of the mystery, a sign of how much more they were inclined to express a direct intuition of the intimately spiritual nature of the created reality that can be analytically resolved in the primordial causes and, through them, into the unity of the Divine Cause.[54] This is why it is above all in the Greek Fathers, inspired and guided by the Pseudo-Dionysius, that there can at times be realized, insofar as it is possible for created being, a mystical penetration into the divine being through virtue and through knowledge, a penetration that is a prelude to the disappearance of this world as the return (*reditus*) of nature to its originating causality and its transmutation into a better state.[55]

This last observation introduces the possibility of advancing to a still higher level of theological knowledge in which the complementary truth of both procedures, the affirmative and the negative, would be fully manifested—the level of the beatific vision, promised from eternity for the witnesses of the faith but also realized once in a single episode, the mystical ascension of John the Evangelist alluded to in the Prologue to his Gospel. The prophet who immerses himself in divine profundity and approaches the supreme truths of theology in order to express them through the language of the revelation of the Gospel is a symbol and an anticipation of the effort with which the highest intuitive capacities of *nous* surpass their creaturely limitations in the beatific vision to gain the one Truth in definitive fashion through a direct identification of the knower with the known. In Eriugena's *Homilia* the three most important apostles symbolize the succession of these cognitive levels: Peter is faith; John, the direct intuitive contemplation of the Truth; and between the two Paul is placed as a symbol of mediated and discursive human intelligence which is capable of being transvalued into intellectual intuition.[56]

Yet even the *vera theologia* of John the Evangelist, promised to the blessed and only to be realized in the eschatological time beyond the division of affirmative and negative theology, is not opposed to these methods. Rather than deprive the preceding levels of human approach to God of truth, it finishes by absorbing both of them into its own more ample and definitive absoluteness. All the preceding theological paths find their verification and conciliation in the light of the promised theology. As explicitly indicated by Maximus, this is the agreement (*concordia, concordate*) that ought to be realized between the testimony of John and that of Paul concerning the possibility of redeemed humans attaining God directly.[57]

In light of this conclusive recovery of the theological process along which the entire creation moves toward being reunited with its Principle, even the contrast between the negatively noetic element of theological wisdom testified to by the Greek Fathers and the affirmative one of dialectical reason represented by the Latins is finally resolved, within an eschatological perspective, with the overcoming of all the temporal accidents and the provisional character of presently diversified levels of human knowing.

If knowing is the natural end of the human soul ("non enim aliud est animae essentialiter esse et substantialiter moveri," that is, to know), and if the natural end of knowing is the contemplation of God, the realization of this finality is entrusted to the whole of human history. It is to be completed by a slow and carefully marked-out evolution of human faculties, darkened for a time by the effects of original sin, but regained and brought back to their effective *energeia* by Christian redemption. Therefore, beyond every apparent contradiction, the teachings of the Church Fathers are always to be proposed as the most secure and rich steps of this history whose promised outcome is the reunification, within the intuition of the unity of the Divine Word, of the fourfold rational division of knowledge of the universe and the relation of the universe to God: "ab ipso, per ipsum, in ipso, in ipsum."[58]

Translated by Bernard McGinn

NOTES

1. *Iohannis Scotti Eriugenae Periphyseon (De divisione Naturae)*, Books, I–III, ed. I. P. Sheldon-Williams (Dublin, 1968, 1972, 1981). Books IV and V can be found in PL 122, 441A–1022D. Citations here will be made according to book and chapter and the column numbers in PL 122 (also found in the Sheldon-Williams edition). The passage referred to here is I, 67–69 (512B–513C). All translations, unless otherwise noted, are from *Eriugena: Periphyseon (The Division of Nature)*, trans. I. P. Sheldon-Williams, revised by John J. O'Meara (Montréal–Dumbarton Oaks, 1987).

2. P I, 69 (513B): "Nil enim aliud videtur mihi esse vera auctoritas nisi rationis virtute reperta veritas et a sanctis Patribus ob posteritatis utilitatem litteris commendata." This definition of Eriugena enjoyed a special historical fortune in following centuries, not only because it was used on more than one occasion by Honorius Augustodunensis (cf. *Clavis Physicae*, ed. Paolo Lucentini [Rome, 1974], 44: "Nil enim aliud est vera auctoritas nisi rationis virtute reperta veritas"; *Liber VIII quaestionum* 1 [PL 172:1185B]: "Nil aliud est auctoritas quam per rationem probata veritas") but also, through the Parisian glossed version of the *corpus dionysiacum* (where it was introduced in the margin of *De divinis nominibus* 1.1), it was taken up by thirteenth-century Scholastics. See Albert the Great, *In I Sent.*, Prol. Mag. (ed. Borgnet [Paris, 1983], vol. 25:11): "Quia sicut dicit Commentator super primum caput de divinis nominibus: Nihil aliud est auctoritas quam rationis reperta veritas, ob posteritatis utilitatem scripto commendata." See also Albert's *III Sent.*, d.23, a.19, obj.4 (ed. Borgnet [Paris, 1984], vol. 28:440): "Unde Iohannis Episcopus diffinit auctoritatem dicens: Nihil aliud est auctoritas nisi rationis reperta veritas, et ad posteritatis utilitatem scripto commendata." The name *Iohannes Episcopus* probably comes from an incorrect reading of the sign which often indicates an Eriugenian text by the first three Greek letters of his name. A few pages prior to this, Albert also attributes another citation to the same person, but I have not yet been able to find this in John the Scot's writings—*III Sent.*, d.23, a.18, ad quaest. 1 (vol. 28:439): "Ita dicit quidam Iohannes Episcopus: Fides locat fideles in veritate, sicut immobile summae veritatis principium." Cf. H. F. Dondaine, *Le 'corpus dionysien' de l'Université de Paris au XIIIe siècle* (Rome, 1953), 86, n. 47, and 137; and M. D. Chenu, *La théologie au douzième siècle* (Paris, 1966), 355, n. 4.

3. Augustine, *De ordine* 2.9.26–11.30 (PL 32:1007–1009). Note especially 1007: "Ad discendum item necessario dupliciter ducimur, auctoritate atque ratione; tempore auctoritas, re autem ratio prior

est" (cf, P I, 69 [531B]: "Rationem priorem esse natura, auctoritatem vero tempore didicimus").

4. Augustine, *De ordine* 2.9.27 (1007–1008): "Auctoritas partim divina est, partim humana, sed *vera,* firma, summa ea est quae divina nominatur. . . . Humana vero auctoritas plerumque fallit."

5. P I, 69 (513B): "Auctoritas siquidem ex vera ratione processit, ratio vero nequaquam ex auctoritate. Omnis enim auctoritas quae vera ratione non approbatur infirma videtur esse, vera autem ratio quoniam suis virtutibus rata atque immutabilis munitur nullius auctoritatis astipulatione roborari indiget."

6. P III, 16 (671A–B): "ad hoc enim praesens ratiocinatio, immo vero *ipsa ratio* perducet . . . , ut ait sanctus Maximus."

7. P III, 17 (672C). The same formula is found in *De divina praedestinatione* 11.3 (PL 122:398C; ed. Goulven Madec in CCCM 50:68.58).

8. See Cicero, *Topica* 4.24; Boethius, *In Topica Ciceronis Commentaria* 6 (PL 64:1168B–1169B).

9. Cf. *De divina praedestinatione* 1.3 (PL 122:358C–359A; CCCM 50:7.47–60). This is a textual citation from Augustine, *De doctrina christiana* 4.2.3 (PL 34:89), on the ambiguity of rhetoric in relation to the necessity and the unity of truth. Cf. *De divina praedestinatione* 1.2 (PL 122:358C; CCCM 50:7.42–44) on the invitation to combat heresy by making use of the combined forces of rationality and patristic authority ("veris rationibus sanctorumque Patrum auctoritate"); and further in 12.5 (404C; 76:123–124) the identification of patristic authority and truth ("si ergo sancti Augustini cedendum est auctoritati, immo per eam veritati").

10. See the volume *Eriugena: Studien zu seinen Quellen,* Vorträge des III. Internationalen Eriugena-Colloquiums, Freiburg-im-Breisgau 27–30 August 1979, ed. Werner Beierwaltes (Heidelberg, 1980). See also I. P. Sheldon-Williams, "Eriugena's Greek Sources," in *The Mind of Eriugena,* ed. John J. O'Meara and Ludwig Bieler (Dublin, 1973), 1–14; Goulven Madec, "Jean Scot et ses auteurs," in *Jean Scot écrivain,* Actes du IVe Colloque International, Montréal 28 aout–2 septembre 1983, ed. G. H. Allard (Montréal-Paris, 1986), 143–86. On Marius Victorinus, see the studies of Gustavo Piemonte, especially, "L'expression 'quae sunt et quae non sunt': Jean Scot Erigène et Marius Victorinus," in Jean Scot écrivain, 81–113.

11. P I, 8 (446AC). The Pauline texts in question are Rom. 11:34 ("quis enim intellectum Domini cognovit?") and Phil. 4:7 ("pax Christi quae exsuperat omnem intellectum"). For the identification of the patristic texts used by Eriugena, see Madec's study, previously mentioned.

12. Cf. P II, 14 (542C–543B).

13. P IV, 12–14 (800B–804C).

14. P IV, 15–16 (812D–816D).

15. P IV, 26 (856B–858A).

16. P V, 17 (888D–889A). The same theme returns also in P V, 38 (1000C–1001A).

17. See especially P V, 8 (876B–880A), where, besides Augustine, Boethius is cited among the Latins with a passage from his *De trinitate.* On Boethius's testimony to Latin resistance to accepting a fusion between corporeal and spiritual nature, see my paper, "Giovanni Scoto e Boezio: Tracce degli *Opuscula sacra* e della *Consolatio* nell'opera eriugeniana," *Studi Medievali,* 3d series, 21.2 (1980): 707–752, whose observations also appear in "A proposito del 'magnificus Boetius,'" in *Eriugena: Studien zu seinen Quellen,* 189–200. On the spatio-temporal interpretation of the condition of the restored creature by Augustine, see P V, 37 (990C–991A). The views of Ambrose and the Greek Fathers contrary to this position are recorded in P V, 38 (995B). In V, 20 (897A) Eriugena notes the opposition of "patristic authority" (unidentified) in relation to his teaching regarding the intelligible and noncircumscribed form of the angels which humans are destined to share after the resurrection. In V, 25 (914B–915A) the same holds for the doctrine of the universal redemption of creatures made possible by human redemption. Here the view of the Pseudo-Dionysius is cited in opposition.

18. P III, 38–39 (736B–739B).

19. See my observations in "La dialettica in Agostino e il metodo della teologia nell'alto medioevo," *Atti del Congresso internazionale su S. Agostino nel XVI centenario della conversione,* Roma, 15–20 settembre 1986 (Roma, 1987), 1:251–282; also in "Il pensiero *convertito:* Il giovane Agostino," *Archivio di filosofia* 59 (1991): 323–337.

20. On this issue, see M. D. Chenu, *Le théologie au douzième siècle,* 360–61; and Martin Grabmann, *Geschichte der scholastischen Methode* (Freiburg-im-Breisgau, 1911) 2:199–213.

21. See Peter Abelard, *Sic et non,* prol. (PL 178:1340D–1349A).

22. P I (441A–B).

23. See, e.g., P I, 8 (447C–D).

24. See P I, 9 (448D), on the different grades of the beatific vision: "A[lumnus]. Verisimile videtur. N[utritor]. Recte dicis *verisimile.* Quis enim de talibus firmarit ita et non aliter esse, dum vires humanae adhuc in hac fragili carne intentionis videantur excedere?" Again, on the question of the universal return, see P I, 10 (451BC): "N. . . . Sed sufficiant ista, si tibi clare lucescunt. A. Lucescunt sane, quantum talia nostris mentibus lucere sinuntur. De re enim ineffabili quis in hac vita

luculenter potest fari ut nil amplius inquirentium appetat deside-
rium?. . ." "N. Caute ac rationabiliter existimas."

25. E.g., P I, 13 (455B): "A. Hactenus quae dicta sunt videntur esse
probabilia." See also I, 33 (478C): "A. Haec quae a te dicta sunt de dif-
ferentia locorum et corporum *verisimilia* esse videntur, sed subtilius
eadem velim repetas."

26. See P I, 13 (457D–458A): "A. . . . Nosse tamen aperte ac
breviter per te velim utrum omnes categoriae, cum sint numero decem, de summa divinae bonitatis una essentia in tribus substantiis et
de tribus substantiis in eadem una essentia vere proprieque possunt
praedicari. N. De hoc negotio nescio quis breviter atque aperte potest
dicere. Aut enim de huius modi causa per omnia tacendum est et sim-
plicitate orthodoxae fidei committendum—nam exsuperat omnem
intellectum, sicut scriptum est: 'qui solus habes inmortalitatem et
lucem habitas inaccessibilem' [1 Tm. 6:16]—aut si quis de ea dispu-
tare coeperit, necessario multis modis multisque argumentationibus
verisimile suadebit. . . ." See also, in the same sense I, 15 (463B–C), also
treating of the theological use of the ten Aristotelian categories. On
the "probabilistic" approach of early medieval theological inquiry, see
my observations in "Theological Ideas and the Idea of Theology in
the Early Middle Ages (9th–11th centuries)," *Freiburger Zeitschrift für
Philosophie und Theologie* 38 (1991): 273–297; and "An Introduction to
the Problem of Method in Early Medieval Theology," in *Knowledge
and the Sciences in Medieval Philosophy*, Proceedings of the Eighth International Congress of Medieval Philosophy (S.I.E.P.M.) (Helsinki,
1990), 3:367–75.

27. See, for example, Alcuin, *Adversus Felicem Urgellitanum* VI, 12
(PL 101:212A), who describes Augustine as "tantus doctor et tam
probabilis"; in the *Adversus Elipandum Toletanum* II,10 (PL 101:267A–
B) he says that the heretic introduces pretended patristic texts into his
works from the "probabilium scripta doctorum." Cf. III, 14 (279D),
where citations of Hilary are set forth as "valde probabilia testimo-
nia"; III, 17 (282A–B), where Augustine is "veridicus, probabilisque
veritatis testis"; IV, 14 (298B) speaks of "in sanctorum Patrum probabilius litteris." In the *Libri Carolini* III, 15 (ed. H. Bastgen in MGH,
Leg. III, Conc. II, Suppl., 134.10), the biblical Tobit is described as
"vir probabilis et Deus carus" insofar as he is strong and able to undergo trials. Again, Beatus of Liébana in the preface to his *Commen-
tarius in Apocalipsin*, ed. H. A. Sanders (Rome, 1930), 2, presents as
"probabiles vires" the Fathers whose texts he included in his exegetical florilegium. The same is true with Agobard of Lyon, *De privilegio
et iure sacerdotii* (PL 104:127B): "sicut probabilium Patrum expositio
probat."

28. Maximus the Confessor, *Ambigua ad Iohannem* 1 (PG 91: 1064A); Eriugena's version can be found in the edition of Edouard Jeauneau in CCSG 18:17.10.

29. P III, 1 (627A–C); cf. P V (935D), where the disciple, confronted by one of the gravest difficulties of the theological teaching of the *reditus* (that relating to the eternity of hell and of the punishment of the damned), seeks rational aid from the Master that cannot be anything else but a probable way of approaching closer to the truth that in itself is not directly attainable: "Succurre itaque deque praedictis tormentorum speciebus, quas divina non mendax promittit historia, *probabilem* redde *rationem.*"

30. P I, 13 (458A), following the text cited above in n. 26, ". . . necessario multis modis multisque argumentationibus *verisimile* suadebit, duabus principalibus theologiae partibus utens, affirmativa quidem, quae a Graecis *KATAPHATIKE* dicitur, et abnegativa, quae *APOPHATIKE* vocatur."

31. P IV, 15 (813D–814B). After having noted the patristic authorities contrary to the spiritualistic negation of any time in Paradise before original sin, Eriugena says: "Sed quia adversus eos . . . non est nostri propositi agere, ea siquidem solummodo, quae nobis *verisimilia* videntur dicere procuravimus, aliorum vero sententiam, qui aliter sapiunt, refellere seu spernere, seu falsam esse pronuntiare . . . ad nos nullo modo pertinet. . . . Recte quippe ratiocinandi via tenenda est, ut neque in dexteram, neque in sinistram deviare videamur; hoc est, neque his, quos summae ac sanctae auctoritatis esse catholica sanxit Ecclesia, detrahamus, neque eos, quos simpliciter intellexisse cognovimus, quoniam intra catholicae fidei sinceritatem continentur, spernamus. . . . Nostrum quippe sensum approbare aut eorum, quos ceteros praecellere arbitramur, aliorum vero sensum reprobare, aut periculosissimum est, aut superbissimum, aut certe contentiosum." The same eclectic and "probabilistic" attitude is displayed in P IV, 16 (816D–817A and 818A–B).

32. Here is the complete passage from P IV, 14 (804D): "Mihi autem et tibi, si placet, sufficiat, sententias sanctorum Patrum de constitutione hominis ante peccatum legere, et quid unusquisque eorum voluit, cauta ac diligenti inquisitione quaerere. Lites autem inter eos constituere, non est nostrum, aut hunc constituere, hunc autem refellere, scientes, post sanctos Apostolos nullum apud Graecos fuisse in expositionibus divinae Scripturae majoris auctoritatis Gregorio theologo, nullum apud Romanos Aurelio Augustino. Et quid, si in hac veluti controversia magnorum virorum quendam *consensum* velimus *machinari,* dicentes, illud corpus, quod Gregorius dicit divina praescientia propter futurum peccatum homini *supermachinatum* ex-

teriusque adjectum, id ipsum ab Augustino animale vocatum . . ." (translations here adapted). See John J. O'Meara, " 'Magnorum virorum quendam consensum velimus machinari' (804D): Eriugena's Use of Augustine's *De Genesi ad litteram* in the *Periphyseon*," in *Eriugena: Studien zu seinen Quellen,* 105–116.

33. See, for example, P I, 68 (512B): "Quid tibi videtur his argumentationibus *machinari* . . . ?" Also P III, 35 (724C): "Plus ergo tenet divina virtus et naturarum ratio quam quod *machinatur* humana cogitatio?" With a negative sense it is used, on the other hand, to describe the wiles with which demons and those opposed to the faith combat the truth, e.g., P IV, 24 (850B and 852A).

34. P V, 36 (970A): "et omne quod vanissimis mortalium opinionibus *machinatum* est, evacuabitur, ideoque penitus interimetur, quoniam nihil est."

35. P II, 16 (548D–549A): "Non enim nostrum est de intellectibus sanctorum Patrum diiudicare, sed eos pie ac venerabiliter suscipere. Non tamen prohibemur eligere quod magis videtur divinis eloquiis rationis consideratione convenire." In the same direction, see P IV, 16 (816D): "Cum his, qui talia volunt, non est nostrum colluctari"; IV, 16 (818A): "Non est nobis colluctandum adversus eos"; V, 8 (877C): "Quorum sententiam non solum non reprehendimus, verum etiam libenter accipimus; theologos autem, qui graece locuti sunt, aliter sensisse non ignoramus"; V, 17 (889A): "Sed quid horum convenientius tenendum sit, non est nostrum diiudicare"; etc.

36. P V, 17 (889A–B): "Unusquisque de talibus disputantium intra seipsum deliberet, quid sibi rationabilius sequendum sit." Cf. V, 20 (897A–B): "Consequens disputationis ordo exigit, ut, quid quisque ecclesiasticorum sapientium, quos legisti—non enim omnes te legisse opinor, quod cuiquam impossible est—de talibus senserit, proferas, ut in arbitrio legentis ponatur, quem velit sequi."

37. Cf. P III, 39 (739A–C).

38. See P III, 30–31 (708B–709B), especially 31 (708B–C): "Non enim debemus divinorum Patrum intellectus ullo modo neglegere seu annullare, praesertim cum non nos lateat eos saepissime simpliciter disputasse capacitatem audientium non satis idoneam ad profundissimos spiritualis virtutis naturalium rationum percipiendos intellectus *praevidentes;* atque ideo non temere dixerim ut opinor deiferum Basilium superna gratia illuminatum simplicius exposuisse sex primorum dierum intelligibilium operationes quas intellexerat, sermonem simplicitati auditorum coaptans. Siquidem omiliariter ad populum locutus est." Cf. 708D–709A: "Non ergo praedictum Patrem debemus arbitrari simpliciter intellexisse quod simpliciter videtur exposuisse. Quis enim audebit divinum luminare reprehendere

dum nesciat quantum in se ipso potuit lucere lumenque suum minus capacibus temperanter voluit distribuere?"

39. E. g., see P V, 37 (986B–987B, 990C–991A, 991C–992A).

40. P V, 38 (1001A): "De auctoribus utriusque linguae non est nostrum contendere: sequatur quis quem vult, *nulli derogans.*"

41. See the explicit indication of this exegetic method, which afterwards will be proper to the whole articulation of books II–V of the work, in P II, 15 (545B–546B).

42. P IV (749C): "Est enim multiplex et infinitus divinorum eloquiorum intellectus. Siquidem in penna pavonis una eademque mirabilis ac pulchra innumerabilium colorum varietas conspicitur in uno eodemque loco ejusdem pennae portiunculae."

43. P IV, 16 (829A–B): "Sed quisquis haec, quae inter nos tractavimus, non dedignatus fuerit legere ac diligenter intueri, eligat ex praedictis sanctorum Patrum sententiis, quod sibi sequendum videtur, videatque, ne incaute nos laceret, aestimans ea, quae a nobis dicta sunt, nullius auctoritatis auxilio esse munita, ac veluti praesumptive contra sanctorum Patrum traditiones machinata."

44. P IV, 23 (849C): "Quod enim a sanctis Patribus satis est explanatum, explanare fortassis videbitur non necessarium, et quod in illorum scriptis plenissime planissimeque invenitur, cur a nobis, forte quis dicet, quasi melius explanaturis repetatur? Quod absit de nobis existimari, cum illorum vestigia vix valeamus consequi."

45. See Maximus Confessor, *Ambigua ad Iohannem* 1, in Eriugena's version (CCSG 18:17.3–7): "Laudantur quidem et fortasis iuste ab omnibus qui bona propter studium doctrinae promptiores amant et disciplinam quae in eis est sollicitiores cogitant, ad meliores et meliorum magistros accedentes, quia per interrogationem sapientum disciplinam reverenter accipientes seipsos ab ignorantia et imperitia et earum opprobrio liberant."

46. See, for example, in P V, 27–28 (931A–934A), an illuminating testimony to Eriugena's way of dealing with patristic sources, in this case a passage from Pseudo-Dionysius (the famous treatment in *De divinis nominibus* IV, 23 [PG 3:724C–725A] of the nonsubstantiality of evil and the impossibility of the corruption of the nature of the demons). This is analyzed by Eriugenian exegesis (*expositio*) in order to identify the dialectical, that is, rational, passages implicit in it.

47. See, e.g., P I (487A–B).

48. On the threefold Neoplatonic gnoseology, see P II, 23 (572C–579A). An essential, though not exclusive, source of this teaching for Eriugena is the *Ambigua ad Iohannem* of Maximus Confessor: see, for instance, 6, 3 (CCSG 18:48.119–50.202). We must not, however, forget that the distinction between rational knowing (*ratio*) and intellec-

tual (*animus, mens, intellectus*) is also amply attested to in the scientific and cultural patrimony of western Neoplatonism, for example, Augustine, *Soliloquia* I, 6, 13 (PL 32:876). On Eriugena's theology as the result of an intellectual unity beyond all the *dissensiones* of dianoetic rationality, I refer to my previous works: "I fondatori di Parigi: Giovanni Scoto e la teologia del suo tempo," in *Giovanni Scoto nel suo tempo: L'organizzazione del sapere in età carolingia,* Atti del XXIV Convegno storico internazionale del Centro di Studi sulla Spiritualità Medievale e VI Convegno della S.P.E.S. Todi, 11–14 ottobre 1987 (Spoleto, 1989), 413–56; and "Oltre la teologia: Per una lettura dell' *Omelia* di Giovanni Scoto Eriugena sul Prologo del Quarto Vangelo," *Studi Medievali,* 3d series, 31 (1990–91): 285–356.

49. See P III, 3 (629AB).

50. This clearly results when Eriugena introduces the true and proper form of conciliation (*consonantia*) between positive and negative theology, one that is expressed in terms of rational discourse but which is completely realized within the intuitive realm of noetic knowing. It consists of predicating adjectives constructed with the prefix *super* or *plusquam,* thus avoiding every theological use of terms that are limited in their semantic capacity because they are opposed to respective contradictory terms—because *esse* is opposed to *non esse,* it is better to predicate the term *superessentialis* of God; cf. P I, 13–14 (459C–460B, and 461B–462D).

51. E. g., P II, 23 (576C–577C).

52. See Brian Stock, "Some Observations on the Use of Augustine by Johannes Scottus Eriugena," *Harvard Theological Review* 60 (1967): 213–220; and "In Search of Eriugena's Augustine," in *Eriugena: Studien zu seinen Quellen,* 85–104; Goulven Madec, "Observations sur le dossier augustinien du *Periphyseon,*" in *Eriugena: Studien zu seinen Quellen,* 75–84: and "L'augustinisme de Jean Scot dans le *De praedestinatione,*" *Jean Scot Erigène et l'histoire de la philosophie,* Colloque internationale du C.N.R.S., Laon, juillet 1973, ed. René Roques (Paris, 1977), 183–90.

53. P II, 32 (611D–613A).

54. P II, 35 (614B–615D).

55. P V, 21 (897B–898C).

56. See *Omelia Iohannis Scoti* 2–4, ed. Edouard Jeauneau SC 151 (Paris, 1969): 208–20. On the first chapters of the *Homilia* and their interpretation in terms of the levels of Platonic tripartite psychology, see my paper "Oltre la teologia." It is probable that this distinction of roles was suggested to Eriugena by the *Quaestiones ad Thalassium* of Maximus Confessor. In the third interrogation, in fact, Maximus proposes a contrast between Peter and John as symbols of *actio* and *con-*

templatio, while in the ninth he distinguishes between the testimony of an anticipation of the beatific vision in John and the descriptive-demonstrative nature of theological procedure in Paul. For these two texts, see the edition of C. Laga and C. Steel in CCSG 7: 55.12–24 (with Eriugena's version on 54.9–19) and 79.2–81.40 (Eriugena's version on 78.1–80.34). In Eriugena's *Expositiones in Ierarchiam Coelestem* 5 (CCCM 31:50.1099–52.1184) the same distinction of cognitive levels, that is, (1) the theology of rationality, (2) the theology of intellect, and (3) beatific "more-than-theology," is confirmed by the interpretation of the anagogic operation completed by the "theosophists" as a distinction of the symbol signifying the truth from the truth itself that is signified through the symbol. The affirmative and negative cognitive levels are, in fact, confined to the limited field of significative language, while only the direct mystical vision, beyond the capacities of both human and angelic intelligences, penetrates the Truth in definitive and complete manner.

57. See Maximus Confessor, *Quaestiones ad Thalassium* 9 (CCSG 7:79.21–26, with Eriugena's translation on 78.18–22): "Concinunt itaque Apostoli, per aestimatam contradictoriam doctrinam sibi invicem conspirantes, ab uno quippe eodemque spiritu moti, unus siquidem [i.e., John] modi futurae per gratiam deificationis fatetur ignorantiam, alter vero [i.e., Paul] speculationis gloriosissimae introducit scientiam." Concerning the word *concordare*, see P II, 31 (602A): "N. Primo igitur de his quae in hac quaestione sibimet videntur contradicere dicendum arbitror. A. Nec alia via quaerendi est. Nemo enim concordantia copulabit nisi prius discordantia diiudicaverit." Concepts such as *concordia, harmonia, consensus, copulatio* play an important role in Eriugena's theology and in his metaphysical doctrine of the *reditus universalis*. Cf. P I, 72 (517C); II, 31 (606D–607A); III, 3 (630C–631A); V, 36 (965D–966C); and *De divina praedestinatione* 17.8 (PL 122:430A; CCCM 50:168–74).

58. See P II, 23 (547B–D, especially 547C–D): "Quid obstat ne similiter intelligamus humanos intellectus indesinenter circa Deum volvi quoniam ab ipso et per ipsum et in ipso et ad ipsum sunt . . . , praesertim cum divina eloquia hominem ad imaginem Dei factum perhibeant . . . ?" The fourfold interpretation of the Pauline formula from Romans 11:36 (*ex ipso et per ipsum et in ipso*), especially significant for Eriugena insofar as it corresponds to the dialectical structure of the fourfold division of nature in *Periphyseon*, is borrowed from the Pseudo-Dionysius; cf. *De divinis nominibus* 4, in Eriugena's version in PL 122:1134A ("et ex ipso, et per ipsum, et in ipsum, et propter ipsum"), in 1136D ("per optimum, ex optimo, et in optimo, et in optimum"), and in 1137C ("ex seipsa, et per seipsam, et ad seipsam . . . , et

in seipsam"), etc. On these correspondences, see my paper, "Über die Natur der Einteilung: Die dialektische Entfaltung von Eriugenas Denken," *Begriff und Metapher*: *Sprachform des Denkens bei Eriugena,* Vorträge des VII. Internationalen Eriugena-Colloquiums, Bad Homburg, 26–29. Juli 1989, ed. Werner Beierwaltes (Heidelberg, 1990), 17–38.

Eriugena's Use of the Symbolism of Light, Cloud, and Darkness in the *Periphyseon*

Deirdre Carabine

THE DIVERSE WAYS IN WHICH ERIUGENA EMPLOYS the theme of light have been given scholarly attention in the past.[1] It is my intention that this essay should complement that aspect of Eriugena's thought through an elucidation of *la métaphysique nocturne* in the *Periphyseon*. In doing so, I do not propose to diminish the importance of the carefully constructed light metaphysics so obviously present in that work. Nevertheless, I do suggest that there exists a certain ambiguity regarding Eriugena's application of some aspects of metaphors of both light and darkness in terms of the ultimate epistemological and eschatological consequences of a radical *apophasis*.

The ambiguity that can be readily detected in following through Eriugena's employment of the light/darkness metaphor is due, at least in some measure, to his reading and assimilation of both eastern and western sources, but it is also a fundamental aspect of the nature of metaphor. Since the mind must use illustrations from things it can understand,[2] it employs metaphor as an effective means of access to what cannot be expressed literally; metaphor cannot, therefore, be retranslated into literal terms, nor can its application be fully effective in every instance. In forcing the mind beyond the literal, a basic tension is revealed between the literal meaning which is obviously denied and the non-literal meaning which cannot be fully affirmed. Literally speaking, God is not darkness in the same sense as God can be said to be light, for the final darkness of *apophasis* is always, paradoxically, "inaccessible light" (1 Tim. 6:16)—and yet the non-literal aspect of the metaphor cannot be denied.

141

In Eriugena's thought, the light metaphor in the service of kataphatic utterances is a means of expressing both the creative movement of the self-manifestation of the hidden[3] and, in epistemological terms, the Platonically inspired development of the ascent of the mind from the darkness of unreality and ignorance to the light of truth. The light metaphor cannot, then, be employed usefully in terms of apophatic utterances unless it is adapted, if not indeed fully reversed. The darkness metaphor, as symbolic of the ascent of the soul from the light of creatures to the hiddenness of God, is a development of the allegorical interpretation of the long climb of Moses up the dark mountain of the *deus absconditus* (see Exod. 20). The Exodus text is interpreted as presenting darkness as a symbol, both for the transcendence of God in its objective sense and also for human "ignorance" in its subjective sense as a prerequisite for the "knowledge" of God.[4] And yet both these symbolic movements, from light to darkness (the scaling of cloud-wreathed Sinai) and from darkness to light (the journey from the depths of the cave up to the light of the Sun, as in Plato's *Republic*), meet in their ultimate conclusion, for the consequence of both is blindness. In the case of the cave dweller, blindness is a temporary state until the eyes become accustomed to the brilliance of the Sun's light; in the case of the mountain climber, blindness or sightlessness would appear to be a permanent condition. However, in the last analysis, the darkness metaphors of *apophasis* are understood only in terms of light, be it the excessive light that permanently blinds the eye of the intellect or the *lux inaccessibilis* which prohibits entry to the restored soul. In the context of the final *resolutio*, the darkness of God is at some level comprehended: the revelation of the hidden leaves behind some residual understanding of itself before returning once again to darkness.

The ultimate question, therefore, to keep in mind during the course of this discussion is this: Is Eriugena's appropriation and employment of the principles of *apophasis* faithful to his Cappadocian and Dionysian sources or is it in any way tempered by his reading of Augustine? We shall see that Eriugena does not shrink from the consequences of a rigorous *apophasis* which is carried through from the "here" to the "there," as Plotinus would put it, by applying the principle of the unknowability of the divine essence to the state of the restored soul. I believe, however, that Eriugena's position differs slightly from that of Dionysius and Gregory of Nyssa, and that these differences (nuanced as they are) can be found especially in his exposition and interpretation of the final "cloud of contemplation." Therefore, in order to appreciate, and indeed evaluate, Eriugena's understanding of the darkness of the divine essence as *lux inaccessibilis*, I begin with some brief remarks on the light/dark symbolism in the Greek and Latin traditions before him.

The Latin Tradition: Augustine

In general terms, the main focus of Augustine's thought can be stated simply enough in terms of his underlying reliance upon a number of key Pauline texts. The Christian life is characterized by faith in the unseen God, the faith which guides us through the night of this world to the light of the vision of God "face to face" in the next (1 Cor. 13:12).[5] That God is not known directly in this life but, rather, through his works (Rom. 1:20) is for Augustine a reminder that the next life will be characterized in terms of a more direct knowledge of God (2 Cor. 5:6–7).[6] Augustine's juxtaposition of faith and sight in terms of darkness and light, based as it is upon the Johannine exposition of the Incarnation, reverses the great apophatic symbols of the *Deus absconditus* of the Old Testament: the pejorative sense of darkness (in epistemological, ontological, and moral terms) as sin, evil, death, and ignorance (the state of the world before the coming of the light) is contrasted dramatically with the notion of light as symbolic of good, salvation, life, and knowledge. The Augustinian reliance upon the light metaphor, in terms both of Incarnation and redemption and also in an epistemological context, appears to render wholly invalid the term "darkness" either as a symbol for the transcendence of God or as a symbol for the human response to that transcendence. The two most powerful symbols of the journey of Moses (cloud and fire), fade in the light of the splendor of the revelation of Mount Tabor. Augustine's use of the light metaphor, then, renders his account of the journey of the soul in every aspect as a journey which is best portrayed in terms of a movement from the darkness of ignorance to the light of truth.

The Greek Tradition:
Gregory of Nyssa and Pseudo-Dionysius

In contrast to the general direction of Augustine's thought, we find that the fourth-century Cappadocian Father, Gregory of

Nyssa, develops a Philonic/Alexandrian theme which was to enter into western thought through Eriugena's use of the works of the Pseudo-Dionysius. Although Philo of Alexandria appears to have been the progenitor of the explicit use of the term "darkness" (γνόφος) as illustrative of the transcendence of God (and indeed also of man's intellectual condition in the face of that transcendence), his pioneering account of the journey of the soul in terms of the movement from light, through cloud, to darkness, had only faint reverberations in the earlier Christian Fathers. For the most part, ignorance and the darkness of Sinai were not understood as the culmination of the order of knowledge, but as the ignorance of the multitude.[7]

Gregory of Nyssa's scriptural inspiration for his conception of the progress of the soul as a movement from light to darkness would appear to rely chiefly on Exodus and the Song of Songs. In the *Life of Moses*, he describes the three stages of the journey of the soul as follows: (1) from light, which is knowledge of created effects; (2) through cloud, which involves *aphairesis* (the removal of foreign matter so that God can be known in the mirror of the soul); (3) and finally to darkness, whereby the soul finally knows and sees God through not-knowing and not-seeing.[8] In one remarkable passage in the *Commentary on Ecclesiastes,* he describes the experience of not-knowing most vividly in terms of putting one's foot over the edge of a high cliff (into the area of the non-concept) and finally pulling back in fear.[9] Although the soul moves back to what it is familiar with, to concepts, it now knows that knowing God consists precisely in not knowing God. However, Gregory's portrayal of the darkness in which God is known is not a negative darkness but a "luminous darkness" (like "watchful sleep" and "sober intoxication"), for the soul has entered into the place where God is (Ps. 17:11), the "secret chamber of divine knowledge."[10] "The true vision and the true knowledge of what we seek consists precisely in not seeing, in an awareness that our goal transcends all knowledge and is everywhere cut off from us by the darkness of incomprehensibility."[11] Thus, for Gregory, cloud becomes the not-seeing and not-knowing of existing things, in order that we might "know" that essence which transcends them. Having entered into the place where God is does not mean that the soul now knows the divine essence, however, for that is impossible, even for the resurrected soul. The way Gregory protects the notion of divine incomprehensibility can be seen in his employment and development of Philippians 3:13 and its transference to the post-resurrection era (what has been called his notion of "infinite progress"). The first Good is in its nature infinite; therefore, the enjoyment of it will also be infinite: more is always being grasped and discovered and the search will never overtake its object.[12] God is, therefore, infinitely knowable and infinitely unknowable. It is in Gregory that we find the darkness of Sinai becoming mystical divine darkness wherein the presence of God is experienced; his essence is never seen, not even in theophany.[13]

Pseudo-Dionysius is perhaps Eriugena's most important source for applying equally the symbols of light and darkness to the divine nature. The light metaphors so abundant in the *Divine Names* are set off against the darkness metaphors of the *Mystical Theology*.[14] With regard to the familiar Dionysian use of the darkness symbolism as it appears in the *Mystical Theology,* I note only the following points.[15] The very powerful image of the soul throwing itself sightless (that is, with an "eyeless mind") against the impenetrable rays of the unapproachable light into unity with the superluminous rays, or superluminous gloom, is based upon the fundamental notion that the soul must voluntarily blind itself through the practice of radical *aphairesis:* the not-knowing of creatures.[16] If the darkness of God is hidden to the intellect by the light in existing things, then that light must be extinguished.[17] The *agnosia* of things then becomes the *gnosis* of God, a knowledge which is, as Dionysius describes it, ἀπερικαλυπτός, without the veil of existing things.[18] This ἀπρόσιτον φῶς (inaccessible Light—see 1 Tim. 6:16),[19] is indeed invisible: it is experienced as darkness because the intellect no longer has eyes with which to see. However, at this point I must note that Dionysius (like Eriugena after him) also uses the term "darkness" in a privative sense.[20] That the term "darkness" can be used in both senses is due not only to the elasticity of the metaphor itself but also to the basic Dionysian rule of thumb, the ὑπερφατική: God is neither light nor darkness, but beyond both.[21]

The Meeting of East and West: Eriugena

I come now to an exposition of Eriugena's employment and development of the light/cloud/dark symbolism, keeping in mind that these metaphors are always *vestigia et theophaniae veritatis*,[22] a means of access to that realm wherein speech and thought are denied full access. The Trinity is contemplated, says Eriugena, at a deeper and truer level than can be expressed in speech, and is understood more deeply than it is contemplated, and it *is*, that is, *exists* more deeply and more truly than it is understood, for it passes all understanding.[23]

We can begin this discussion of Eriugena's use of *nubes* and *tenebrae* with some brief reminders of the general focus of his employment of the light metaphor.[24] First, in terms of the cosmic drama of salvation and redemption, light symbolizes the procession of the light of the Father, in Christ, who illumines the hidden places of darkness and ignorance.[25] After the expulsion from paradise, the human condition of darkness and ignorance stands in need of illumination and redemption.[26] Second, the use of the light metaphor in an epistemological context portrays God as the *lux mentium*,[27] enlightening the ignorant mind with the brightness of pure knowledge.[28] Third, the light metaphor is also used as an expression for the diffusion of all things from their causes into created effects. The more Neoplatonic character of this theme, inspired by the Dionysian interpretation of a phrase from James 1:17 ("the Father of lights"),[29] explains the primordial causes in their effects as "brightness" and "day" and in their hidden nature as "night" and "darkness."[30] Eriugena's comments on the first day of Genesis interpret creation as a movement from darkness to light, from the unknown to the known.[31]

Eriugena's use of the light metaphor, then, in all three aspects, involves an understanding of the term "darkness" as symbolic of ignorance, damnation, evil, sin, hell, and privation. How can he then adopt the term as a symbolic expression for the transcendence of God's nature? The answer, of course, rests in the fact that Eriugena, following Dionysius, asserts that although we can speak of God in terms of light or darkness, he is neither.[32] Apart from the necessary transcendence in dialectical terms of all conceptual and symbolic representations of God, there is no confusion in Eriugena's mind in applying the terms "darkness" and "ignorance" both to God and to the human condition. The reason is that the understanding of God as light (and indeed of Christ as the "light of the world") belongs to an inner, secondary account, of theological analysis in the *Periphyseon*. The description of humanity moving from the light of paradise to the darkness of damnation after the fall, and its complementary movement from the light of Christ either to the darkness of the excellence of the divine nature or to the darkness of hell (Eriugena repeats the interpretation of Ambrose in his *Commentary on Luke* that "outer darkness" is hell)[33] is, I believe, situated within the overall, more general, understanding of the movement from the original dark hiddenness of God into the light of manifestation and back once again to darkness.

It is in this sense that we find Eriugena using the term darkness to describe the primordial causes in the absolute purity of their unfathomable depth: they are *tenebrosae abyssi*.[34] Even when the primordial causes are revealed in the light of manifold forms, they remain always in a dark abyss: *in secretissimis divinae sapientiae semper sedeant*,[35] for the causes, in true Neoplatonic fashion, both remain in themselves and proceed into all things.[36] Darkness, then, can be used as an expression either for the excellence of the divine nature,[37] or as symbolic of the condition of human nature before redemption. This is the predominant meaning of the use of darkness in the *Homily*.

I have shown that Eriugena does not diverge significantly from his Dionysian source in his employment of the light/darkness metaphor. It is, however, in his expression of the cloud symbolism that we find some notable differences emerging.

Although Eriugena is often thought of in the same terms as Gregory and Dionysius with regard to *apophasis,* it is surprising to note that he does not (except for one fleeting mention in book V)[38] make use of the cloud of Sinai as expressive of the ultimate ontological and epistemological condition of the restored soul. Instead, we find him focusing upon the clouds of the New Testament, the clouds of the Ascension and Transfiguration, but more especially: (a) the cloud of heaven upon which the Son of Man will come (Dan. 7:13 and Matt. 26:64); and (b) the clouds into which those who have died with Christ will be taken up to meet with the Lord in the air (1 Thess. 4:17).[39] Although Eriugena does make use of the Dionysian notion of cloud, it is the context which sets his employment of it apart from the Areopagite's thought. The eschatological dimension of Eriugena's discussion puts it at one remove from the more immediate spiritual and epistemological significance to be found in Gregory of Nyssa and in Dionysius.

The most significant and comprehensive discussion of the cloud symbol can be found in book V of the *Periphyseon*.[40] Using both Ambrose and Maximus, Eriugena comments on the clouds into which the saints will be taken up. Repeating Maximus, he explains that each saint will have his own cloud wherein he will see and rejoice in theophanies; he rejects Ambrose's notion that only the patriarchs will have clouds. The rather interesting, and indeed most unapophatic, description of the cloud from Ambrose's *Commentary on Luke* is repeated by Eriugena: the cloud of light which moistens the mind with the dew of faith and is sent by the Word.[41] The other clouds, those upon which the Son of Man will come, are understood to be the celestial substances which always attend Christ in contemplation through theophany.[42]

Clouds would appear, therefore, to symbolize the means of experiencing theophany; because God is invisible in himself, he can be seen only in cloud: *Deus enim omnino nulli creaturae visibilis per seipsum est, sed in nubibus theoriae videtur.*[43] The ascent into the "cloud of contemplation" is explained by Eriugena as the highest theophany, the vision of God "face to face,"[44] wherein each will "see" God according to capacity.[45]

Clouds, as the "theophanies of the righteous,"[46] would appear to be the final resting place of the soul, for the transcendence of the divine nature is *inaccessibilis*. Or is it? At 920A of *Periphyseon* V, Eriugena quotes the Letter of Dionysius to Dorotheus, where cloud and darkness are called *lux inaccessibilis*. Entry into the cloud, therefore, is entry into inaccessible light: the final stage of the restoration of the elect is described as entry into the darkness of "inaccessible light."[47] The *accessus* to the *inaccessibilis* is, however, limited, in the sense that God is known and seen by not being known or seen: the resurrected soul knows *that* God is, not *what* God is, even in the highest theophanies.[48] Access to the inaccessible is permitted. Theophany itself is, in some measure, the apparition of the unapparent;[49] the ineffable light is present to all intellectual eyes, but it is not known as to *what* it is, only *that* it is.[50] Ignorance, in the superlative sense, is the not-knowing which is ineffable wisdom.[51] There is also access to the inaccessible primordial light of the Father through Christ: *per quem ad principale lumen, Patrem accessum habemus.* Although no one has seen the Father, to have seen the Son (*paternum lumen*) is to have seen the Father.[52]

Although Eriugena uses the Dionysian theme of cloud and darkness as expressive of the situation of the restored soul, we do not find him developing the Areopagite's notion of blindness or sightlessness. There is one brief mention in *Periphyseon,* book II, where, quoting Maximus, he says that through perfect ἀορασία one can attain to God,[53] but for the most part, that blindness wherein the sightless intellect experiences God is absent from Eriugena's thought. Even his use of the term "theophany" carries with it something of the sense of vision: the eyes of the intellect are open, even though they do not see the hidden essence of the divine nature. In this sense, I believe that Eriugena's understanding differs slightly from that of his Greek predecessors.

I come now to the final point I wish to make concerning Eriugena's use of the cloud metaphor, one that concerns his appropriation of Gregory of Nyssa's development of Philippians 3:13 in eschatological terms. According to Eriugena, the quest for God is endless, for God is indeed found in theophany, but is not found as to what he is in himself.[54] His comments on Isaiah 6:2, where the angels hide their feet and faces with their wings (theophanies), are expanded in a direction which emphasizes their infinite search, always being beaten back by the radiance of divine splendor.[55] While this idea is certainly true to Gregory's formulation, nonetheless there exists a difference between Eriugena's notion of hiding one's eyes from the divine radiance and Gregory's notion of being unseeing in the "luminous darkness" with God. The metaphor changes for Gregory from sight to touch when the soul closes its intellectual eyes and enters into the place where God is. For Eriugena it does not.

In conclusion, I suggest that perhaps this difference between the two thinkers reflects on Eriugena's part, at least in some measure, his acceptance of the light-dominated thought of his greatest Latin authority, namely, Augustine. In this sense, Eriugena would appear to have brought together the diverse elements of eastern and western thought on the subject of the final "vision" of God (although to see the light/darkness symbolism as representative of a clear-cut division between East and West runs the risk of distortion). In the Nyssean/Dionysian sense, the blinded intellect entering into unknowing union with God contrasts forcefully with the Augustinian interpretation of the ultimate vision of God "face to face." Eriugena understood both only too well, and he would appear to have effected a compromise whereby the vision of God is vision "face to face," even though that vision is mediated via theophany.

In the last analysis, it is Eriugena's emphasis on the concepts of vision and sight along with his individual use of the cloud symbolism which places him alongside Augustine more than with Gregory or Dionysius. I believe, however, that it is the expression of his thought which is more Augustinian than Dionysian, for Eriugena's *apophasis* is no less radical than that of either Gregory or Dionysius. In fact, Eriugena's understanding of the absolute incomprehensibility of the divine essence is more elitist even than that of Gregory of Nyssa, for only the elect pass beyond the cloud into the darkness which is itself inaccessible Light.[56]

NOTES

1. See, most recently, J. J. McEvoy, "Metaphors of Light and Metaphysics of Light in Eriugena," in *Begriff und Metapher*, ed. W. Beierwaltes (Heidelberg, 1990), 149–167.

2. P III 650D–651A.

3. See McEvoy, 161.

4. See V. Lossky, *In the Image and Likeness of God* (Oxford, 1974), 31–43.

5. Augustine, *Enarrationes in psalmos*, Ps. 142 10.

6. Augustine, *De Trinitate* VIII 4 (6); and *In Ioannis evangelium tractatus* 109 2 (3). For Augustine's employment of apophatic themes, see D. Carabine, "Negative Theology in the Thought of Augustine," in *Recherches de théologie ancienne et médiévale* 59 (1992): 5–22.

7. See H. C. Puech, "La ténèbre mystique chez le Pseudo-Denys l'Aréopagite et dans la tradition patristique," *Etudes carmélitaines* 23 (1938): 46–49; and V. Lossky, *Essai sur la théologie mystique de l'église d'orient* (reprint, Paris, 1990), 33–34.

8. Gregory of Nyssa, *Vita Moysis* II 164.

9. Gregory of Nyssa, *In Ecclesiasten*, sermo 7.

10. See Gregory of Nyssa, *Super cantica canticorum* 11. Cf. *Vita Moysis* II 86–87 and *Super cantica canticorum* 6.

11. Gregory of Nyssa, *Vita Moysis* II 87 (6–9).

12. Gregory of Nyssa, *Contra Eunomium* I 219.

13. Gregory of Nyssa, *Super cantica canticorum* 11.

14. E.g., Pseudo-Dionysius, *De mystica theologia* I 4, II 4, III 1, IV 4, IV 5.

15. See Puech, "La ténèbre mystique," for an invaluable account of the Dionysian use of the symbol of darkness.

16. See, e.g., Pseudo-Dionysius, *De mystica theologia* I 1, and *De divinis nominibus* IV 11.

17. See Pseudo-Dionysius, *Epistola* I.

18. Pseudo-Dionysius, *De mystica theologia* I 3.

19. Pseudo-Dionysius, *Epistola* V.

20. See especially Pseudo-Dionysius, *Epistola* XI.

21. Pseudo-Dionysius, *De mystica theologia* V.

22. P II 614C.

23. "Sed haec altius ac verius cogitantur quam sermone proferuntur et altius ac verius intelliguntur quam cogitantur, altius autem ac
verius sunt quam intelliguntur; omnem siquidem intellectum super-
ant" (P II 614C). Eriugena is repeating here an Augustinian formula:
see *De Trinitate* V 3 (4), VII 4 (7); *De civitate dei* X 13.

24. I direct the reader to the exposition mentioned in n. 1, above.

25. P II 564B; III 656D, 664D, 684A; and V 963C. See also *Homélie sur le Prologue de Jean* XI (SC 151:256, 258–260).

26. P III 683C; V 924C, 1002C–D, 1009C, 1018A.

27. P II 684A.

28 P II 683C and 691B. See also P V 1017A, 988C–D; III 651A;
Hom. X 289B, XII 290B–C, and XVII 293A–B. Ignorance used in the
pejorative sense as representative of the human condition before the
coming of the light can be found at P III 708D; IV 761A, 777C, 781C,
813B; and V 867C.

29. See P II 565C; III 684C; as well as the first chapter of the *Expositiones in Ierarchiam coelestem* (CCCM 31:1–19).

30. P III 692B–693A.

31. P III 619B and ff.; IV 781A and ff.

32. P I 460B; see Pseudo-Dionysius, *De mystica theologia* V.

33. See P V 936C and 946A.

34. P II 550C; and III 692B–693A.

35. P II 551B.

36. Eriugena's account of this notion is situated within the context
of his discussion of Genesis 1:1. See, e.g., P II 552A.

37. See P III 681B; and IV 773C. The only use of darkness in this
sense in *Hom.* is found at XIII 219B.

38. P V 999A. He does refer once in the *Commentary on John* to vision via the cloud (see *Comm.* I XXV [SC180:124–126]).

39. At this point, I should note that Eriugena also uses cloud
symbolism in a privative sense: the cloud of fleshly thoughts and
the cloud of error and faithlessness of the Antichrist (see P III
683C; V 996A–B).

40. P V 998A and ff., and also at 945D–946A.

41. See P V 1000A.

42. P V 1000B–1001A.

43. P V 905C. See also P V 945C–D.

44. P V 926C–D. See also *Comm.* I XXV [SC 180:124–126].

45. P V 876B and 945C–D.

46. P V 913C, 945C–946A, 982C.

47. P V 1020C–D. On the theme of "inaccessible light," see P II 579B, 551C; III 633A, 668C.

48. P V 919C, 1010D.

49. P III 633A; II 557B.

50. P III 668C. See also P IV 771B–C: God is more honored in ignorance than in knowledge.

51. See P I 510B; II 590C–D, 593C–D, 597D–598A; and IV 771C.

52. *Expositiones in Ierarchiam* 2 (CCCM 31:29).

53. P II 534C.

54. P V 919A–D.

55. P III 668A–C and 614D–615A.

56. The Dionysian exhortation to Timothy not to divulge mystical secrets to the uninitiated (see *De divinis nominibus* I) may have been responsible for this aspect of Eriugena's thought.

Biblical and Platonic Measure in John Scottus Eriugena

James McEvoy

THE NOTION OF MEASURE makes most people today think sponta-
neously of the scientific and technological domains, but in premodern times rather of corn, wine, oil, and their exchange at the
marketplace, where the measure in its various forms was a fundamental requisite of everyday life. In premodern life, architects and
builders had, of course, their yardlines, set squares, and measuring rods, incorporating units that must have varied greatly from
people to people and place to place, but which engendered notions
of accuracy achievable by counting, in ways that foreshadowed the
incomparably more accurate standards of the contemporary age,
with its strictly defined, purely conventional units that have long
since lost any relationship to the body and its members. Time, also,
was an object of measurement—though the reader of, say, brilliant ancient discussions of time, such as those to be found in Plotinus or Augustine, is struck at once by the fluidity—sometimes
literally so, as in the case of the hydratic clock!—of, for instance,
the hours of the day. The month and year fared better, because of
the regularity of the lunations.

I. The Premodern Senses of "Measure"

It may prove instructive to begin our reflection upon the
measure theme in Eriugena by returning to the experiences
which shaped the literal sense of the numerous metaphors and
concepts that mark both the biblical and the philosophical traditions of which Eriugena and also we ourselves are the heirs.
For measurement forms part of the fundamental stratum of ancient classical and European languages, for reasons that are easy
to appreciate.

153

This preliminary reflection has the advantage of evoking the rich experiential and linguistic associations of the measures used throughout antiquity, especially perhaps in ages before money became "the measure of all things," or at least of all commodities, insofar as there is still any distinction left between thing and commodity.

Perhaps the simplest measure of all was a cup or can, used—as it still was in my childhood, in Ireland—to measure liquids like milk and oil, or products such as barley and grain. The cup itself was the measure; so was the fill of its content ("a measure of corn"). In barter societies it is easy to imagine its use, always provided that agreement could be reached to exchange, say, three cups of wine as the equivalent of one measure of grain. The variability of harvests would lead to fluctuations in the application of the measure, but without destroying the value of the measure itself, as the standard for each product's distribution; the variation would affect the number of fills of oil reckoned by the market to be the equivalent of a different number of measures of, say, wine, at a given season. Thus, as soon as we have a measure at all, we have at once the practice of counting, by adding or multiplying the unit measure. Measure and number are inseparable notions right from the start, and they begin with equality, or one, since an equal or equivalent exchange of different things (or of a commodity against a unit of money) is what the recourse to a measure is meant to provide.

The second measure, the scales in balance, is a development of the first, for the balance scales (in Latin, *statera*) is in essence nothing else than two cups or cans suspended to balance when empty, and hence also when full. In this device the notion of weighing is obviously the central one, for a quantity is measured—and hence rendered definite or determinate—either by equality of content on both sides of the balance or by reference to the weights placed on one side of the scale. The operation can be repeated so many times, or the weights varied on the basis of a unit—the tiniest weight used—to give almost any desired result. And so, to the ideas of *measure* and *number* is added that of *weight;* which recalls at once the statement in the Old Testament Book of Wisdom (11:21) that "God created all things in measure, number, and weight."

By the way, the same triad turns up, not so very surprisingly perhaps, in the *Statesman* of Plato, a fact which has given rise to a learned hypothesis[1] concerning the presence of Platonism in the

Alexandria which saw the composition, around the middle of the first century B.C., of the biblical work.[2] However, "we have no need of that hypothesis": it is simply *de trop*. Platonic or general Greek intellectual influence there may well be in some later books of the Old Testament—just as in earlier portions there is Egyptian influence—but the triad of number, weight, and measure is too much a part of traditional experience, written as it is into the very scales themselves, to require explanation when found in different cultures.

The scales became an image of justice, for evident reasons, and even of the cosmological justice at work in the annual regulation of opposing qualities—hot and cold, dry and wet—in the seasonal rhythm. And since that justice was widely attributed to the sun and its light, the sun became in the Old Testament *sol iustitiae*, and in Greek classical philosophy the symbol of justice. The moral sense of measure so prominent in the Greek mind, and encapsulated in the proverb "the measure is best" (*metron ariston*), is, I take it, derived from the balance of the scales; for a measured action or attitude avoids excess, that is to say, too much on either side: μέτρον is a mean, a *medietas*, hence right action must be measure, or even the *aurea mediocritas* of Horace—how words change their meanings over time in the sphere of moral discourse!

The third measure applied to lengths, of land to be divided, say, or of stones or wood to be cut, and was used by surveyors, architects, and builders. It is the measuring rod, or κανών, in Greek. I suppose that the rod itself may sometimes have functioned as the unit; but then the practical requirement of measuring lengths shorter than itself must quickly have led to systems of its internal calibration, into four, or six, or ten or more. Perhaps, mathematically speaking, six would have represented the optimal choice, since it is divisible by one, two, and three, whereas ten is divisible only by one and five; that is why six was adopted as the basis of Babylonian measurement and of astronomy, in particular, giving us still 360 degrees to the circle and 60 minutes to the hour. The calibrated measuring rod, or ruler, is used to lay off so many of its own lengths against an extended object, to yield an accurate measure. Plato called this kind of measuring μετρητικὴ τεχνή, and he sought to transfer to the domain of right and wrong judgment of actions the values of accuracy and objectivity it incorporates. Aristotle thought of the canon when he claimed, in *Metaphysics* 10, that we measure something in order to know it better—meaning

by that, more determinately, more accurately. This perception it
was which led him to discuss whether knowing is more like measuring, or like being measured.

Is there a notion common to these three measures? All three
create or establish a relationship between two things: an object for
exchange (or a project of building), for example, and some objective standard, a rule and measure: *regula et mensura,* as Aquinas
will say, when thinking of the creative ideas of God as the true
standard for created being and activity. The act of μετρεῖν posits a
standard of reality and objectivity to overcome the false effects of
passion, bad judgment, illusion, relativism, and arbitrariness.

The notions of measure give rise to their own opposing states,
for an object that is not measured, or that is not capable of being
measured, has no definite limit that can be known, and an act that
knows no measure is indefinite, lacking in limit, uncircumscribed
and unbalanced (the French word *démesuré* expresses these and
similar meanings). On the other hand, however, two realities may
be deemed incommensurable—the heavens and the earth, the
creator and the creation—because they do not stand in a relationship to any third thing that might supply a common standard to
both; they are related asymmetrically as incommensurables.
Again, two or more things, when measured against a standard,
can be said to be measured together, so that the Greek notion of
συμμετρία is given, and also that of ἀναλογία, since the operation
is constituted by the reference of each element to a common factor,
or λόγος. In this case (and here one thinks of the Pseudo-
Dionysius) each of the various realities will have its own particular
relationship to the standard, while at the same time the plurality
in question will be related, as plurality or multiplicity, to the One.
Aristotle had a similar idea in *Metaphysics* 4, 2; Aquinas was to express the Aristotelian notion of "equivocity including reference to
one" in terms of the analogy *plurium ad unum.* In this usage the
central or transcendent value of the measure, its degree of univer-
sality, will be highlighted.[3]

II. Biblical Motifs

It is not surprising to find among the Proverbs of the Old Testament the castigation of unjust dealing by the deceitful use of
weights and measures in commerce: "Diverse weights and diverse

measures, both are abominable before God" (Prov. 20:10).[4] In Job, measuring becomes a cosmological metaphor, for the creation is the product of the wisdom and understanding (Job 28:20) of God, "who made a weight for the winds and weighed the waters by measure" (28:25). But the weighing and measuring of the creatures, although the work of a wise mind and the expression of its plan, are not as such available to the creature, for the mind of God is far beyond any created understanding and to question the mighty wisdom from which all things proceed is temerarious. When Jahweh answers Job in the theophany of a whirlwind, it is with a question full of rebuke and reproach against the presumption that Job has shown: "Where wast thou when I laid the foundations of the earth? Tell me if thou hast understanding. Who hath laid the measures thereof, if thou knowest? Or who hath stretched the line upon it?" (Job 38:4–5).

In the Book of Wisdom, which comes at the very end of Old Testament times, we find a reflection which was to attract much attention in Christian exegesis, above all from St. Augustine. God, it is said, "ordered all things in measure, and number, and weight" (11:21). In the context of a song in praise of divine wisdom this phrase may be said to have a double meaning, for it can refer to God's actions in providential history, preserving and chastising his people with the measure of wisdom, and it can also refer to the creation itself, the work of might and wisdom combined (11:18; 22–23). But if verse 21 can be read as applying to both creation and the economy of salvation, it must be admitted that patristic exegesis, and in particular the influential agency of Augustine, withdrew the verse from salvation history and sought in it enlightenment concerning the relationship of the universe to its wise creator. Thus the double sense affirmed by the context became the single sense bearing upon the characteristic of the divine creator of being or nature.

Jesus used the simile of a measure of wheat, a generous measure which his followers are to use generously, in the awareness that the measure employed for giving will be the same used for the return: "Give and it shall be given to you: good measure and pressed down and shaken together and running over. . . . For with the same measure that you shall mete, withal it shall be measured to you again" (Luke 6:38; cf. Matt. 7:2). The context—the Beatitudes and the love even of enemies—suggests the nature of the

measure: just as God loves and pardons without measure, so must
the disciples of Christ love and pardon without calculation, or in
the measure that they have received, which means, in reality, without measure.

In the Gospel according to John, the Baptist speaks thus of the
Christ: "For he whom God has sent, speaketh the words of God:
for God doth not give the Spirit by measure [ἐκ μέτρου]. The Fa-
ther loveth the Son; and he hath given all things into his hand"
(John 3:34–35). The Christ, accordingly, will have the Spirit of
God in him without measure.

St. Paul comes back several times to the image of the measure
generously given by the God of redemption. Paul is content to measure the worth and the range of his own apostolate, not by comparison with that of others, but solely with reference to "the God
of measure": "But we will not glory beyond our measure; but according to the measure of the rule which God [ὁ θεὸς μέτρου] has
measured to us, a measure to reach even unto you" (2 Cor. 10:13).

We must assume that John Scottus was familiar with the references to measure in the New Testament, each one of which highlights some aspect of the reality of the redemption. There are,
however, two scriptural passages which we have not yet considered
and which, attracting his attention with particular force, were expounded by him in book V of the *Periphyseon*.

In Ephesians 4 Paul reflects upon unity in the one Spirit, that
unity which makes all believers into the body of Christ but which
allows at the same time for diversity of spiritual gifts: "But to every
one of us is given grace, according to the measure of the giving of
Christ" (4:47). The gifts in their diversity are given to build up the
one body of Christ, "until we all attain the unity of faith, and of
the knowledge of the Son of God, unto a perfect man, unto the
measure of the age of the fullness of Christ" (4:13).

Eriugena's extended commentary on this passage, and on the
doctrine of the headship of Christ in the Letter to Ephesians, is
occasioned by his dismay at the naive form of belief in the resurrection of the body (P V, 994B–995B). He comments on the Greek
words of Eph. 4:13, εἰς μέτρον ἡλικίας, arguing that they cannot
be construed to refer to the fullness of the age of Christ's body,
attained in the thirtieth year of his age, as though each human being is to rise again in the size and height his or her body attained
in the flower of youth (as Augustine maintained would be the
case). How should those who died before their time, or decrepit

or defective in body, rise in a perfect body of thirty years of age? The suggestion is wayward and inadmissible, thinks Eriugena. He makes appeal to the context of verse 13, claiming that the body of Christ of which Paul speaks there is the Church. Now the measure and fullness of the Church's spiritual time is identical with its spiritual head (994C) who is the end and consummation of all things. The Church is the "corpus et plenitudo eius [sc. Christi] qui omnia in omnibus adimpletur" (Eph. 1:23). Hence the measure and fullness of the time of Christ will no longer be seen by the eyes of the body but perceived instead from within the unity of the body under its head, and the spiritual time, the fullness of all virtues, will be accomplished in eternal blessedness. The literalist misunderstanding of the Apostle's reference to "the measure of the age" cannot be defended, for it is not the true meaning of the Apostle himself. In this way Paul's reference to "the measure" in the context of his headship doctrine became a moment of importance in Eriugena's teaching on the return of all things through Christ to that perfect unity in which nothing is lost, all is consummated, and the physical as physical, having achieved its purpose in the overall redemptive plan, makes its return to unity by passing upward into the spiritual.

"And he that spoke with me had a measure [$\mu\acute{\epsilon}\tau\rho o\nu$] of a reed of gold, to measure the city and the gates thereof, and the wall" (Rev. 21:15). It must, I think, be this verse that John Scottus has in mind when he refers to Christ as the measuring rod "because he rules and measures all things" (P V, 981C). The passage in which this idea comes up is the meditation on Christ the tree of life in the center of paradise (980D–982B). Eriugena develops a mystical sense of the building of the Temple of Solomon in order to support his own allegorization of the tree of life: all men are placed according to their degree within the natural paradise of eschatology, as within the outer precinct of the Temple, but only those sanctified in Christ shall enter the Temple, wherein everything is a type of Christ: the altar of incense, the ark, the altar of sacrifice, and indeed the measure by which all things (in the eschaton) are measured (981C).

III. Plato and Neoplatonism

Broadly speaking, it was Plato who first developed notions associated with measure and made them a constitutive part of his philosophy.[5] Four dialogues are of particular importance for the theme, namely, *Protagoras, Philebus, Theaetetus* and *Laws*.

The young Socrates approaches Protagoras with two questions: What does a Sophist teach? Can virtue be taught, much as an art can be? Now when Plato addresses the question How are we to live? we can generally expect that the life of pleasure will be taken up and considered, as a dialectical starting point. Socrates leads the discussion from the idea that it is good to live pleasurably, towards a disjunction between pleasure and pain, on the one hand, and good and evil, on the other, as quite different sets of scales for the weighing of experience. If we go by pleasure and pain, admitting no other criterion, then questions of worth are replaced by excess and defect in comparison, or greater and less: "Like a practiced weigher, put pleasant things and painful in the scales, and with them the nearness and the remoteness, and tell me which count for more" (*Protagoras* 356C). Socrates at once moves away from this calculus to the relativity of objects of sight and sound, of thickness and number, depending upon their nearness to and distance from the perceiver, and asks whether, if the safety of our life lay in choosing, say, large things rather than small, we would choose to rely upon the art of measurement (μετρητικὴ τέχνη) or upon the perceptual impact of appearances (ἡ τοῦ φαινομένου δύναμις, 356D). The force of truth is poured into the discussion, for true measurement annuls perceptual relativity and ends the confusion which that engenders. In that case our salvation would be assured by ἐπιστήμη, that is to say, by measurement, and the numbering on which that is based. The point of the parable, needless to say, is that life does depend upon right choices in the area of pleasure and pain, and that there must be an art and science (τέχνη καὶ ἐπιστήμη) which guides us with truth.

Philebus is linked with *Protagoras* (as well as with *Gorgias*) by the discussion concerning pleasure and the true good of life. Pure pleasure is opposed to any limit; like pain, it is limitless. If, however, the good life consists in a mixture of pleasure and reason, supposing that pleasure has a part in reason, as Socrates maintains it does, then knowledge must be given a place in human life. We come back, then, to the place of "numbering, measuring, and weighing" in the arts (*Philebus* 55E), and we must distinguish between arts which, like building, are more mathematical and accurate, using instruments of measurement, and those like music, on the other hand, which have less accuracy in them. We should also distinguish between pure mathematics (which is exact) and applied (which is less so).

In the life mixed of contemplation and pleasure, the highest pleasure attaches to the highest knowledge (63). The nature of mixture naturally reintroduces measure and proportion (μέτρον καὶ συμμετρία), which are at once allied with beauty (κάλλος) and virtue (ἀρετή) and with "the power of the good." The good can be made visible only through beauty (συμμετρία) and truth (ἀλήθεια); μετριότης, measure, forsakes once and for all the limitless and immoderate (ἄμετρον) nature of pleasure, since measure is internal to mind and knowledge. The crowning accolade of measure follows at once (66A): the eternal nature has chosen μέτρον and the moderation and balance which it confers (τὸ μέτριον), together with το καίριον, the fitting, and all such terms as the very first of goods; after which, in second place, come proportion (σύμμετρον, the effect of measure), beauty, perfection, etc.; in the third place are νοῦς and φρόνησις; and in the fourth, the arts and sciences. The highest pleasures follow this hierarchy faithfully. All are the offspring of the ἀγαθόν, which in itself remains invisible.

In the *Theaetetus,* Plato confronts, in its sharpest delineation and formulation, that relativism which he always attributes to Protagoras. The identification of perception with knowledge is "the description which Protagoras used to give." "Man is the measure of all things, of those that are, that they are, and of those that are not, that they are not" (152A). Plato may be expected to invoke the art of measurement, which promises rescue from the power of appearance—and so indeed he does (154B). Throughout the maieutic passage (150C), the dictum of Protagoras is undermined by the Socratic profession that "it is the God who compels me to act as midwife" (150C), and by the implicit suggestion that the human cannot be the ultimate measure of anything: a higher kind of weighing and measuring always has the last word. Socrates indeed asks the youthful Theaetetus, "Do you think Protagoras's 'measure' applies any less to gods than to men?"(162C).

In the *Laws* the opposition of the human and the divine measure becomes fully articulate. The Athenian Stranger opens his address to those who are to found a new colony with the acknowledgment that "the god holds the beginning and end and middle of all things that exist" (715E). That is the god's nature and also the nature of divine *dike,* which is the criterion for human life, whether in its folly and abandonment by the god or in that likeness to the god which is the aim and achievement of those who are the god's acolytes, since only what follows the measure can be "dear" or "like" to what has the measure within it (ἐμμέτροις); "but let the god be for us the measure of all things, in the highest degree, much more than any man they talk of " (716C). The conclusion may be drawn from what Plato says, that the man who is temperate and ordered will be loved by the god, for his measure will be attuned to the divine measure.[6]

It is in Plotinus, as one might expect, that the Platonic thought concerning the invisible divine measure of all things finds an eminently dialectical expression. Immanent to the thought of Plato is the implication that the divine measure of being is the highest causal agency, the framer of the universe, the one who allots to each kind of thing a share in the good. This thought is made explicit by Plotinus: the One is the first principle and the universal cause of being, the absolute measure of all that exists, μέτρον οὐ μετρούμενον (*Enneads* V, 5,4). At *Enneads* I, 8,2 the One is designated μέτρον πάντων καὶ πέρας. In genuinely Platonic fashion, Plotinus draws the notion of measure towards form, limit, and intelligibility—the work of reason—allying it with number as a principle of order in the universe.

It fell to Proclus to give the most systematic treatment of the Platonic theme of measure.[7] His thoughts on this subject are drawn by the very movement of procession and reversion into a meditation upon that causality of higher being which measures their products by unity and number, and upon the participation of the effects in the causes according to the measure of their being and their place within the whole hierarchical order of the cosmos. Procession and reversion, the ideas which predominate in his thought, are linked by a common measure, for as a being proceeds so it reverts: the measure of its reversion is set by the measure of its procession, so that what proceeds into existence as intellect must make its return through consciousness of the Good, its cause. The measure of being is also the measure of activity. Unity defines and measures all the manifold of existent things, drawing them away from indetermination; that which possesses unity tends of its nature to measure and determine the things in which it is active as cause, hence each divine being is a measure of beings (*Elements*, proposition 117). Every cause furnishes the measure to the product, and it is in this that the superiority of cause to effect is apparent. Variation as between different beings is not due to the divine and unitary but to the varying capacity of the effects, each of which participates in being according to the measure of its own presence to the divine. No good quality can be found in derivative beings that is not present and preexistent in the divine, as in the measure.

IV. Pseudo-Dionysius

Chapter 4 of *The Divine Names* is a contemplation of the name Good and the names most closely associated with it—Light and Beauty among others. Plotinus's image of the Good as pouring forth a multiplicity of rays into being is adopted (through the agency of Proclus) and the variety of the receptions of being-light are enumerated, beginning with the pure intellects in their different orders. Human souls participate according to their measure in the illuminations of the good, as in their different ways do living things and material, unsouled things. This is the same hierarchy as that of Proclus. Measurement and order are given to the visible cosmos by the sun, the image of the archetypal good that is the source and creator of all order; and Ps.-Dionysius gathers into a single phrase the Platonic and Neoplatonic symbols of the transcendence of the source over the product: "the Good is the μέτρον of the universe and its eternity, its numerical principle, its order, its power, its cause, and its end" (chap. 4,4). All creatures in time are measured by eternity (chap. 10,3) and participate in unity and being according to the analogy or receptive capacity of their being, which likewise ensures their place in the hierarchical outpouring of things, their activity, and the way of their turning back towards their source. God is the measure of being (chap. 5,8): all that is, is measured through him, the one universal μέτρον; but he himself, being superessential, is unmeasurable.

It is a central truth, in the eyes of Dionysius, that God is the transcendent and universal measure, just as he is the transcendent, universal source of order (ταξιαρχία). René Roques has noticed that Dionysius never employs the term μέτρον of created beings, preferring to apply to them the composite word συμμετρία, which signifies, at least by implication, the common measure to which all creatures must be traced back.[8] In this way all that is measure in beings must be referred back to the absolute measure, or the measure in itself, the divine measure, as image to archetype. In the view of Roques, analogy and symmetry are two aspects of a complex idea. Both signify the relationship of the intelligence to God, but each does so through its own specific meaning. From the side of the divine, symmetry and analogy designate the maximal ideal measure of participation assigned to each being in a way fixed by God; in that sense the two terms denote predeterminations, divine ideas. On the other hand, the individual intelligence has to equate itself with the gift offered it by its own being, activity, and location within the universal order, as determined and distributed by the divine wisdom. Hence the second aspect of analogy/symmetry relates the intelligent creature as a free being to the attainment of its true place within the providential order of things, as by its free initiative it responds to God's creating and redeeming love.

V. St. Augustine

In the thought of Ps.-Dionysius regarding measure, order, symmetry, and analogy it was the transmission of the Platonic heritage through Proclus which was the defining element, and in fact the biblical references to measure receded behind the philosophical.[9] Augustine, on the contrary, seems almost to have aimed at uniting the biblical motifs with the Platonic, which he appears to have met with only in their Plotinian form. In consequence of this aim, Augustine's development of the measure themes in the two forms available to him, and his ingenious and original intertwining of the biblical with the Plotinian, makes up by far the richest patristic meditation on the notions that are the object of this inquiry. As we shall see, John Scottus was attracted to this aspect of Augustine's thinking and drew consistently upon a number of its major developments. In particular, he was to adopt the Plotinian inflection accorded by Augustine to the biblical triad of created *mensura*, *numerus*, and *pondus*, which yielded the dialectical formulation, *mensura sine mensura, numerus sine numero, pondus sine pondere*, to designate God as the source of all created order, a source who nevertheless can only be thought of as in himself the beyond of all that is constituted "in measure, number, and weight."

"Deus omnia disposuit in mensura, numero et pondere" (Wisdom 11:21). No patristic author returned to this idea for inspiration more frequently or in more varied contexts than did Augustine. Each member of this triad has a definite kernel of meaning in his thought, and the triad itself makes up a strand in the counterpoint of triadic formulas employed by Augustine. The terms of the triad vary, frequently in a way that relates the triad explicitly to the very central Augustinian idea of order: *mensura, numerus, ordo; summa mensura, summus numerus, summus ordo; naturae moderatae, naturae formatae, naturae ordinatae. Ordo* can even be replaced by *caritas,* a possibility replete with the development of Augustine's entire intellectual and spiritual life. *Modus* is a synonym for *mensura,* and in his treatise on the Good,[10] *modus, species,* and *ordo,* which may be regarded as a triad that encloses that of *mensura, numerus,* and *pondus,* are declared to be "tamquam generalia bona . . . in rebus a Deo factis," in other words transcendental qualities of being that has been created good—for, of course, the *De natura boni* is directed against Manichaean dualism. From God is every measure, great or small, that is expressed within the creation. As the unique source of being, good, and order, however, God must be above all measure, species, or order, since it is from him that all measure, form, and order come to be. Augustine seeks thus to vindicate the inherent goodness of being, and he closes the first part of his work with praise of God, who has no limit, no opposite, and no measure (I, 22).

In *De Genesi ad litteram* IV, 3,7 Augustine will claim that measure, number, and weight are not as such created but are in reality the imprint in creatures of the divine nature, since God should be thought to be *mensura, numerus,* and *pondus* in the original and absolute meaning of the terms, which are thus employed to give expression to a metaphysics of intrinsic participation. In this perspective, each creature, though distinct from the creator in being, participates in him by its form, so that each according to its own level within the created order is a trace and a sign of its creator.[11] However, the creator in himself can be signified only through the negation and transcendence of creaturely existence and form, as absolute measure ("mensura autem sine mensura est, cui adaequatur quod de illa est, nec alicunde ipsa est") or measureless measure, at once the measure from which each measure proceeds and the measure which is not itself constituted as universal measure by anything other than itself; hence it is without measure. Similarly, the divine nature must be thought of as absolute number, forming all without having been formed; and absolute "weight" (IV, 4,8), since it draws all things to itself without being drawn to any other being.

VI. Eriugena: Thinking East and West Together

In Eriugena's thought both the biblical themes surrounding measure and the Platonic motifs are present and are taken up actively into his personal reflection. Something has already been said concerning his reception of the biblical, especially the New Testament, doctrine: in the economy of redemption God is a God of measure (just as he is in creation), and Christ, the head of the Church, is the pleromatic measure into whom redeemed humanity is to be incorporated, the measure of the heavenly temple itself. In what follows, the themes of creation "in measure, number, and weight" and of the measureless creator will be at the center, for it is to these that Eriugena accords the most persistent attention. Now these themes offer us an opportunity to observe his creative reception of the philosophical and religious tradition of the eastern and western parts of the undivided Catholic Church, in a single well-defined area of thought.

It was essentially through two authors, Augustine and Dionysius, that John Scottus received the ancient measure teaching in a certain fullness. Other authorities undoubtedly contributed to the nourishment of his reflection. Origen, for instance, is quoted at length to show the way in which God will be "all in all," and in this passage the idea is invoked of God as the "mode and measure" of all movements of the redeemed spirit (P V, 929B). Origen here expounds a spiritual development of a thought that can probably be found in Plato: the spiritual man will take as the measure of thought and action God himself, referring every thought to the divine measure and taking the divine measure as the balance in which alone right action is to be weighed. A further source, although not one of any great consequence for the measure theme, may be found once again in a quotation from a Greek writer: Gregory of Nyssa holds that the sun is the measure of light and darkness (P V, 917A; cf. *De Imagine*, ed. Cappuyns, pp. 243–244). Apart from these two references, however, neither of which is more than an occurrence of the word "measure" within a quotation, John depends wholly and exclusively upon Augustine and Dionysius for the measure themes with which he works as a speculative thinker.

We should acknowledge, of course, that Eriugena has certain interests and some ideas which do involve the notion of measurement but which are not prominent, nor even really present, in the two authors mentioned. Take, for instance, the idea of the return of time and space (P V, 890A). Time is defined as the exact and natural measure of movements and pauses, and since it subsists only in measurable motion, the ending of physical motion will entail the ending of time. It is not clear to me that this idea can be firmly pinned to a source (such as the teaching of Augustine relative to time, and the movements and pauses of the human voice, in *Confessions* XI), in the same way that can be done regarding the assertion that place and time must be understood to be prior to all the realities and occurrences within them, precisely as the *modus, id est mensura* of all they contain, for at this point, of course, Eriugena himself refers us to Augustine's *De musica* (VI, 5,8). His interest in measurement comes once more to the fore in his long discussion of the geometric measure for the dimensions of the earth (P III, 725Bff.) and for determining the distances between earth and moon (P III, 715Bff.). However, it is not the mathematical-calculative interest of Eriugena but his reception of the metaphysical and theological notions surrounding measure that will be the subject of the present discussion.

The triad measure, number, and weight turns up five times in *Periphyseon*. Each of its occurrences will be examined. Now it is without any doubt through his reading of Augustine that Eriugena's attention was brought to bear on Wisdom 11:21. In Augustinian fashion, he glosses the three terms by adding a fourth: "id est in *ordine*" (P V, 1013A). It is interesting to remark that this addition may just reflect a parallel reading of *The Divine Names*, where God is affirmed to be μέτρον τῶν ὄντων . . . καὶ ἀριθμὸς καὶ τάξις (chap. 4, 697C). In Augustine and Dionysius, after all, we have two Christian authors each of whom develops the same faith by using current Neoplatonic categories, so that the coincidence occurring here is not altogether surprising. Order was a significant theme of each writer, and each was influenced in characteristic ways by the Neoplatonic theme of differentiated order, or hierarchy. John could draw upon their ideas about measure without having to reconcile these in advance, because quite simply there were no conflicts to be reconciled, though, of course, there was a distinctive reflection of the authorial personality of each, when measure was under discussion. Both Augustine and Dionysius recognized the need for variety and inequality in creation. Eriugena asks why God did not make an equal distribution of contemplative power among the angelic orders and answers by the scriptural authority, "God made all things according to measure, and number, and weight—that is to say [he adds] in order." No beauty is possible, either in music or in the creation at large, without differences, though of course differences interrelated by rational proportions (P V, 1013A). No authority is referred to in this brief question and answer. The Dionysian nature of hierarchy and analogy seem to hover close, but equally Eriugena may be thinking of Augustine's idea of order as "parium disparfor mque rerum sua cuique tribuens loca *dispositio*" (cf. the *disposuit* of Wis. 11:21).

On two occasions Eriugena appeals to Wisdom 11:21 as a scriptural authority affirming the fundamental role played by mathematical number in the creation universally. It is natural that in both these contexts the emphasis falls, within the triad, upon the second member, number. When we consider the perfection of the number six, *Alumnus* asks, how could we possibly think that this "exemplar in which God made his works" could have had a temporal beginning? And he at once answers: "Siquidem non de solo senario, de universo vero generaliter omnium numerorum dictum est: Omnia in mensura et numero et pondere fecit Deus" (P III, 656B). The intellectual numbers must be held to precede spaces and times, and must be reckoned to be among the realities that are both eternal, in the Monad, and made, in differentiated multiplicity. The same Platonist realism of Eriugena is given forthright expression in the discussion of arithmetic, that science of the numbers by which we count, not of those which we count (P III, 651A). Arithmetic thus understood is the foundation and cause of the other mathematical sciences—geometry, music, and astronomy. Even more generally, however,

> etiam omnium rerum uisibilium et inuisibilium infinita multitudo iuxta regulas numerorum quas arithmetica contemplatur substantiam accipit, teste primo ipsius artis repertore Pithagora summo philosopho qui intellectuales numeros substantias rerum omnium

uisibilium et inuisibilium esse certis rationibus adfirmat. Nec hoc
scriptura sancta denegat quae ait omnia in mensura et numero et
pondere facta esse. (P III, 652A9–15)

We have here in a novel form Eriugena's conviction that a profound
agreement unites true philosophy with true religion. Pythagoras,
"the supreme philosopher," would have found his doctrine of the
universal causality of number in the creation confirmed from
the Old Testament. None of Augustine's multiplied references
to Wisdom 11:21 makes this connection, which is probably Eriugena's own.

The discussion of the divine knowledge and ignorance shows
another example of Eriugena's drawing the measure theme, and
the text from the Book of Wisdom, close to a very central preoccupation of his own (P II, 589B–590B). The infinite knows itself
beyond the polarity of finite and infinite, beyond any possible categorical knowing. Since the divine nature is "nothing" with respect
to created beings and essences, it cannot know itself in any finite
thing, and in this sense it does not know "what it is," for it is not a
"what." *Modus et mensura* are to be found as definite limits set to
any being to which we can apply literal predicates. Eriugena tells
us how we are to understand the two words: "Aliquo nanque modo
quo finitur concluditur, aliqua mensura quam superare non potest
lineatur" (589D15–16). Each creature is enclosed within some *limit*
that bounds it and is confined by a definite measure which it cannot overstep. This ontological rule is verified in the lowest beings,
which cannot extend the measure of their being either beneath or
above them; in the highest, because the highest intellectual creature has only "nothing" beyond it, nor can it be lowered to become
a creature it itself is not; and, finally, in the middle beings, which
are at the balance point of order and are held there by their nature. God, however, understands that he is none of these but
knows himself instead as the *supra* of all the grades of nature, as
their *infra* and as their *intra*, and as embracing (*ambire*) all, since all
are within him and nothing is outside of him.

Two additions, following closely upon each other in the Rheims
manuscript, give a distinctive relief to this passage. The first follows the thought of the *modus et mensura* that delimits each created
thing: "Ac per hoc nulla creatura est siue uisibilis siue inuisibilis
quae non intra terminos propriae naturae in aliquo coartetur in
mensura et numera et pondere." The parallel addition is placed a

few lines later, at the conclusion of the statement on the divine self-knowledge: "Solus enim ipse est mensura sine mensura, numerus sine numero, pondus sine pondere, et merito quia a nullo nec a se ipso mensuratur numeratur ordinatur nec in ulla mensura in ullo numero in ullo ordine intelligit se esse quoniam in nullo eorum substantialiter continetur cum solus uere in omnibus super omnia infinitus existat."

Now it is at least in part the thought of Augustine which inspires both these additions. We have seen how Augustine aligned the triad upon the order of creation, and how he applied the Plotinian dialectical formulation concerning the "universal, unmeasured measure" to each member of the Wisdom triad: *mensura sine mensura, numerus sine numero, pondus sine pondere*. Regarding *numerus*, John Scottus had already employed this dialectic of the divine transcendence in book I, to affirm that God and his action are not two things, but one: "Deus enim numerum in se non recipit quoniam solus innumerabilis est et numerus sine numero et supra omnem numerum causa omnium numerorum" (P I, 518A12–14). In fact, already in *De praedestinatione* he had absorbed this same element of Augustinian dialectic and applied it with a similar aim:

> "quid mirum de ipsa ineffabili causa omnium, quae dum generibus, formis, indiuiduis numerisque careat, ab ea tamen est omne genus, omnis forma, omne totum, omnis numerus, quoniam ipsa est prima uniuersitatis essentia . . . Ab ea est omne totum, quae in se ipsa ubique tota est; ab ea omnis numerus, quia in se ipsa est multiplex sine fine, sine numero numerus."[12]

Augustine's influence is tangible in the dialectical manipulation of the triad, but the same surely cannot be said of the argument pursued by John Scottus to the effect that "no one, not even God himself, can measure, number, or order him, since he does not understand himself as being in any measure, in any number, or in any order." The thought that God both truly is and truly is not, or the conception of God as the "nothing of all things," together with the consequent impossibility of a divine quasi-categorical self-knowledge, is part, not of the Latin, but the Greek patristic heritage, wherein "the nothing of all" was adopted by Dionysius from Proclus. Divine infinity was scarcely thematized by the Latin Fathers, although it is not wholly absent from Augustine. Be that as it may, Eriugena's most characteristic ways of developing and expounding the divine infinity derived very decidedly from the Greek side of his intellectual experience.

In the most dialectically intensive and emphatic adaptation made by Eriugena of the Wisdom triad, measure, number, and weight are pressed into service to express the teaching on theophany. It is with an examination of the great passage in the third book that this study must close (P III, 633 A–B).

The Wisdom motif here turns up in the context of the dialectical unity of all that is: this is the setting which gives its sense to the notion of theophany (P III, 632D1–633A11). By an inexhaustible outpouring the Good causes all things and indeed is all things; the positing of creation is not the setting up of things "outside" of the Good in finite independence but is to be thought (as indeed it comes about) as a bringing forth from the Good itself (*a se ipsa*) within the Good (*in se ipsa*) and in the direction of the Good (*ad se ipsam*). For nothing can be outside of the all-ambiting cause, while within it there is nothing that truly exists save the Good itself—for only the Good truly exists. Things that are otherwise said to be are its theophanies, and they also are *in* the Good, in the truth of their existence.

The positive designation of the Good as *est, est omnia, sola vere est* invokes implicitly the fourth member of the fivefold division of nature, as developed in the first book (P I, 445B5–445C10), the division *secundum philosophos* (meaning the Platonists) into what is contemplated by intellect and "is said truly to be," and what is subject to generation and dissolution "and is truly said not to be." In what immediately follows, namely, the series of antitheses which locate the theophany with respect to its source and end, and hence designate theophany *as* theophany, the transition is silently made from the fourth member to the very first of the fivefold division (P I, 443A19–23), that division which in its turn repeats and makes explicit the most fundamental division of all, the one with which the work opens (P I, 441A), "in ea quae sunt et in ea quae non sunt," where by "the things that are" are meant all that is intelligible to sense or intellect, whereas all that transcends all understanding is designated as "what does not exist." This passage from positive to negative designation of the transcendent provides the major key to the comprehension of the antitheses through which the dialectical identity of theophany (positively enunciated in what follows) and God (negatively designated) is expressed:

Omne enim quod intelligitur et sentitur nihil aliud est nisi non
apparentis apparitio, occulti manifestatio, negati affirmatio, incomprehensibilis comprehensio, [ineffabilis fatus, inaccessibilis
accessus,] inintelligibilis intellectus, incorporalis corpus, superessentialis essentia, informis forma, immensurabilis mensura,
innumerabilis numerus, carentis pondere pondus, spiritualis in-
crassatio, inuisibilis uisibilitas, illocalis localitas, carentis tempore
temporalitas, infiniti diffinito, incircunscripti circunscriptio et caetera quae puro intellectu et cogitantur et perspiciuntur et quae me-
moriae sinibus capi nesciunt et mentis aciem fugiunt.

God is the whole of what truly is, for, argues Eriugena (with
Ps.-Dionysius), God both makes all things and is made in all things;
hence all that is the object of understanding and of sense is nothing other than theophany. There follows the series of designations
(nineteen in all) consisting of linguistic antitheses, each couple of
which, despite (or, in truth, because of) the literal contradiction it
expresses between its two terms, offers us a way of thinking dialectically the unity of God and creation. Three of these antitheses
are composed from the triad *mensura, numerus, pondus,* but it will
be helpful to learn how the mind is to work on them and through
them if we begin our examination from the first three couplets:
non apparentis apparitio, occulti manifestatio, negati affirmatio. If these
literal contradictions are to give way to dialectical understanding
of the totality, then they must be read in the light of the movement
of the Eriugenian dialectic understood in its entirety. Now the nature of that movement has already been indicated by Eriugena
himself, when, introducing the sense of the antitheses that are to
follow he employs the triplet *in se ipsa . . . a se ipsa . . . ad se ipsam,*
a formulation which is paralleled elsewhere by the words *principium et medium et finis* (P I, 451D25), and which reproduces at one
remove (that of Dionysius) the Proclean triad of πρόοδος, μονή,
ἐπιστροφή. In fact, the appearance of literal contradiction as between the members of each of the antitheses (e.g., *non apparentis
apparitio*) is due to a reading of the genitive (*non apparentis*) simply
as an objective genitive, as though *apparitio* were the noun qualified by *non apparentis.* The sense of dynamic ontological movement
that is opened up by the threefold formula *in se ipsa, a se ipsa, ad se
ipsam* makes of *non apparentis* a subjective genitive, and therewith
the designation of the source of theophany.

Now the first element of each of the antitheses is in each case negative either in form (*non apparentis; incomprehensibilis; informis*), or at any rate in meaning (*occulti; spiritualis; carentis pondere*), whereas the second is positive; and the positive term, which designates in each case the theophany, must be read as emerging from the negative and returning to it, just as positive attribution in general, in the thought of Eriugena, must give way to the truer negative or apophatic approach to the divine, as it is in itself. On this understanding we should have to paraphrase the first three antitheses somewhat as follows: "coming out of the non-appearing there is the appearing, which moves ineluctably to its goal that is also its source; coming out of the unrevealed is the showing-forth, which will return to its origin; coming out of the negated is the affirmation, which will in turn go back, by negation, to the negated."

"The negated" can now be seen to carry two interrelated meanings. God negates himself *as* infinite by the fact of producing out of himself something which, as affirmation, is not himself but is at the same time a positive statement (or theophany) that remains inseparable, in both its existence and its significance for finite intellect and reason, from what it signifies. However, for the theophany to effect its return it must become once again that which it itself, as affirmation and positive value, is *not;* and the mind that attempts to follow the trajectory and read the meaning of the *apparitio* may do so only by a negative movement of transcendence.

We may apply a similar scheme of understanding now to the triad of antitheses which has its origin in Wisdom 11:21 and in Augustine's reflections upon that biblical verse. Augustine's *mensura sine mensura* presented contraries which did not include a literal or even apparent logical contradiction. It is possible, after all, to think of examples of a measure (such as the standard meter) which measures all other meters but is not measured by any of them. The same holds true for a number which has no number producing or governing it, for unity is that number. In Eriugena, on the other hand, we can observe an intensification of the opposition, an intensification which is deliberately pushed to the literal contradiction pertaining as between something that cannot be measured (*immensurabilis*) and a measure related to it. In the style of Eriugena's thought, needless to say, this contradiction between the two terms, though real in a static conception of logic, will be made the springboard of a movement of thought that seeks to transcend contradiction by tending towards unity, but of course unity in infinity.

The attempt must now be made to paraphrase the three sets of antinomies based upon measure, number, and weight, even though the effort to do so must sacrifice entirely the poetic and suggestive character of the formulas. Poetry, after all, is what is lost when poetry is translated.

Immensurabilis mensura

Out of the reality that cannot be measured, either by any other reality or even by itself, and which is therefore negative for categorical understanding, there comes forth a finite measure, something positive that can be apprehended as commensurate with concepts. This measure must be apprehended as being theophanic in character and hence as the only means the human (or angelic) mind has for affirming that before, and behind, and also beyond the apprehended measure, there is that which has already measured the apprehended measure, there is that which contains and conserves it, and which at the same time draws the measure back to itself. However, since the measure is not and cannot be the measure *of* its own origin, it is only by the negation of its measured nature and its measuring capacity (for conceptual apprehension) that its source can be posited as its contradictory opposite, the unmeasurable; and as both containing the visible measure and being at the same time beyond all and every possible measure.

Innumerabilis numerus

Out of the only reality that cannot be made many in itself (being the simple Monad) there comes into being a number, or a plurality that stands in a positive relationship to conceptual thought. This plurality becomes the road by which the mind may affirm that before the plurality (as its source) and behind it or beneath it (as its support), but also beyond it (as its goal), there is the Monad, which has multiplied itself in order to produce number: the Monad which in its turn contains the multiplicity it has sent forth and which draws that multiplicity back to unity. However, the numerous things that exist cannot, in the plurality which they form, be the number of their unique origin; it is only through the negation of the plural that the non-multipliable can be posited as the contradictory of what has been multiplied. Moreover, the Monad in itself cannot be constituted by or from the multiple (since, after all, the One in itself is not uni*fied* or unit*ed*), any more than it can be grasped on the basis of the conceptual starting point of the multiple; for the Monad is not the opposite of multiplicity, rather is it in truth the multiplicity which is the opposite, or the negation, of unity. The One can be posited only as the beyond both of the non-one (the plural) and of the non-multiplied, which is to say that it can be posited only as the One which, while remaining unknown in its own unity, is both the source of all multiplicity and that to which all multiplicity will return.

Carentis pondere pondus

Coming from the reality which alone is not drawn out from itself by any correlative *other* and which knows no gravitational attraction towards any other, there is a *pondus,* a created universe which never leaves its source but remains always within the gravitational field, as it were, of its own origin, and is furthermore drawn forward to rejoin that origin. Now what is subject to gravitation cannot as such give a true representation of that which has no attraction or gravitation but is beyond all and any drawnness. In its own nature this beyond is not the simple negation of the gravitational, but as the reality which alone is not drawn out of itself to other things it is beyond all that is not in precisely that same condition.

VII. Indebtedness and Originality of Eriugena

The biblical and the Platonic themes of measure offer an opportunity to observe John Scottus Eriugena at work, assimilating and developing a complex tradition which he received at first hand from the Bible, from St. Augustine, and from the Pseudo-Dionysius. The major speculative interest attaches to his employment of Wisdom 11:21, even though he also shows awareness of the measure theme as found in St. Paul and in the Apocalypse.

Eriugena was indebted to Augustine for a series of that great doctor's meditations on Wisdom 11:21. Augustine was led in great part by his own anti-Manichaean polemics to develop the doctrine of a good and orderly creation "in measure, number, and weight." Under the influence of Plotinus, he spoke of *mensura sine mensura, numerus sine numero, pondus sine pondere,* thus seeking to express the transcendence of God and the asymmetrical relationship which pertains between God and the creation. On the other hand, Augustine's ethical development of the measure teaching (*mensura/modus/modestia*) does not appear to have touched Eriugena. As between Augustine and the Ps.-Dionysius, there was a broad coincidence of doctrine concerning the measure theme, a general agreement which stemmed from a common biblical inheritance and from their shared tendency to adopt and adapt Neoplatonic ideas in order to express a Christian meaning. Concerning the measure, the differences are largely of style rather than substance, and there was in this instance no conflict to be reconciled between Christian East and Christian West. On the other hand, Ps.-Dionysius did not make explicit use of Wisdom 11:21, but Eriugena did receive his thought (which was itself derived from Proclus) concerning symmetry and analogy. Above all, Ps.-Dionysius, together with Gregory of Nyssa and Maximus Confessor, taught Eriugena to view the entire sensible and intelligible creation as a theophany, inseparable in both being and significance from its divine source. Eriugena showed himself quite original in adapting the Augustinian dialectical thought based upon Wisdom 11:21 (*mensura sine mensura . . .*) to express the theophanic nature of creation, its circular movement from its creator and back to him, the dialectical identity of creation with the uncreated, and the superior truth of negation over against affirmation. Other points of originality have been noted (his keen interest in mathematical measurement, and the relationship which he posited between Pythagoreanism and Wisdom 11:21), but Eriugena's chief originality in respect of the ancient measure theme lay in the blending of central Augustinian and Dionysian motifs; and the marked presence especially of the latter at one of the high points of Eriugenian dialectic (P III, 633B) lends to his thought a distinctive flavor of Greekness not to be found before his time in western and Latin Christian speculation. Eriugena's handling of the measure theme cannot be reduced to his source reading: here as elsewhere, his thinking displays a manifestly original quality.

NOTES

1. Plato, *Statesman* 284D. See I. Peri, " 'Omnia mensura et numero et pondere disposuisti': Die Auslegung von Weish. 11:20 in der lateinischen Patristik," in *Miscellanea Mediaevalia* 16/1:1–21, here 16.

2. For a general discussion of the theme of divine measure, see J. McEvoy, "The Divine as the Measure of Being in Platonic and Scholastic Thought," in *Studies in Medieval Philosophy*, vol. 17, ed. J. F. Wippel (Washington, D.C., 1986), 85–116.

3. See ibid.

4. The translation used in this section is by Bishop Challoner (Rheims, 1582), which has the merit (and, it may be said, the advantage, regarding the discussion in English of medieval authors) of adhering closely to the Vulgate.

5. For a somewhat fuller discussion of the measure theme in Plato, Plotinus, Proclus, Ps.-Dionysius, Augustine, and Aquinas, see McEvoy, "The Divine as the Measure of Being."

6. On Aristotle's ideas about measure, see ibid.

7. See especially Proclus, *The Elements of Theology*, ed. E. R. Dodds (Oxford, 1963).

8. R. Roques, *L'Univers dionysien* (Paris, 1954), 59–64.

9. No comprehensive account exists as yet of the motifs associated with measure in the thought of St. Augustine. The most important studies are referred to in McEvoy, "The Divine as the Measure of Being," at 96n and 101n.

10. Augustine, *De natura boni*, in PL 42:551–572.

11. See the critical notes to Augustine, *De Genesi ad Litteram*, lines 1–7, in *Oeuvres de s. Augustin*, vol. 48 (Paris, 1972), 635–639.

12. John Scottus Eriugena, *De praedestinatione* 2,3 (ed. G. Madec, CCCM 50:13–24).

Humans and Animals:
Aspects of Scriptural Reference in Eriugena's Anthropology

JEAN PÉPIN

THE PRESENT ARTICLE PROPOSES TO CONTRIBUTE to the study of Eriugena's anthropology. Since this is a vast subject, one can only hope to undertake a small portion of it here. Given that some form of limitation is inevitable, my study derives its inspiration from an analysis of texts rather than themes. I shall attempt to evaluate the anthropological significance of the first few pages of *Periphyseon*, book IV, in which the author tries his hand at the exegesis of Genesis 1:24 on the creation of terrestrial animals. Since these pages are well known for the support they lend to Eriugena's anthropology,[1] I shall submit them here to a reading of a different kind. Rather than reducing their exegetical discourse to a theoretical construct in order to extract their underlying anthropological framework, I shall situate these texts in the tradition of biblical commentary. Remaining thus inside their exegetical discourse, I intend merely to provide them with some footnotes. But if we can reveal the identity of Eriugena's sources or his so-called *auctoritates*,[2] we shall indeed have made considerable progress in understanding his anthropological thinking. We shall also be able to see how this anthropology combines eastern and western sources.

The few columns of *Periphyseon* IV under review here are not exclusively exegetical, for they also contain developments of a theoretical nature. Although Eriugena's text lists the theoretical reflections after the exegetical ones, I shall reverse this order here for reasons of clarity.

I. *Periphyseon* IV 5 (754D–755B):
The Hierarchy of Creatures

After having made a strong claim that the entire human soul is present in each one of its functions, be they high or humble (P IV, 754C), Eriugena highlights the different names which the soul adopts for each of its roles. Traveling into the higher regions of the divine essence, it is named intuition, spirit, or intellect. When applying itself to created things, the soul is called reason. Receiving the species of sensibles through the body's senses, it is called sense and, guaranteeing nourishment and growth to the body through invisible movements, vital motion.

The four functions of the human soul are thus, in descending order, intellectual intuition, discursive reasoning, sensitive life, vegetative life. The first two of these the soul shares with the angels, the last two with the animals. Thus the totality of (living) creation finds itself assembled in the human person, making him a microcosm of sorts. But humans also have bodies. It therefore follows that the human person gathers into himself not just four but all five levels of creation. From low to high, human nature is throughout corporeal, vegetative, sensitive, rational, and intellectual.

This is in essence the content of this coherent passage, with the microcosmic representation of human nature inducing Eriugena to pass from four to five terms. The above summary left out certain elements, however, which are found in the Latin text:

Siquidem dum circa diuinam essentiam uehitur [sc. humana anima], et mens, et animus, et intellectus; dum rerum creatarum naturas causasque considerat, ratio; dum per sensus corporeos species sensibilium recipit, sensus; dum in corpore occultos suos motus iuxta similitudinem irrationabilium animarum peragit, nutriendo illud et augendo uitalis proprie motus solet appellari [. . .] Constat enim inter sapientes, in homine uniuersam creaturam contineri. Intellegit enim et ratiocinatur, ut angelus; sentit et corpus administrat, ut animal; ac per hoc omnis creatura in eo intelligitur. Totius siquidem creaturae quinquepertita diuisio est. Aut enim corporea est, aut uitalis, aut sensitiua, aut rationalis, aut intellectualis. Et haec omnia omni modo in homine continentur. Extremum quidem subsistentiae ipsius corpus est; deinde seminalis uita corporis administratiua, cui praeest sensus; deinde ratio, quae inferioribus se naturae partibus dominantur; supremum in his omnibus animus obtinet locum.[3]

As for the hierarchical structure of the created world, there is a clear analogy between this Eriugenian passage and two passages from Gregory of Nyssa, i.e., *De hominis opificio* VIII (PG 44:144D–145B) and XIV (176A). In these two Greek texts we find the same five ontological levels, namely, in ascending order, the body without life, the living body without sensation, the living sensible without reason, the living sensible with reason, and finally the level where intellect reigns. The similarity with Eriugena's differentiated ontology is clear. This need not surprise us, since we know that Eriugena had a good knowledge of Gregory's treatise, which he had translated just earlier under the Latin title *De imagine*.[4] Several technical Aristotelian terms (or words of the same family) appear in Gregory's Greek text. If we compare the above passage from the *Periphyseon* with Eriugena's own translation of these two Gregorian texts, we find enough evidence to conclude that in the *Periphyseon* Eriugena essentially adheres to his earlier translations, which he sometimes quotes literally.[5]

While we can find the same five ontological levels in Gregory, he actually sees them as four ascending degrees, of which the last one, the rational level, is doubled into a rational and an intellectual one. Although Eriugena's translation does not use the adjective *intellectualis*, in *Periphyseon* IV 5, we find the intellect coupled with the four other terms, which thus makes 4 + 1 = 5 degrees. This is clearly an Eriugenian innovation. One suspects it to have been influenced by his reading of Augustine, to whom the distinction *intellectus–ratio* or *intellectualis–rationalis* was familiar. To find the first pair, one could turn to Sermo 43, in which Augustine not only distinguishes between two faculties of the soul but also stresses their inequality by affirming that the possession of *ratio* is a prerequisite for the use of the *intellectus*.[6] The same distinction in adjectival form is found in *De trinitate* XII, where Augustine integrates it with the famous opposition between *sapientia* and *scientia*.[7]

We have seen how in comparing the different faculties of the human soul with the different levels of the created universe, Eriugena comes to adopt the notion of human nature as a microcosm: "Constat enim inter sapientes, in homine uniuersam creaturam contineri." He restates this claim on numerous occasions. It appears this doctrine was also suggested to him by Gregory of Nyssa, who describes it in very similar terms.[8]

II. *Periphyseon* IV 5 (754A–B): The Oneness of the Human Soul

Prior to the passage at *Periphyseon* IV 5 (754D–755B), Eriugena had argued against the hypothesis that there are two souls in the human person: one which is vegetative, sensitive, and imaginative, i.e., an animal soul, and one which is made of reason and intellect, i.e., created in the image of God. The Disciple objected that such a duality would be an absurd consequence of their previous analyses. The Master then reassures him: only the rational soul is cojoined to the human body in a mysterious manner:

> Duas animas in uno homine nec ratio, nec divina auctoritas sinit me arbitrari [. . .] Vnam uero eandemque rationabilem animam humano corpori ineffabili modo adiunctam hominem esse assero.

In *De hominis opificio* XIV (176A–B) Gregory of Nyssa had counted differently, as he distinguished between the plants' purely vegetative soul and the animals' vegetative and sensitive soul. It was to refute the possibility of a mixture of three souls in the human person that Gregory made his statement. Gregory's particular nuance notwithstanding, it is from his own perspective that Eriugena read this expression in the *De imagine*.[9]

III. *Periphyseon* IV 4–5 (748C–749D): Genera and Species

The account of the creation of plants and animals in Genesis, when read according to different versions of the text, reveals different details. Taking, for example, the Greek translation of the Septuagint, one reads in chapter 1, verses 11 and 12, the phrase κατὰ γένος καί καθ' ὁμοιότητα, "according to genus and according to likeness," followed next by a single κατὰ γένος, "according to genus." Only these last two words recur: twice in Gen. 1:21 (once in the plural: κατὰ γένη), and five times in Gen. 1:24–25. Behind this lies the Hebrew turn of phrase l^e mînēhû.[10] Prompted by this stereotypical Hebrew expression, the Greek translators apparently felt confident enough to introduce a light diversity.

For their part, the commentators who later came to work on this Greek text were reminded of Aristotle's teaching on genus and species. Some glossed γένος therefore as εἶδος (e.g., Basil, *Homilia in Hexaemeron* VIII 2, PG 29:168B–C). Prior to this Philo had substituted ἰδέα in the sense of "species" (*De opificio mundi* 13, 43–44). Struck by Genesis's two accounts of the creation of animals (cf. 1:24 and 2:19), however, of which he saw the first as the creation of genera and ideas, and the second as the creation of species, Philo restored the word to its original meaning of "idea" in *Legum allegoriae* II 4, 12–13. In an even more ingenious fashion, others such as Didymus the Blind in *In Genesim* 1, 11, regard καθ᾽ ὁμοιότητα here as an indication that species is inferior to genus.[11] Aristotle's binary scheme must have carried much weight in the minds of early Christian exegetes, for they even traced it in passages of the Septuagint where the word "species" never occurs.

In the oldest Latin translation of the Bible, the *Vetus Latina*, which itself displays various forms, we sometimes find no corresponding parallel for καθ᾽ ὁμοιότητα, yet one also finds the substitute *similitudinem* or *secundem similitudinem*.[12] The equivalent most often used for κατὰ γένος or γένη is *secundum* [. . .] (or *ad*) *genus*, though on occasion one will read *secundum suam* (or *in*) *similitudinem* (Gen. 1:11–12).[13] Although there is no special significance about this, there is an important discrepancy with Jerome's Vulgate. Jerome replaces κατὰ γένος or γένη not just with forms of the noun *genus*, but almost equally often we read: *secundum speciem suam* (1:12), *in species suas* (1:21), *secundum species suas* (1:24), *iuxta species suas* (1:25).[14] This last instance is unique in that it reveals the introduction into the biblical narrative not just of a word but of an abstract concept, namely, *species*, which was absent both from the Hebrew and the Greek text. Jerome's use of this term appears to be an attempt to construe the philosophical system *genus/species* and integrate it with a textual pattern of Semitic provenance which was unfamiliar with such concepts.

Given the widespread use that was made of the Vulgate, the consequences of this innocent manipulation had to be enormous. It is necessary to remind ourselves of these data if we want to comprehend Eriugena's exegesis first of Gen. 1:24 and next of Gen. 1:20. I shall consider three important passages:

1. P IV 4 (748C–D)

Quoniam itaque in hac omnium communi terra omnia animalia secundum corpus et animam causaliter et primordialiter creata sunt
[. . .], quid mirum, si diuino praecepto iubeatur, animam uiuentem, hoc est animal uiuens producere, ut, quod causaliter occulte
in causis et rationibus habebat, hoc in genera et species aperte produceret? Et uide, quomodo naturalem rerum consequentiam diui-
num nobis manifestat eloquium. Producat, inquit, terra animam
uiuentem in genere suo. Primo genus posuit, quoniam in ipso
omnes species et continentur et unum sunt, et in eas diuiditur
et multiplicatur per generales formas specialissimasque species.
Quod etiam ostendit dicens: Iumenta et reptilia et bestias terrae
secundum species suas [Gen. 1:24].

2. P IV 5 (749A–B)

. . . si quis uoluerit, potest etiam alio modo intellegere quod scriptum est: Producant aquae reptile animae uiuentis, et uolatile super
terram [Gen. 1:20], ut non solum simpliciter, quemadmodum superius tractatum est, intellegat pisces et uolatilia de hoc uisibili
atque tractabili humidoque ac frigido aquarum elemento creata
esse, uerum etiam altiori sensu ex abditis profundisque naturae
sinibus, in quibus causaliter et primordialiter facta sunt, in genera
et species deducta.

3. P IV 5 (749C)

Vis autem seminum, quae in eis [sc. terra et aqua] sunt, operante
illa uita, quae nutritiua dicitur, secundum leges et rationes insitas,
quantum sinit diuina prouidentia, in diuersas species herbarum,
surculorum, animalium, per genera et formas ex secretis creaturae
sinibus erumpit.

These passages contain the author's reflections on the notions of
genera et species (in 3, *species per genera*). I want to highlight the following points in relation to them:

The divine commandment *producat terra* (Gen. 1:24) indicates
that the earth in which the animals have been created will bring
these animals from their states as primordial causes (*causaliter et
primordialiter*, 1 and 2) into their states of genera and species (*in
genera et species*, 1 and 2). What is said of the *producat terra* must
also apply to the *producant aquae* of Gen. 1:20. Unsatisfied with the
obvious meaning (*simpliciter*, 2) which he had mentioned before,[15]

Eriugena moves on to a deeper meaning. Although the words *genus* and *species* are now absent, we are again dealing with a creation (in this case of the reptiles and the birds) on the level of primordial causes followed by their coming into being in *genera et species*.

The distinction between the two states of *causaliter et primordialiter* and *genera et species* is as lucid as that between hidden and manifest. On the one hand we have the hidden (*occulte*, 1), the depths (*ex abditis profundisque naturae sinibus*, 2), the secret places (*ex secretis creaturae sinibus*, 3), while on the other hand there is a great openness (*aperte*, 1).[16] The *productio*, which reflects God's command to the waters and the earth, signifies to Eriugena the passage from one state to another. Moreover, the Latin word that he takes up here (*produceret*, 1) means to make appear. Two verbs close in meaning bring out the same idea of a passage, i.e., to burst forth (*erumpit*, 3), and to make descend (*deducta*, 2).

By employing the terms *genera* and *species* the biblical narrative (Gen. 1:24, see 1) depicts the natural unfolding of events: *naturalem rerum consequentiam*. For Eriugena this means that the Bible displays an accordance with the elementary doctrine of genus and species as he perceived it, and that appropriate terminology is in order (in 1): *in genere species continentur, genus multiplicatur per species*. Apparently, there are *generales* and *specialissimae species*.

After the transition from primordial causes to their manifestation in genera and species we come to the third text. Here we witness the movement by which the seeds and their powers (*uis seminum*) in earth and water, in accordance with the reasons implanted in them, create different vegetative and animal species (*in diuersas species*) by means of genera (*per genera*).[17]

Other Eriugenian Texts on Genera and Species

When combining all this half-exegetical and half-speculative information, we get a fairly coherent doctrine of creation. Our first task should now be to see if we can find confirmation of it in the rest of Eriugena's oeuvre, especially in the *Periphyseon*. We noted the idea, for example, that all animals are created *causaliter et primordialiter* in the "earth," which is common to all (1). This may be integrated with Eriugena's preferred reading of Gen. 1:1, in which he takes *caelum et terram* to mean that the primordial causes of intelligible and sensible things are created by the Father in the Son, here called *principium*, before the rest of creation.[18]

If we turn now to the exegesis of Gen. 1:20, so crucial in Eriugena's construction of doctrine as analyzed above, we find a surprisingly concise and clear explanation of this text as early as the end of book III: "So much for the creation of the fishes and flying things in their primordial causes. Their procession into their genera and species follows."[19]

In an earlier passage of book III Eriugena had used not only the same themes as at the beginning of book IV but also the same terms. Rather than on Gen. 1:20 or 1:24, Eriugena's focus here was on the exegesis of Gen. 1:11–12. We mentioned this text, which narrates the creation of seed-bearing herbs and trees,[20] as the third pericope in which the Vulgate employs *genus* and *species*. In his exegesis Eriugena refers explicitly to the *primordiales causae* and *genera et species*. The following points are worth mentioning:[21]

The "force of the seeds" (*vis seminum*, cf. text 3), as the Fathers used to say, has been created in the primordial causes.

Every visible manifestation of nature receives "the original causes of its generation" (*originales causas generationis suae*) exclusively "from the hidden recesses of the natural and substantial form" (*ex occultis naturalis et substantialis formae sinibus*). Whereas the first statement pertains to the invisible level of the creation of plants, Eriugena's statement here affects both the visible and invisible level. The "hidden recesses," the "substantial form," the "original causes" all pertain to the invisible level. We have already noted how the "hidden recesses" exercised that function in 2 and 3, and the *originales causae* can easily be reduced to the *primordiales causae*. It follows that we should try to prove the same with regard to the *naturalis et substantialis forma*.

Such an interpretation of the "substantial form" is indeed confirmed when we read that this form was previously called "dry land" and "earth."[22] It has been noted how for Eriugena the "earth" points to the primordial causes.

Under these circumstances, the divine command of Gen. 1:11 (*Germinet terra*, etc.) clearly aims at the generative "procession" (*per generationem procedat*), by which the "seminal force" (*uis seminalis*) passes from its original state in the "causal reasons" (*in [. . .] rationibus causaliter*), and the "primordial causes" (*primordialium causarum*) to the state of effects in the world of sensible forms (*in [. . .] species sensibiles*).

Thus far book III's exegesis of Gen. 1:11 (*Germinet terra*) corresponds exactly with the exegesis of Gen. 1:20 (*Producant aquae*)
and Gen. 1:24 (*Producat terra*) at the beginning of book IV. As
a result of divine will, different plants and animals are seen to
leave the hidden state of their creation in the primordial causes
to become manifest. As in book IV, one expects that Eriugena's
exegesis uses as its point of departure here the same terms of *genera et species*. One only needs to recall the unique formula of text 1:
"ut, quod causaliter occulte in causis et rationibus habebat, hoc in
genera et species aperte produceret." Yet the end of book III presents a rather different picture, for *genera et species* are here seen as
the place where things exist in a causal and invisible state before
they break forth to become manifest to the senses: "scriptura
genera et species manifestissime declarat, in quibus causaliter et
inuisibiliter subsistunt quaecunque per generationem in quantitatibus et qualitatibus in notitiam corporalium sensuum erumpunt."[23] Although there is a clear discrepancy with book IV, this is
not to say that book III and book IV are generally at odds with
one another. We have previously seen how the phrase of P III 40
was in complete accordance with book IV.[24]

The *Periphyseon's* internal inconsistency on the interpretation of
genera et species may perhaps be resolved if we turn to other pages
of the work. For this, however, we would have to overstep the
boundaries of our present study, the success of which has been
that it diagnosed the problem. I here simply wish to add that Eriugena's homily on the prologue to St. John's Gospel sheds no light
whatsoever on the text of P III 28. On the contrary, using very
much its own terms—"For his generation from the Father is itself
the creation of all causes and the working and making of all things
that proceed from the causes into the genera and species"[25]—this
text points unmistakably to the creation of the primordial causes
in the Word, in accordance with the same doctrine that we found
in P II 15.[26] With *genera et species* being used to describe a "procession" from the causes, the homily clearly foreshadows the use
of these words in the beginning of book IV.

Porphyry, Maximus the Confessor, Eriugena

The most important reference text on genera and species during the period of late antiquity and the early Middle Ages was un-

doubtedly Porphyry's *Isagoge*. In this short text one finds remarks that may well have influenced some of Eriugena's views on this matter. As was shown above, Eriugena hesitated whether to situate *genera et species* on the level of the invisible primordial causes or in the visible, concrete world. This clearly reflects Porphyry's reluctance when he, after having enumerated the problems he will pass by in silence, cites as one of these the question whether genera and species are corporeal or incorporeal realities, i.e., separated from sensible things or residing in them. The resemblance between the two authors becomes even more striking when one reads the *Isagoge* in Boethius's translation,[27] with which Eriugena was familiar.[28] As for the less original remark in text 1 that all species are contained in the *genus* (*in ipso omnes species et continentur*), which is thus multiplied (*multiplicatur*) by them[29]—the same words and ideas are found in the *Isagoge*.[30] Finally, in the same context of *genera et species*, text 1 made use of adjectival forms, including one superlative, *generalis et specialissimus*. These adjectives, *generalis et specialis*, represent the Greek γενικός and εἰδικός. Although absent from Aristotle's vocabulary, these Greek adjectives, including the superlative, are found in the *Isagoge*. Boethius translated them with the same adjectives as Eriugena.[31] It is thus only through a comparison with Boethius that we can reach an understanding of what Eriugena means when he states that the genus is multiplied *per generales formas specialissimasque species*. We are apparently dealing here with two levels of species: one *generalis*, which serves at the same time as species for its genus and genus for a species, and one *specialissima*, which is only species. In other words, *genus* and *species* are relative notions.

Eric Perl has referred me to two important passages on genera and species in Maximus's *Ambigua* (2nd series = *Ambigua ad Iohannem*). I have translated the first passage from Maximus's Greek as follows:

> From the beginning the substance of all things is moved in the reason and manner of expansion and contraction [κατὰ διαστολὴν καὶ συστολήν]. It is in effect moved from the most general through the mediation of the more general genera towards the species [ἀπὸ τοῦ γενικωτάτου γένους διὰ τῶν γενικωτέρων γενῶν εἰς τὰ εἴδη]. Through the mediation of these and in these the substance of things finds a natural division, progressing until the most special species [μέχρι τῶν εἰδικωτάτων εἰδῶν] that pose an end to the ex-

pansion as such and circumscribe its being in light of its downward boundaries. On the other hand, the substance contracts itself by abandoning the most special species and passing through the more general species [ἀπὸ τῶν εἰδικωτάτων εἰδῶν διὰ τῶν γενικωτέρων] and returns to the most general genus [μέχρι τοῦ γενικωτάτου γένους] which poses the end to the contraction as such, defining its upward boundaries.[32]

Even upon a superficial reading, this passage is very clear. Expansion and contraction are two movements which, for Maximus, form the rhythm of all physical and spiritual life. They are portrayed here as part of a logical or biological ladder of genera and species: most general genus, more general genus, more general species, most special species. Through a play of comparative and superlative terms, this structure not only displays more subtlety than Porphyry's, but it also receives an entirely different application. Still, it is likely that the *Isagoge* served as its point of departure. Since Eriugena's Latin translation of Maximus's text stays on the whole remarkably close to the Greek,[33] the conclusion seems justified that it is through Maximus that Eriugena was informed about the content of the *Isagoge*.[34]

The second Maximus passage leads to the same conclusion. Here we find the same adjectives γένικός and [ε]ἰδικός, as Maximus demonstrates how distinct realities become unified on every level: the genera according to their substance, the species according to their genus, the individual things (τὰ ἄτομα) according to their species.[35] Maximus's text presents itself as a commentary on Dionysius's *De divinis nominibus* XIII 2 (PG 3:977D–980A), which he goes on to cite. Yet while Dionysius makes mention of genus and species, he does not mention individual things. Maximus must therefore have found these elsewhere, probably in the *Isagoge* where they are listed next to genera and species.[36] Through his translation of this Maximian text,[37] Eriugena thus reveals that he has had contact with the Porphyrian legacy. His use of the sequence genus–species–individual may well be a result of this mediated inspiration.[38]

Patristic Precedents

Precedents, if not sources, for Eriugena's ambiguity concerning the status of *genera et species* can also be found in the literature of the patristic age. By surmising that the primordial causes of all things are created in the Word, Eriugena puts himself in the Jewish and Christian tradition of Alexandria. It is from this perspective that Origen read the famous verses of Ecclesiastes on the antiquity of everything that would seem new. If we take a closer look to see which realities Origen considers eternally preexistent in the Word, we find that they are precisely genera and species.[39] Thus we have a prefiguration here of the most uncommon of Eriugena's two theses, that of P III 28.

Another one of Eriugena's predecessors on exactly the same point is Augustine. Assuming that the formula *secundum genus* in Scripture was not mentioned casually but with good reason, Augustine took it to mean that the beings whose creation is first mentioned here would already have been in existence before. Could it be that their *genus* was among the number of transcendent reasons, after whose model beings here below are created?[40] This Augustine exegesis closely anticipates Eriugena's conception of the two moments of creation: in the primordial causes and in sensible manifestation. Placing *genus* on the first of these two levels, this exegesis also joins Origen in that it corresponds with one of Eriugena's two options.

We have previously noted Eriugena's observation in P III 28 that the dynamism of plants, created in the primordial causes, was commonly named "force of the seeds" by the Fathers: "quae uirtus uis seminum a sanctis patribus solet appellari."[41] As is often the case when Eriugena speaks about the *patres,* he probably means only Augustine here. Augustine appears to have effectively narrowed the scriptural use of *secundum genus,* as his definition presupposes the *seminum uis* as well as the transmission of likeness.[42] As part of the same discussion about plants, the text of P III 28 also uses the corresponding formula *uis seminalis.* This "seminal force" is apparently contained in the creation of the primordial reasons. Thus we have what seems to be a new borrowing from Augustine's vocabulary.[43]

In his exegesis of Gen. 1:24 Eriugena admires the fact that God's command to the earth mentions *genus* before *species.* He regards this as a manifestation of the natural unfolding of things, *naturalem rerum consequentiam.*[44] This last point appears to be a reference to an ancient cosmological notion, which is present in Gregory of Nyssa,[45] where Eriugena probably found it. As to the existence of a right order according to which the genera were created before the species, this theme goes back much further, namely, to Philo of Alexandria.[46]

IV. *Periphyseon* IV 5 (751A–752B): The Three Species of the Animal Genus

This passage takes its starting point in the Disciple's astonishment as he reads in the Bible how the earth brings the first human to light alongside the earthly animals, while it is clear that only the human is created in the image of God and will dominate these animals (750C–D). To justify this biblical paradox, the Master develops a fairly long, but interesting, argument. I have singled out the most remarkable points:

A. To understand man's being created in the genus of the animals, one needs to study the tripartite division of this genus in *iumenta, reptilia, bestiae* (Gen. 1:24).

B. On the third and the fifth days of creation, which both also mention *genera et species*, there is no division into genus and species. On the third day (the creation of plants) Eriugena lists only one genus alongside undistinguished species, and on the fifth (creation of fish and birds) we find only one genus with a single species. Eriugena goes on to take this single species for a genus, since it is impossible to have a division into a genus and just one species.

C. On the sixth day, however, we encounter the creation of a genus as well as its division into three species. To find support for his view, Eriugena refers to the Vulgate text of Gen. 1:24 and also to the Septuagint,[47] which is in fact the "European" text of the *Vetus Latina*.[48] The only reason why Eriugena wants a double citation here is to replace the *iumenta* mentioned in the Vulgate with the noun *quadrupedia*.[49]

D. This tripartite division of the animal genus points to three movements, the sum of which belongs exclusively to the human, who is the only rational animal. The three movements are:

  a. Movements submitted to human reason. These are indicated as *iumenta* and *quadrupedia*. They signify the movement of the five corporeal senses, which are fittingly called *iumentum adiutorium*, as they lend a helping hand to the rational soul, but are also called *quadrupes,* after the objects of sensation which consist of four elements.

b. Movements which are opposed to reason. These are conveniently termed *bestiae.*

c. Hidden movements through which that part of the soul that is responsible for growth and nourishment governs the body.[50] Since these movements are both relaxed and latent, they are rightfully called *reptilia.*

We shall now turn to the text of P IV 751A–752B. Interspersed with the divisions we just summarized, the whole passage runs as follows:

[A] ut intellegas [. . .] quod in uniuersali animalium genere homo conditus sit, hoc maximum suscipe argumentum, tripertitam uidelicet huius generis diuisionem in iumenta et reptilia bestiasque. Quae diuisio non sine causa facta est, ut aestimo. [B] Nam in aliis diebus, id est in tertia et quinta, in quibus genera et species commemorantur, nulla diuisio generis in species introducitur, sed simpliciter aut solum genus et indiscretae species, ut in tertia, qua herbarum surculorumque genera speciesque de terra oriri iubentur [Gen. 1:11–12], aut solum genus et una species ipsius, ut in quinta, piscium quidem genus reptile, auium uero uolatile [Gen. 1:20] uocans, neque hoc neque illud in species diuidens. Nam in eo quod dixit: Creauitque deus cete grandia [Gen. 1:21], magis speciem pro genere intellegendum est posuisse, quam genus in speciem diuisisse. Quomodo enim diuisio generis in unam speciem posset fieri, dum omnis diuisio non minus quam in duobus inuenitur? [C] Sexta autem die non solum generis conditio, uerum etiam trina diuisio ipsius in species narratur. Dixit, inquit, deus: Producat terra animam uiuentem in genere suo, iumenta, et reptilia, et bestias terrae secundum species suas [Gen. 1:24]. Vel secundum septuaginta interpretes: Dixit deus: Educat terra animam uiuam secundum genus, quadrupedia, et reptilia, et bestias secundum genus, et factum est sic. [D] Haec itaque, ut arbitror, tripertitio totius uitae terreno corpori adhaerentis [. . .] triplicem motum insinuat. Et quidem ternarius ille motus in homine solo, qui solus est rationabile animal, intellegitur, [a] quosdam quidem motus suos rationi subditos habens, qui iumentorum seu quadrupedum uocabulo significari uidentur. Verbi gratia, mouet quinquepertitum corporis sensum disciplinaliter in cognitionem sensibilium rerum solerti earum intellegentiae studio. Qui motus non irrationabiliter iumentum dicitur; non enim paruum adiutorium rationabili animae praestat ad contemplationem ueritatis sensibilium omnium [. . .] Est etiam quasi quidam quadrupes motus sensuum subditus rationi. Siquidem omne, quod per sensum cognoscimus in natura sensibilium rerum, hoc ex quattuor elementis est compositum, aut in ipso composito constitutum [. . .] Non immerito igitur corporeus sensus quadrupedis uocabulum accepit, quoniam omne, quod sentit, non aliunde nisi ex quattuor elementis originem ducit. [b] Quosdam uero ex inferiori natura sumptos recte dixeris irrationabiles, hoc est rationi resistentes, ut est furor, et cupiditas [. . .] Et quoniam hi motus ex irrationabilibus animalibus humanae naturae inserti sunt, non incongrue bestiarum appellatione significantur [. . .] [c] Sunt praeterea in animali rationabili occulti quidam motus, quibus maxime corpus sibi coniunctum administrat, et sunt in auctiua et nutritiua parte animae constituti. Qui quoniam naturali facilitate sua peragunt officia, et quasi latenter, [. . .] reptilium appellationem non irrationabiliter meruere.

Origen and his Tradition on the Motus Animi

Above, in A and B, Eriugena has expressed some basic notions concerning the relation of genera and species. His remarks undoubtedly have their origin in contemporary school logic which must have been influenced in some fashion by Porphyry's *Isagoge*. In this work one finds that a genus cannot serve as a predicate for a single species, but only for a plurality of different species. One reads also that humans belong to the genus of animals, that the same terms may be seen as either genera or species, and that in certain cases there is no division at all into genera and species. We encountered these same issues in terms similar to Porphyry's in the above citation from the *Periphyseon*. The similarity becomes even more striking when we compare this passage with Boethius's translation of the *Isagoge*.[51]

A significant feature of the above passage is Eriugena's view that the three kinds of animals of Gen. 1:24 indicate different human "movements" (*motus* is repeated several times in D, a and b). Essentially the same exegesis is found in Origen, who holds that not only the animals of Gen. 1:24 but also the fish and the birds of Gen. 1:20, and even the beasts repeated in Gen. 1:28 refer to movements, be they of our minds, our bodies, or our flesh. This indeed is what we read in Rufinus's Latin translation of two passages from Origen's first homily on Genesis.[52]

It is tempting to dismiss these Origenian findings as only a meager result. Yet this would mean that one bypasses the fragmentary character of his exegetical oeuvre, especially where Genesis is concerned. Still, we can perhaps compensate for the relative lacuna by turning to the later Origenian tradition. As far as Genesis is concerned, the principal representative of this tradition is Didymus the Blind. Reading in Gen. 1:21 that the great whales have been created "according to their genera," Didymus makes the observation, for a reason which is only too clear, that in writing "genus" the holy author actually meant to say "species."[53] This could well be the Greek formula that lies behind the phrase *speciem pro genere* of Eriugena's text at B. Whether or not this is the case, it is at least noteworthy that both authors were inspired to such a remark by the same biblical verse, i.e., Gen. 1:21. Like Eriugena, both Didymus and his paradigm Origen incorporated elements of school logic into their exegesis.

Ambrose is hardly any less dependent on Origen's exegesis. He interprets the beasts and the birds in accordance with another one of their biblical roles, as they are brought before Adam to receive their names (Gen. 2:19).[54] Ambrose considers these animals, among which the *bestiae*, to represent our *inrationabiles motus*. This is precisely the profound meaning that Eriugena detects in the *bestiae* of Gen. 1:24, according to the text at D, b. A few lines further down, Ambrose comes to the end of the following verse (Gen. 2:20), which reveals how the first man lacks a helper like unto him (*similis adiutor*), a transitional verse which leads up to the creation of woman. Since Ambrose considers the first man a symbol of the intellect, the help he receives is thus that of sensation. Given that Eriugena is unconcerned with Gen. 2:20, at least in the texts studied in this article, it is all the more revealing that he lifts parts of Ambrose's exegesis to apply them to a biblical verse which they were not meant to elucidate. For it is clearly in accordance with Ambrose that he characterizes the movement that sets the bodily senses in motion as assisting the rational soul, *qui motus [. . .] adiutorium rationabili animae praestat* (text at D, a). In sum, Eriugena's biblical reference is not, as for Ambrose, the term *adiutor* of Gen. 2:20, but rather the term *iumenta* found in Gen. 1:24 (Vulg). I wish to add that Eriugena knew this passage of Ambrose's only too well, for he does not hesitate to quote it literally as part of a longer citation.[55] It is thus highly probable that Eriugena was already under the influence of Ambrose here, in the manner that we reconstructed just now.

Origen's influence on the exegesis of Augustine is clear, though much more limited. Even if it is hard to trace the paths of this influence, one is inclined to see it at work ever since Augustine composed his first commentary on Genesis. Here he gives a spiritual interpretation of the fish, the birds, and the reptiles, seeing them as our passions and as *motus animi* which resemble these animals.[56] Origen used the same exegesis, which is even more recognizable because it can be distinguished from that of others (among whom is Eriugena). Augustine and Origen agree in that they base their common interpretation on God's command that man dominate the animals (Gen. 1:28), rather than on earlier verses. In saying that we ought to curb (*subditos haberemus*) our *motus animi*, however, this same text of Augustine's also foreshadows Eriugena, who sees the biblical animals as images of the movements submitted to human reason: *motus suos rationi subditos habens* (text at D, a).

Augustine and Isidore

Eriugena's exegetical indebtedness to Augustine goes far beyond this one example. We have already commented on the role of numbers in Eriugena's arguments: three kinds of animals, three movements, five corporeal senses, four elements. It was to be foreseen that, since these numbers are not synchronized, they would cause problems. An example is the word *quadrupedia* which indicates the highest level of movement, which is submitted to reason and geared towards knowledge of the sensible world. Thus this movement relates to the five corporeal senses. Yet this creates a difficulty, for how can a word like *quadrupedia*, based as it is on *quattuor* (four), be connected with the five senses? Eriugena finds an artificial solution in that the object of sensible knowledge is ultimately composed of four elements. He concludes his comments in D, a: "Non immerito igitur corporeus sensus quadrupedis uocabulum accepit, quoniam omne, quod sentit, non aliunde nisi ex quattuor elementis originem ducit." Augustine's commentary on Gen. 1:20–21 contains an echo of a similar attempt to conflate distinctions: that of the five bodily senses and that of the four physical elements.[57] He does not identify the authors, but mentions only the extreme subtlety of their analysis. He himself does not adopt it, however, for once he has learned that sensation is a matter of the soul of which the body is a mere instrument, he loses all interest. Still, he has shown us how this harmonizing effort in fact operates: one assigns to every sense a particular element as its proper object. Because the number of the senses is not the same as that of the objects, water becomes object of both the sense of smell and that of taste. Although efforts of this kind are often found among philosophers,[58] we do not find the same desire to parallel the five senses with the four elements, which makes Augustine's information so valuable. As for Eriugena, his exegetical preoccupation causes him to be interested above all in confirming their underlying correspondence, without pausing to give a detailed demonstration. The fact that he had an active memory of the *De Genesi ad litteram* is the most viable explanation for this.

We insisted above on the influence of school logic as codified by Porphyry. Another area of interest for Carolingian culture was the art of etymology, as is testified by Isidore of Seville, who was another one of Eriugena's well-known sources.[59] This encyclopedist was interested in the Vulgate reading of *iumenta,* which he linked to *iuuare* and consequently to *adiutorium.*[60] However mistaken this connection may be in terms of modern scholarship, this etymology must have been on Eriugena's mind when he wrote: "Qui motus non irrationabiliter iumentum dicitur; non enim paruum adiutorium rationabili animae praestat" (text D, a). A similar observation can be made when we see Eriugena, apparently convinced that the "reptiles" of the Bible signify the movements of the vegetative soul, justifying this interpretation from the fact that these movements are hidden and invisible: *occulti quidam motus, et quasi latenter* (text D, c). Isidore had used the same characteristics for the progression of the serpents.[61]

Conclusions

Thus we reach the end of a long list of parallels between some exegetical passages of the *Periphyseon,* for the main part dealing with book IV, and extracts from earlier philosophical and theological works. These parallels are unequal both in scope as well as meaning. As for their scope, in most cases we have been dealing with parts of a sentence, and most often simply with words. Some similarities pointed merely to an analogy *ad sensum*, though these ought not to be completely neglected. As for their interpretation, we found great differences as well. Eriugena's Latin translation of some of the Greek texts that we compared precedes the composition of the *Periphyseon*, where he quotes them extensively. This is the case with Gregory of Nyssa's *De hominis opificio*, and Maximus the Confessor's *Ambigua*. Since no one knew these works better than their translator, there is a definite chance that Eriugena was directly inspired by them with regard to the points enumerated above. The same could very well be true for some Latin works with which he was familiar, such as Ambrose's *De paradiso* and Augustine's *De Genesi ad litteram*.

Other texts belong to the culture of the period, be it as its foundation, such as Porphyry's *Isagoge*, or as its mirroring reflection, such as Isidore's *Etymologies*. It is quite possible that Eriugena read these, the *Isagoge* perhaps in Boethius's translation. It could also be that he became familar with their contents, at least in part, during his own school training. With regard to other important authors the situation is far from clear. This is, for example, the case with Origen, who seems to have made a crucial decision in the history of exegesis by transforming Philo's interpretation of biblical animals into *motus animi*. A case such as his, however, brings back the problem of lost works and obscure traditions.

Whatever the consequences of these parallels and comparisons may be, they are far from exhausting the substance of Eriugena's text. Several of his exegetical positions still keep their secrets locked, and thus may well have been his own creation, such as the interpretation of *quadrupedia*. On the other hand, even in the case of direct influence, Eriugena never felt compelled to follow slavishly the text of his probable source (except when he gives large citations), but he rewrites it in his own manner. This is not to say that where he had actually translated the texts elsewhere (*De imagine, Ambigua ad Iohannem*) he did not remain loyal to his lexical choices. This option enhances the possibility of detecting his sources of influence.

Translated by Willemien Otten

NOTES

1. See, e.g., Brian Stock, "The Philosophical Anthropology of Johannes Scottus Eriugena," *Studi medievali*, 3d series, 8 (1967): 12–15; Willemien Otten, *The Anthropology of Johannes Scottus Eriugena*, Brill's Studies in Intellectual History, vol. 20 (Leiden: E. J. Brill, 1991), 132–137.

2. Cf. Goulven Madec, *Jean Scot et ses auteurs: Annotations érigéniennes* (Paris: Études augustiniennes, 1988) which is an indispensable tool for those interested in Eriugenian *Quellenforschung*.

3. Although it is difficult to find three English nouns to translate *mens, animus, intellectus,* their common distinction from *ratio* proves sufficiently that we are dealing here with the difference between intellectual intuition and discursive reason. The "species of the sensibles" (*species sensibilium*) which the soul, called sense here, "receives through the corporeal senses," are derived from Aristotelian psychology. Eriugena's phrase has a remarkable parallel in *De anima* II 12, 424 a 17–18: ἡ μὲν αἴσθησίς ἐστι τὸ δεκτικὸν τῶν αἰσθητῶν εἰδῶν (see Hicks's commentary on this, 415–416). The affinity with Aristotle is no less apparent when one considers "the proper name of vital motion by which the soul is commonly called when it nourishes the body and makes it grow," for *De anima* II 1, 412 a 14 reads: ζωὴν δὲ λέγομεν τὴν δι' αὑτοῦ τροφὴν τε καὶ αὔξησιν (cf. also III 12, 434 a 22–26). Furthermore, in II 2, 413 a 22–25 Aristotle uses the idea of different bearers of *life* such as *intellect, sensation,* [. . .] and also the *movement of nutrition* [. . .] and *growth.* Eriugena calls the movement of nutrition and growth also *vitalis proprie motus.* In the *Homily* on the prologue to St. John's Gospel, the term *motus vitalis* is found in a slightly different sense (X 9, ed. Jeauneau, SC 151: 246). The wealth of Aristotelian parallels is no proof that Eriugena read Aristotle.

4. Around 862–864, according to Maïeul Cappuyns, "Le *De imagine* de Grégoire de Nysse traduit par Jean Scot Erigène," *Recherches de théologie ancienne et médiévale* 32 (1965): 205. The *Periphyseon* is dated around 864–866: cf. *Iohannes Scotti Eriugenae Periphyseon (De divisione naturae)*, ed. I. P. Sheldon-Williams, book I (Dublin: The Dublin Institute for Advanced Studies, 1968), 7.

5. Gregory of Nyssa, *De imagine* 8, ed. Cappuyns, 217, 7–14, and 17–20: "Necesse est enim etiam in germinibus *uitalem* quandam uirtutem sensus expertem intelligi [. . .] Nam [. . .] nutrit et auget [. . .] Perfecta uero in corpore uita in rationabili, humana dico, formatur [PG 44:145A: καθορᾶται !] natura et nutritiua est et sensualis, et rationem participat, et animo ministrat [νῷ διοικουμένῃ] [. . .] corporalium uero hoc quidem uniuersaliter expers est uitae, hoc autem

uitalem participat operationem, iterum uitalium corporum, hoc quidem sensui coniungitur, hoc autem expers est sensus. Deinde sensuale iterum secatur in rationale et in irrationale." (Note that despite several errors on the part of the venerable translator, Gregory's Greek goes on to confirm the "intellectual" value of *animo*.) For *De hominis opificio* XIV, cf. *De imagine* 15, 230, lines 17–21. One will notice that these texts have already been quoted extensively in P III 292, 4–23 (735D–736B). The dilemmas involved in this hierarchy of creation can be visualized as follows. The five levels are clear:

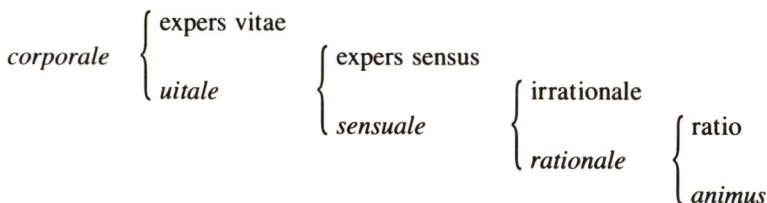

$$
corporale \begin{cases} \text{expers vitae} \\ \\ uitale \end{cases} \begin{cases} \text{expers sensus} \\ \\ sensuale \end{cases} \begin{cases} \text{irrationale} \\ \\ rationale \end{cases} \begin{cases} \text{ratio} \\ \\ animus \end{cases}
$$

6. Augustine, *Sermo* XLIII (3) 53–55, ed. Lambot, CCSL 41: 509: "Sed aliud est intellectus, aliud ratio. Nam rationem habemus et antequam intellegamus, sed intellegere non valemus, nisi rationem habeamus."

7. Augustine, *De trinitate* XII 15 (25) 14–44, ed. Mountain-Glorie, CCSL 50 A: 379: "Si ergo haec est sapientiae et scientiae recta distinctio ut ad sapientiam pertineat aeternarum rerum cognitio intellectualis, ad scientiam uero temporalium rerum cognitio rationalis, . . ." Note that Eriugena must have had knowledge of this Augustinian prooftext, for he appears to refer to it in P III 48, 28–50, 6 (629A–B); cf. G. Madec, 101.

8. Gregory of Nyssa, *De imagine* 30, p. 257, 26–29: "Hoc igitur ab omnibus confesso omnia elementa quae in mundo considerantur in nobis esse . . ." (follows a syntactical error by the translator). Gregory's position on this point is fairly nuanced. In *De hominis opificio* 30, 241B–C (which we have just quoted in Eriugena's translation) and in *In inscriptiones psalmorum* I 3, ed. McDonough, 30, 24–31, 16, and 32, 16–33, 6 (cosmic music and human music), Gregory displays a positive reaction, while in *De hominis opificio* 16, PG 44: 177D, he is negative. Eriugena is positive throughout. So *Homily* XIX 15–16, ed. Jeauneau, SC 151: 294: "homine [. . .] in quo omnis creatura adunatur"; P II 18, lines 18–21 (531A): "Homo [. . .] creatus est ut nulla creatura siue visibilis siue intellegibilis sit quae in eo reperiri non possit." See Jeauneau, SC 151: 295, n. 3, and the valuable Appendix VII: "A propos de l'homme-microcosme," 336–338.

9. Gregory of Nyssa, *De imagine* 15, p. 230, 21–25: "nemo ex his opinetur tres animas commixtas esse in humana concretione, in pro-

200   *Jean Pépin*

priis circumscriptionibus consideratas ita ut conformatione mul-
tarum animarum humanam esse arbitretur. Sed uera quidem
perfectaque anima una in natura est, intellectualis et immaterialis."
Eriugena's own translation of this passage from Gregory clearly influenced him in the *Periphyseon*, for he cites it with a large part of its
immediate context in P IV 11 (792C). He had already quoted its few
preceding lines in P III 292, 19–23 (736A–B). Cf. G. Madec, 40–41.

10. *Mîn* is a rare term with a disputed meaning, cf. Monique
Alexandre, *Le commencement du Livre: Genèse I–V, La version grecque
de la Septante et sa réception*, Christianisme Antique 3 (Paris: Editions
du Cerf, 1988), 128. Alexandre makes reference to Henri Cazelles,
"Myn = espèce, race ou ressemblance?" *Travaux de l'Institut catholique
de Paris*, 10 = Ecole des L.O.A. de l'I.C.P., *Mémorial du Cinquantenaire*
(Paris, 1964), 105–108; and Paul Beauchamp, *Création et séparation:
Etude exégétique du chapitre premier de la Genèse*, Bibliothèque des Sciences Religieuses 1 (Paris: Aubier-Montaigne, 1969), 240–247: "Le
sens du mot mîn (Gen. 1:11, 12, 24, 25)."

11. Didymus the Blind, *In Genesim* 32, 10–11, ed. Pierre Nautin,
SC 233:88 in a fragmentary statement: καθόλου φυτόν, δηλοῖ δὲ διὰ
τοῦ καθ᾽ ὁμοιότητα τὸ εἶδος. A similar formula, in a more complicated but better reading, is found in 49, 6–9, ed. Nautin, 128 (regarding Gen. 1:24). For the reactions of Greek commentators, see
Alexandre, 130.

12. Certain exegetes will use the duplication *secundum genus/secun-
dum similitudinem* (Gen. 1:11) for their own theological purposes. Ambrose connects the first two words of Acts 17:28: "cuius et genus
sumus" with the last two of Gen. 1:26: "Faciamus hominem ad imaginem et similitudinem nostram" (*Exameron* III 7, 31, ed. Schenkl,
Corpus Scriptorum Ecclesiasticorum Latinorum 32 I: 79, 26–80,
11). Thus he gives Gen. 1:11, "utinam imitaremur hanc herbam," a
moral interpretation.

13. Cf. *Vetus Latina: Die Reste der altlateinischen Bibel,* ed. Bonifatius
Fischer, 2: *Genesis* (Freiburg: Herder, 1951), *ad* 1, 11–25, 15–25. The
information given here concerns only the essentials; in reality the situation is more complex.

14. Cf. Alexandre, loc. cit.: "On notera que la Vulgate en 1, 12 a
'genus,' puis 'species,' pour le même mot!"

15. This is a possible reference to the end of book III 300 (739D sq).

16. Note Eriugena's subtlety here: the scheme that expresses the
duality of primordial causes vis-à-vis genera/species is the same as
that of simplicity (*simpliciter*) and profundity (*altiori sensu*) which reflects the duality of apparent vis-à-vis hidden meaning. For these
themes and their imagery, especially the inaccessible "recesses" (*sinus*)
of nature and creation, see Jeauneau's excellent article "Le 'caché' et

l'"obscur'," *Quatre thèmes érigéniens* (1978), reprint in E. Jeauneau, *Etudes érigéniennes* (Paris: Etudes augustiniennes, 1987), 221–242.

17. The phrase *illa vita, quae nutritiua dicitur* in text 3 stems probably from Gregory of Nyssa, *De imagine* 8, 217, line 13. See n. 5 above: "uita [. . .] nutritiua."

18. P II 48, 35–37 (546 A–B): "primordiales totius creaturae causas quas pater in unigenito suo filio qui principii appellatione nominatur ante omnia quae condita sunt creauerat intellegamus," etc.; P III 188, 34–190, 1 (690C); P III 192, 23–26 (692A): "Nos autem primordialium causarum conditionem siue uisibilium siue inuisibilium in factura caeli et terrae in principio [. . .] uolentes intellegere."

19. P III 304, 28–30 (742A): "Hactenus de conditione piscium et uolatilium in primordialibus causis, eorum uero in genera et species processio sequitur." On this issue of animal creation Eriugena could hardly have drawn a clearer distinction between on the one hand the level of the intelligible model in the Word and on the other the level of concrete manifestation. To indicate the transition from one level to the next, *processio* is an excellent term which points to the terminology at the beginning of book IV.

20. See for this point also P IV (749C–D [text 3]).

21. P III 220, 24–222, 8 (704C–705A): "[Gen. 1:11] Virtutem herbarum lignorumque in primordialibus causis conditam per haec uerba propheta commemorat, quae uirtus uis seminum a sanctis patribus solet appellari [. . .] quoniam omne quod in natura rerum uisibiliter apparet non aliunde nisi ex occultis naturalis et substantialis formae sinibus, quam aridae uel terrae uocabulo significatam praediximus, originales causas generationis suae recipit, propterea scriptum est: Germinet terra herbam uirentem, et caetera, ac si aperte diceretur: Vis seminalis herbarum et lignorum, quae in intimis substantiarum rationibus causaliter creata est, in formas et species sensibiles per generationem procedat, quae processio primordialium causarum in effectus suos sequentibus scripturae uerbis explanatur: Et factum est ita, et protulit terra herbam uirentem et ferentem semen iuxta genus suum lignumque faciens fructum et habens unumquodque semen secundum speciem suam [Gen. 1:11–12]. Videsne quemadmodum diuina scriptura genera et species manifestissime declarat, in quibus causaliter et inuisibiliter subsistunt quaecunque per generationem in quantitatibus et qualitatibus in notitiam corporalium sensuum erumpunt?"

22. Cf. P III 218, 37–38 (704A): "arida, hoc est occulta substantialis forma."

23. Sheldon-Williams's translation of this passage clearly reveals the contradiction with the other texts: "the divine Scripture reveals most clearly *the genera and the species in which there subsists causally and*

invisibly whatever things [my italics] break forth through generation in quantities and qualities into the knowledge of the corporeal senses" (P III, 223). It is important to add that the Vulgate does not reveal a changed use of *genus* and *species* in Gen. 1:11–12 as opposed to Gen. 1:20–21 and 24–25. The biblical text does not therefore justify Eriugena's manipulation of terms.

24. See above, n. 19 and related text.

25. *Homélie* VII 5–7, ed. Jeauneau, SC 151:232: "Nam ipsius [sc. verbi] ex patre generatio ipsa est causarum omnium conditio omniumque quae ex causis in genera et species procedunt operatio et effectus." The homily's English translation is taken from John J. O'Meara, *Eriugena* (Oxford: Clarendon Press, 1988), 163.

26. P II 48, 35–37 (546A–B). See above, n. 18 and related text.

27. Porphyry, *Isagoge*, translatio Boethii, ed. Busse, Commentaria in Aristotelem Graeca IV 1:25, 10–13: "de generibus ac speciebus illud quidem siue subsistunt siue in solis nudisque intellectibus posita sunt, siue subsistentia corporalia sunt an incorporalia, et utrum separata a sensibilibus an in sensibilibus posita et circa ea constantia, dicere recusabo." Cf. the end of the passage in P III 28 (see above, n. 21): *subsistunt, corporalium sensuum.*

28. Cf. G. Madec, 32.

29. See above, text 1.

30. Porphyry, *Isagoge,* ed. Busse, 26, 21–23: "principium quoddam est huiusmodi genus earum quae sub ipso sunt specierum, uideturque etiam multitudinem continere omnem quae sub eo est."

31. Ibid., 29, 9–11: "Est autem generalissimum quidem, super quod nullum ultra aliud sit superueniens genus, specialissimum autem, post quod non erit alia inferior species."

32. Maximus, *Ambigua*, PG 91: 1177B12–C9.

33. Maximus, *Ambigua ad Iohannem* VI (37), 1390–1397, ed. Jeauneau, CCSG 18:92: ". . . et mota est et mouetur, ea ratione et modo qui est per diuisionem et collectionem. Mouetur enim a generalissimo genere per generaliora genera in species, per quas et in quas diuidi consueuit, proueniens usque ad specialissimas species, quibus terminatur secundum ipsam diuisio, esse ipsius deorsum uersus circunscribens, et colligitur iterum a specialissimis speciebus per generaliora regrediens usque ad generalissimum genus, quo terminatur secundum ipsam contractio, sursum uersus esse eius consummans."

34. This hypothesis is confirmed when we look at P III 28 (above, n. 21). Eriugena integrates the theory of genera and species here with the consideration of quantities and qualities (*in quantitatibus et qualitatibus*), which cannot be found in the *Isagoge.* Maximus (loc. cit., 1177C–D), however, followed by his translator (1399–1409, pp. 92–

93), applies to these two Aristotelian categories all previous statements regarding the category of substance.

35. Maximus, *Ambigua*, PG 91: 1312B–D.

36. Porphyry, *Isagoge*, ed. Busse, 2, 17–20.

37. Maximus, *Ambigua ad Iohannem* XXXVII, 150–172, ed. Jeauneau, CCSG 18:185.

38. See, e.g., P III 208, 30–31 (699B); 216, 37, and 218, 3 (703A); III 28, 218, 26–27 (703C); etc.

39. Origen, *De principiis* I 4, 5, ed. Koetschau, Die Griechischen Christlichen Schriftsteller 22: 68, 8–13: "Si ergo singula, quae sub sole sunt, fuerunt iam in illis saeculis, quae fuerunt ante nos, cum nihil recens sit sub sole (Eccl. 1:9–10), sine dubio omnia uel genera uel species fuerunt semper (πάντα τὰ γένη καὶ τὰ εἴδη ἀεὶ ἦν)" (the Greek words in parentheses are preserved by Justinian, cf. Koetschau's apparatus). Crouzel comments on this as follows in SC 253:81: "Les genres et les espèces sont des idées (générales) au sens platonicien." Note that Eriugena commented on the same formula attributed to Solomon: see P II 21, 78, 31–80, 18 (560B–561A). He is led to this by Maximus, *Ambigua*, PG 91:1412CD = Eriugena's *Ambigua ad Iohannem* LXVII, 87–94, ed. Jeauneau, CCSG 18: 257–258.

40. Augustine, *De Genesi ad litteram* III 12, 18, ed. Josephus Zycha, Corpus Scriptorum Ecclesiasticorum Latinorum 28: 76, 28–77, 4: "Non frustra etiam lectorem mouet, utrumne passim et quasi fortuito an aliqua ratione dicatur: secundum genus [Gen. 1:24–25], tamquam fuerint et antea, cum primo creata narrentur. An genus eorum in superioribus rationibus intellegendum est, utique spiritalibus, secundum quas creantur inferius?" Although Augustine describes this exegesis, he ultimately rejects it. Since the phrase *secundum genus* occurs only in the creation of plants, why is it not used for the earlier creatures, for their *aeterna et incommutabilis ratio* must definitely have been operative in the wisdom of God? (ibid., 77, 4–9). With the context showing that Augustine gave *secundum genus* minute attention, it is not surprising that Eriugena does the same. In III 12, 19, Augustine is interested in *secundum similitudinem*, but not at all in *secundum speciem*, since he did not read the Vulgate!

41. See n. 21, above.

42. Augustine, *De Genesi ad litteram* III 12, 19, ed. Zycha, 78, 1–3: "Hoc est ergo secundum genus, ubi et seminum uis et similitudo intellegitur succedentium decedentibus." This parallel has not yet been noted by Eriugena's editors. We noted *vis seminum* in P IV 5 = text 3 above. With regard to the word *uirtus*, it is used in a similar sense in *Homélie*, X 22, ed. Jeauneau, SC 151:248: *seminum uirtus.* See also Jeauneau's editorial note on p. 250.

43. Augustine, *De Genesi ad litteram* X 21, 37, ed. Zycha, 325, 7–8: "posse inde aliquid sumi, quod non habeat illam uim seminalem, sed tantum corporalem substantiam." This formula translates an aspect of the λόγος σπερματικός, a notion probably of Stoic origin to which practically all patristic theories of creation are indebted. In the same context Augustine speaks about *ratio seminis* (325, 12). Compare Philo, *De opificio mundi* 13, 43: the fruits contain the σπερματικαὶ οὐσίαι made from invisible λόγοι; Didymus, *In Genesim* 48, 23–24, ed. Nautin, 126: the order given to the earth in Gen. 1:24 signifies that it stored the power to bring forth animals, for in it resides "a seminal reason" (λόγου σπερματικοῦ).

44. P IV, 748D = text 1, above.

45. Gregory of Nyssa, *De imagine* 8, ed. Cappuyns, 217, 24, and 29: per eandem consequentiam (ἀκολουθίαν), consequenter progrediente natura.

46. Philo, *Legum allegoriae* II 4, 12–13: πρὸ γάρ τῶν εἰδῶν ἀποτελεῖ τὰ γένη, etc.

47. It is no longer the time of the *Expositions on the Celestial Hierarchy* XIII 4, 374–375, ed. Barbet, CCCM 31:176, where Eriugena wrote: "Septuaginta enim pre manibus non habemus, quod sequitur Dionysius."

48. Cf. the edition quoted above (n. 13), ad loc., 23–24.

49. An identical maneuver which may have inspired Eriugena can be found in the Venerable Bede, *In Genesim* I, 668–696, ed. Jones, CCSL 118A: 23. Bede cites first Gen. 1:24 in the Vulgate, then *iuxta antiquam sane translationem* (line 691, i.e., the *Vetus Latina*) to arrive at the reading of *quadrupedia*, of which he makes no further use. In an editorial note, ad loc., Jones thinks this translation is derived from Augustine, *De Genesi ad litteram* III 11, 16.

50. We have already pointed out, above, the Gregorian inspiration behind these two functions of the vegetative soul. There is no need to return to this theme here.

51. Porphyry, *Isagoge,* ed. Busse, 27, 18–19: "genus autem non de una specie praedicatur sed de pluribus et differentibus specie"; 28, 7: "erat autem hominis genus anima"; 29, 12–13: "et genera et species sunt eadem"; 30, 24: "nunquam diuiditur in species."

52. Origen, *In Genesim homiliae* I 11, ed. Baehrens, Die Griechischen Christlichen Schriftsteller, 29: 13, 6–11: "Et illa quidem, quae de aquis producta sunt [cf. Gen. 1:20], diximus debere motus et cogitationes mentis nostrae, qui de profundo cordis producuntur, intellegi. Nunc uero hoc, quod dicitur: producat terra animam uiuam [. . .], exterioris hominis nostri, id est carnalis et terreni motus arbitror in-

dicari"; I 16, ibid.: 20, 5–8: "in piscibus et uolatilibus uel animalibus et repentibus terrae [cf. Gen. 1:28] ea mihi uidentur indicari, de quibus nihilominus superius diximus, id est uel quae de sensu animae et cordis cogitatione procedunt, uel quae ex desideriis corporalibus et carnis motibus proferuntur." Note the parallel with Eriugena's text D: *uitae terreno corpori adhaerentis*. In the second of his texts, Origen extends his exegesis to include Gen. 1:28, where God gives Adam the order to govern the animals. This has a parallel in P IV 5, 750D–751A.

53. Didymus, *In Genesim* 43, 8–19, ed. Nautin, 112–114: Πρόσσχες δὲ ἔτι καὶ τῷ ἐποίησεν ὁ θεὸς τὰ κήτη τὰ μεγάλα [Gen. 1:21] [. . .] Σαφὲς δὲ καὶ τὸ κατὰ γένη αὐτῶν [ibid.], νοουμένου ἐνταῦθα τοῦ εἴδους ἀντὶ του γένους. The Alexandrian exegete gives a similar explanation in *In Genesim* 178, 2–3, ed. Nautin, II, 86, where he introduces a pair of all the animals into Noah's Ark "according to their genus" (Gen. 6:19–20).

54. Ambrose, *De paradiso* 11, 51, ed. Schenkl, Corpus Scriptorum Ecclesiasticorum Latinorum 32 I: 308, 11–19: "Bestiae autem agri et uolatilia caeli, quae adducuntur ad Adam [Gen. 2:19], nostri inrationabiles motus sunt [. . .] Propterea nullus inuentus est menti nostrae similis adiutor [Gen. 2:20] nisi sensus, hoc est αἴσθησις." According to Schenkl's observation, ad loc., this whole exegesis stems from Philo, *Legum allegoriae* II 2, 5, and 4, 9–11. One should add: eventually through the mediation of the lost Origen.

55. In P IV 18, 831D–832A; 24, 849A. Note also 832D: "Intuere, quemadmodum Ambrosius sensum Origenis approbat"; cf. Madec, 21, 57–58.

56. Augustine, *De Genesi contra Manichaeos* I 20, 31, PL 34:188 (on Gen. 1:28): "recte tamen intellegitur etiam spiritualiter, ut omnes affectiones et motus animi, quos habemus istis animalibus similes, subditos haberemus." Cf. also *De musica* VI 11, 32: the φαντασίαι are what the memory retains *de motibus animi*. These last words probably correspond to a Stoic notion, cf. Stoicorum Veterum Fragmenta II 54:22,4: ὅ τι ἂν δύνηται κινεῖν τὴν ψυχήν.

57. Augustine, *De Genesi ad litteram* III 4, 6, ed. Zycha, 66, 10–13: "sunt etiam, qui subtilissima consideratione quinque istos manifestissimos corporis sensus secundum quattuor usitata elementa ita distinguant, ut oculos ad ignem, aures ad aerem. . . ." Cf. III 5, 7, ed. Zycha, 67, 14–16: "quoniam sentire non est corporis, sed animae per corpus, licet acute disseratur secundum diuersitatem corporeorum elementorum sensus esse corporis distributos." For the famous principle *sentire non est corporis*, etc., cf. Augustine, *De quantitate animae* 23, 41: "sensus quo anima per corpus utitur."

58. Augustine, Cf. *De Genesi ad litteram*, ed. A. Solignac, *Biblioth. augustinienne* 48, complementary note ad loc., 615–619.

59. Cf. G. Madec, 44.

60. Isidore, *Etymologiae* XII 1, 7: "Iumenta nomina inde traxerunt, quod nostrum laborem uel onus suo adiutorio [. . .] iuuent [. . .] Vnde et iumenta appellantur ab eo quod iuuent homines."

61. Ibid. XII 4, 3: "Serpens autem nomen accepit quia occultis accessibus serpit, non apertis passibus."

Part 3

EASTERN SOURCES
AND INFLUENCES

Unity and Trinity in East and West

WERNER BEIERWALTES

I

THE PHILOSOPHY OF LATE ANTIQUITY was motivated by the endeavor to investigate both the concept of unity and that of tri-unity, the latter as a form of unity *and* plurality. The adoption in manifold forms, as well as the transformation into a new thought structure, of Plato's central question justifies the characterization of this philosophy as *Neo*platonism. The central tenet of Neoplatonism is the concept of a unity which is construed in terms of the search for the one ground and origin of the differentiated many, a concept which was to remain fruitful in the subsequent history of thought, and by no means as mere historical reminiscence. This line of thought determined one of the major philosophic intentions of medieval and modern thought—the latter from Spinoza and Leibniz up to the Idealism of Fichte, Hegel, and Schelling.

Since its beginning, Christian theology was, and is, decisively involved in its own special form of a similar concern: the philosophical relationship between unity and trinity. The systematic analysis of this question is the necessary presupposition for the working out of a form of reflection which at least approximates to the central Christian belief in the Trinity or Tri-Unity of God. The Trinity—the three essential appearance-forms of the one God—is revealed by the New Testament as a basic truth and is experienced and adored as a mystery *stricto sensu* similar to the Incarnation. Nevertheless, this concept was a continual challenge to strenuous reflection. It was not that the incomprehensible should be made comprehensible, but rather that the attempt should be undertaken to work out a conceptual approximation of the mystery. Reflection should be a circling delineation of the Trinity which makes faith in the Trinity intelligible, justified by reflection, binding and communicable.[1]

During the long-lasting and momentous process of the hellenizing of Christianity, the conceptuality of Greek metaphysics substantially conditioned the dogmatic formalization of Christian truth, whether consciously or unconsciously. Thus, we find many theological tenets which only through philosophical reflection and theoretical form came to be what they are, or at least through philosophy gained a convincing character for faith as a whole. This is particularly true for the question of creation as the unfolding of the divine Will and Goodness, for the ideas as the structures of divine Thought, for the concept of God as identical with absolute Being in the sense of a reflexively moved immutability, for the concept of a hypostatic unity of God and man in Christ, for will and freedom, *arché* and *logos*, eternity, time and history, and the issue of the approach towards knowledge of God through affirmative, symbolic, and negative theology.

None of these theological tenets is more intensively determined by, and so deeply interwoven with, philosophical concepts and theories than the Trinity. Its intelligibility depends upon more or less developed concepts of unity, singleness, simplicity, and also on the three-ness that indicates a characteristic difference in the unity, but which nonetheless should not be understood as numerical in the mathematical sense. It also involves conceptions of difference and characteristic individuality as elements in the unity and, at the same time, the inseparability, nondistinctness, or even "equality" through which the characteristic three form the Trinity in itself: ". . . in his igitur tribus quam sit . . . inseparabilis distinctio, et tamen distinctio, videat qui potest."[2]

No less decisive for the reflexive form of the Trinity is the ontological meaning of the concept of relation which founds and carries the reciprocal interpenetration of *tri-* and *un*-ity: Trinity as a correlative unity which is itself only through self-relatedness. Such a unity, since it is Being in the most intensive sense, is essentially comprehensible and expressible. It is both unfolding in itself and thinking itself, reflecting spirit: the Trinity is a self-reflexive circle whose unity constitutes itself timelessly as thinking, as willing—and as loving—itself. Besides this open, clear, conceptual basis, and along with the hitherto hidden philosophic implications, the concepts of *usia* (i.e., *essentia*), *physis* (*natura*), *hypostasis* (*substantia*), and *persona* play a considerable role in the reflexive form of trinitarian theology.

The enumeration of the philosophical issues with respect to trinitarian speculation shows that the correlation of philosophy and theology was clearly necessary, if the latter were to endeavor to move beyond a naive reproduction of Scripture, or to avoid being caught up in mere fideism. The connection between philosophy and theology as a reflexive unity was preserved throughout the development of the trinitarian idea in different ways. On account of the difficulties, indeed the paradox, involved in the thought that within the trinitarian unity *both* difference and equality should be present, the struggle to find an orthodox concept of the Trinity inspired energetic refutations of heretical positions and formulations. These formulations sought to express a shifting ratio of unity to multiplicity against the dominance of the One (i.e., identity) or of the Other (i.e., difference) in the same. These generally polemical discussions identified a group of conceptions which were all held to be heretical or possibly heretical (in order to maintain ecclesiastical and political unity) and therefore were repressed: Subordinationism, Monarchism, Tritheism, Arianism, Sabellianism, and finally the lamentable discussion between the western and the eastern churches concerning the *filioque* which eventually led to schism. It is not the concern of philosophy to sit in judgment upon the truth or falsehood of these conceptions; its task is rather to investigate the issues under discussion and to search for the possible evidence of philosophical involvement in the matter.

In the context of this long-lasting "serious game" played out between philosophy and theology in order to develop a concept of the Trinity, I wish to turn to—among others—John Scottus Eriugena. It was not least in this dimension of his thought that he can be seen as a mediator between the East and the West. In order to clarify both the difficulty and the productivity of this mediation, I shall develop the elements of Dionysius Areopagita's trinitarianism as the presupposition for my discussion of Eriugena. First, however, we must turn to a short recapitulation of the Neoplatonic conception of unity as the starting point and philosophical presupposition for the formation of the theological concept of Tri-Unity.

II

Today it is undisputed that the philosophical structure of Dionysius's thought has its origin in Neoplatonism. This is evident from the ontological orientation of his hierarchical thought, from his stress on the immanent self-realization of the triadic principle, and from the drive towards abstraction which is decisive for his *theologia mystica* and which plays such a great role in Neoplatonic thought about the One,[3] as well as in the form of life which is bound up with this thought.[4]

Since the origin of this thinking is to be found in Proclus's exegesis of the Platonic *Parmenides*,[5] wherein he modifies and yet develops Plotinian concepts, both Proclus and Plotinus can be employed to study the concept of the first One and its metamorphoses in relation to plurality. Both consider unity at its most intensive and absolute form as the "autark," abiding within itself, origin of reality as a whole.[6] Insofar as this unity is a dimension of the many, differentiated from the other yet related to each other, the origin is the One eminently. In itself it is the absolute exclusion of the many in the sense of any difference from that world which it causes.

Since being, being-some-thing, and relationality should be thought of as forms of immanent and outwardly acting otherness and thus implying plurality and inner and outer relations, the One is free from being, from immanent form limiting itself towards any other. It is without inner relationality and thus without thought or language. It is "before the some-thing,"[7] and as such it is nothing of all, different from all, free and unconfused, alone ITSELF, the absolute beyond, that is, the ἐπέκεινα.[8] Precisely on account of such an emphasis upon difference, transcendence, and nothingness, in the case of the One there arises a paradox which withstands argumentative solution: How does this relationless One pass over into a new being, that is to say, "its own" being in the form of difference and relationality? This is the fact which reason has to assume when confronted with the given structure of reality which it has to analyze, and when reason re-flects or turns back to the origin of this very fact. This negation of being, form, *some-thing*, relation, and thought cannot be thought of as mere emptiness or as a diminishing of reality. It should point to the very fullness of the One identical with the Good, on the basis of whose all-mightiness (as the most intensive unity and simplicity)[9] it has sublimated and embraced all difference in the manner of absolute *in*difference. Or rather the One does not "have," but eminently "is." Thus the One or the Good gives in fact that which it does not "have." Therefore, the full being of the One first comes to be expressed through this paradox which attempts to present its double aspect (one being and action) as one reality. It is (naturally, non-spatially) both nowhere and everywhere, at once all and nothing. *All*, because the world is through and from the One and exists only because the origin is continually active as beginning and sustaining. At the same time the One is *nothing* (i.e., *no*-thing) of all, because despite its constitutive unfolding in being, it remains itself absolutely: thus both *in* all and *above* all: ITSELF.

On the basis of its goodness and thereby the freely giving sharing of itself in its coming forth or emergence into being, the One sets or founds the first real otherness. This stands as relative selfhood directed towards the First and the One as the thoroughly other; it is related to the One by virtue of the One's immanent presence in the otherness. Thereby, and through the act of individuation and separation, the One enables the existence of plurality in the dimension of self-relationality, while still reflecting back towards the dimension of the origin. The reflection, or bending-back of this dimension of otherness and plurality towards the founding One should be understood as the thinking of its own manifold structure. Plotinus calls this the timeless Spirit (*nous*). The thinking of this Spirit is the relationality of the many, of the individual beings which are the ideas, amongst each other in a dimension which is nevertheless directed towards the One. Since these may be considered as the *being* of Spirit, the Spirit thinks its own being in these, that means, it thinks itself. As opposed to the superessential, free from difference, relationless, nonthinking One in itself, the *nous* is the Second as unfolded form, stage, or, in respect of the forthgoing of the One, phase of unity. *Nous* is being, differentiated in itself, determined through relation and through thought about itself *and* the One. In itself it is the reflexive unity which determines and limits itself as its own hypostasis. This second, in-itself-relational-One is, in comparison with the absolute One, only analogous unity; it constitutes unity by thinking through its immanent plurality and otherness, notwithstanding the retention of difference. By means of the reflection that constitutes unity in this second One, likeness to the absolute One itself dominates in this realm, despite the tendency that any difference has towards its own autonomy.

This form of immanently relational thought, thinking itself and yet reflecting towards its origin, is the philosophical model of the

Christian unity in tri-unity: the Trinity. Both forms of unity developed by the Neoplatonists were placed within a new concept of unity in Christian trinitarian speculation, historically and thematically. When we consider the matter philosophically, the Christian concept of God as the absolute and as the universal origin has its roots in the relationless, transcendent One. Yet, as an inwardly relational being, God has his roots in the second, i.e., in the reflexive One, so that he could be conceived as an inner trinitarian movement of thinking (*intellectus, sapientia*), speaking (*verbum*), willing and loving, (*spiritus sanctus*).[10]

If it is correct to assume, and I am convinced of this, that Dionysius's concept of the divine oneness is philosophically determined by the essentially distinct concepts of the absolute *non*being-One and the being-One as developed in Proclus's *Parmenides* commentary,[11] one may be able to judge adequately the difficulties which he faced in trying to combine both with the intention of producing a concept of the Trinity which is at least approximately appropriate for the Christian theological tradition.

III

At least since the time when Ferdinand Christian Baur clearly and repeatedly stated as a *communis opinio* that Dionysius did not have a real affinity with the doctrine of the Trinity (despite his particular references to the doctrine),[12] it has been said that Dionysius has no "explicit doctrine of the Trinity."[13] It has also been argued that the Trinity is a rather alien element in his thought, and that the unity of the Trinity is merely "a particular case of the metaphysical"—an inwardly concentrated and yet outwardly creatively oriented, self-overflowing, causal unity and goodness.[14] Thus, as this argument continues, trinitarian reductionism for Dionysius is the result of the attempt to "legitimate himself theologically without compromising himself philosophically by insisting upon three consubstantial hypostases of one divine being."[15] The essential cause of this alleged reductionism is said to be Dionysius's philosophical roots in the late Neoplatonic speculation of Proclus. Within Dionysius's thought, the attempt to transform the Neoplatonic One into the Christian conception of the tri-unity or an internally unified three-ness was such a determining factor that it is certainly justified to ascribe a certain prevalence to the One. Certainly, Dionysius cannot be said to have a trinitarian "system," despite his affinity to triadic systematization as a structural principle of thought. His thinking does not concentrate upon the inner-worldly unfolding of the divine tri-unity in connection with, let us say, the Incarnation of Christ, so that he would have been sensitive to the "economic" aspect of the Trinity, according to which the trinitarian Persons of the Son (*Logos, Sophia*) and the Holy Spirit come together effectively, constituting the world and forming the Christian community. Notwithstanding this, the very fact that Dionysius thinks so emphatically in terms of the One, or Unity, as the highest, most powerful name for God—if the unnameable, above all names (Philippians 2:9) should indeed be named—means that his endeavor to see the divine unity as nevertheless trinitarian, the Trinity "derived" from the unity,[16] or the unity as an internally relational Trinity, deserves the utmost attention.

Motivated and led (I do not wish to say forced) by the language of Holy Scripture about Father, Son, and Holy Spirit and their kinship,[17] Dionysius conceives the absolute divine unity—the One—also as an internally relational tri-une oneness. He thereby combines two philosophically clearly divisible strands of thought into one—a unity that appears, at least philosophically, paradoxical because it entails the attribution of *both* negativity and positivity to one and the same object. In accordance with the first hypothesis of Plato's *Parmenides*, the eminent (first) One is absolutely transcendent with respect to everything that subsequently arises; it is pure, superessential, internally relationless simplicity. The second form of unity, which arises from the absolute One and in self-knowledge turns back to it, in contrast to the first is differentiated within itself. This latter unity is a web of relational being which participates in the origin. It is related, both correlatively and subordinately, in thought to itself, and also to the origin which corresponds to the second Platonic hypothesis as a "being-One." This allows it to receive those relational predicates which are denied to the superessential One in respect to its absolute relationlessness. The putting together of both these dimensions must be considered as intending to abolish or lessen the realm of difference between these two forms of unity, insofar as God with *all* his attributes must be thought of as pure unity. First, one might consider the use of all the Proclean negative predications, extended by some biblical negative predications, so that God could be thought of as the "superessential elevated nothing of all."[18] In addition, Dionysius increases the absolute otherness of the divine One through the effusive use of the basically negative prefix *super:* the divine unity must be thought of as "above" the One, or "Super-Unitary,"[19] in order to avoid the identification with the One as principle and element of plurality (number), and thus to distance radically the One from any kind of plurality.

At the same time—herein one sees the paradox—the implications of the "being-One" are valid for God or the divine unity in the same intensity. This is because "He who is" (the name God confirmed in Exodus 3:14, "I am that I am"),[20] as unchangeable being himself ($\alpha \mathring{v} \tau \grave{o} \ \tau \grave{o} \ \varepsilon \mathring{i} v \alpha \iota$), is abiding identity in himself and yet also is difference in the sense of constituting being and giving it a share of his absolute Goodness. He is the Cause of all.[21] Despite all the differences from thought in the realm of plurality, he is absolute Self-thinking,[22] a thinking which embraces the ideas. The divine ideas constitute an intelligible framework of the world, before the world[23]—unitary and unifying in divine thought—and they are identical with "Wisdom," "Logos," "Life," and "Light," so as to ensure congruity with Scripture.

It is only by means of such a paradoxical telescoping of the superessential, absolute One into a unity which in itself is differentiated and essentially relational that a reflective concept of the Trinity is possible. Given the tendency towards a comprehensive radical negation pointing to the absolute divine transcendence, the problematical tension in the relation between unity and trinity is scarcely surprising. This may, indeed, be the reason why Dionysius only suggests a process of trinitarian self-constitution and does not really analyze the properties of the processive hypostases, neither philosophically nor from the biblical and theological point of view.[24] Perhaps he said more about these matters in the lost Theological Outlines.[25]

Notwithstanding the prevalence of the One as opposed to the other determinations in the whole of the Dionysian predication about the Godhead, he did find a formula for the Trinity in which the dominance of the unity is suspended for the sake of a relational perichoresis of the three in a being and thinking unity. I venture to say that the chiasmus in the following formula emphasizes the unity of the three within the Trinity: unified through difference and differentiated through unity—"There is distinction in unity and unity in distinction" (*ἡνωμένα τῃ διακρίσει καὶ τῃ ἑνώσει διακεκριμένα*).[26]

The threeness of the divine hypostases is unconfused unity which maintains the distinctive property of each (*οἰκεῖον, ἴδιον*), a unity, therefore, which through its immanent activity is itself. In his concept of "unity in difference" or "difference in unity" Dionysius gives particular emphasis to the following issue: all predications which in Scripture are about the three Persons or hypostases or which we attribute to the incomprehensible by our own concepts should not be fixed upon one hypostasis but should be ascribed to the trinitarian Godhead as a whole. Thus, they are aspects or elements connected with one another of one interrelated divine being.[27] This is to say that the whole Godhead as Trinity is in the same intensity One, Goodness, Being, Eternity, Identity, Difference, Rest, Motion, Sovereignty, Beauty, Wisdom, Thought, Life, Light, and is also the universal, superessential Cause (Origin or Source exuding itself) of all being.[28] Precisely the last characteristic of absolute Causal-Being shows that the Trinity comprehends all other named attributes in a supercategorical, transcendental way, and at the same time comprehends[29] the tendency "outwards" as creative ideas or archetypes of the world, "unified," "unitary," or "unifying" as *ἐναρχικὴ τριάς*,[30] that is, as primal unified Trinity. This is a Trinity which is the origin of its unity *in* itself or *from* itself. It is the unity of the two different aspects of the same: absolute transcendence of the properties in the Godhead and the intention towards a creative unfolding whereby the unified opposites within the origin disperse themselves into pluralities. Thus, the unitary divine Being which is conceived and moved by difference and relation may be thought of as a unity of opposites. This includes the inner unfolding of the internally differentiated hypostases and perspectives as the one and abiding same,[31] despite its unfolding in the world. "Opposites" characterize here not the difference of the hypostases as such, but their transcendent, internal, unifying, abiding Superessence in relation to the creative emergence from itself into an actual otherness, namely, the polar-determined world in which the creative power (*θεογόνον, γονιμότης*) derived from the divine Goodness is realized.[32]

The concept and reality of distinction and difference (*διά-κρισις, διακεκριμένα, διαίρεσις*) of individual attributes in God is the necessary precondition for the understood unity of opposites and for the relational unity of the Trinity, both of which should be thought of as the whole of the Godhead. Despite his emphasis on the unity—"because in the Divine the unity rules over the difference (distinction) and it is beforehand" (i.e., before the creative unfolding),[33] the distinction remains active and conscious for the reflexive grasp of the Trinity. The difference of the hypostases brings out the characteristic property primarily of one of the three—εὐδιακρίτως καὶ σαφῶς καὶ εὐτάκτως[34]—and marks the individual identity of the three in relation to each other. Thus, differentiating identity allows no inversion with each other (ἀντι-στροφή, οὐκ ἀντιστρέφει πρὸς ἄλληλα),[35] no reciprocal sublimation of the particular individuality: the Word is as the Son of the Father only himself, and not in his propriety identical with the Father (ἰδικῶς, ἀμιγῶς, ἀσυγχύτως).[36] Unity pervades or includes the three particulars (each proper hypostasis) into a One which unifies the different and differentiates the unified without separation. The relationship of the unified-differentiated should be thought of as a reciprocal being-in-another,[37] without the one becoming the other in a part of the whole,[38] and as a whole, they are indeed in the other as in the whole.[39] The Dionysian trinitarian formula follows the maxim: "One may neither separate the unified [διαιρεῖν] nor confuse the distinct [συγχεῖν]."[40] On the one hand, the relational being-in-another of the three toward the unity or as one preserves the particular identity and, on the other hand, the self-distinction of the particulars conditions and determines in the self-unifying relation the whole nature of the Godhead.

At least once Dionysius points to an inner self-explication in the Trinity, a movement which springs from the Father as Principle and Source. From hence springs forth the Son and the Spirit as "offspring arisen from God, and also, as it were, the blossoms and the superessential lights of the God-begetting Godhead."[41]

The timeless theogonia[42] allows the begetting of the Son and Holy Spirit directly from the Father. A procession of the Holy Spirit in the sense of *filioque*,[43] according to which the Holy Spirit is not begotten only by the Father, but equally by the Father and the Son (consubstantially), is not developed. The metaphors "offspring," "blossom," "light," may suggest a hierarchical difference in the origination out of the source which would contradict Dionysius's conviction concerning the equal interrelatedness of the three. But he claims that predications about each individual hypostasis are valid for the whole, and he stabilizes the equality by means of predicates like unity, identity, totality, community, equally divine, and equally good (although not with the correspondingly orthodox concept "consubstantial").[44]

In Dionysius's trinitarian discussion each personal characteristic in the Trinity remains relatively abstract. The inner-trinitarian being and action of the particular Persons are simply mentioned in a few basic words but are not actually analyzed. Also, he draws no specific, significant consequences from the scriptural passages which he quotes at the beginning of the second chapter of *De divinis nominibus*, but, by drawing upon these texts, he merely shows that the statements for one hypostasis are valid for the whole. Only by means of such an analysis would Dionysius's stated claim concerning the "equality" of the particulars (that is, the particular hypostases) for the whole Trinity have achieved a clear contour and a persuasive power transcending that of mere postulation.[45]

IV

Eriugena's reflective investigation of the concept of the Trinity, attempting to seek and find coherence with scriptural assertions about Father, Son, and Holy Spirit, is not to be found mainly in any one place, as is the case with St. Augustine. It is, rather, placed argumentatively within discussions about other topics, primarily in the treatments of the *causae primordiales*, the primordial causes. They constitute the first time-free phase of the self-unfolding of the *principalis causa* or the *principium sine principio* "within itself," which, identical with *Verbum* and *Sapientia*, presents the ontological presupposition for a constitution of the world as theophany, as a "second" real unfolding of the origin. The context of this discussion is decisive for Eriugena's development of the Trinity.

It is inappropriate to maintain that for Eriugena the Trinity has merely a "subjective meaning," "merely in human consciousness,"[46] or that it is a nonobligatory, mere metaphor which evades thought.[47] Eriugena discusses the differences of terminology between the Greek trinitarian formula from Dionysius, Gregory of Nazianzus, and Maximus the Confessor and the Latin conception which Augustine, among others, showed him. Although the linguistic differences which Eriugena emphasizes may suggest a difference in the concept, in fact they only point to different linguistic perspectives, which are partly determined by translation, but which nonetheless point to the same one thought from which the one faith lives: "Una eademque fides est in omnibus quamvis significationum diversitas videatur."[48]

Even though Eriugena in his concept of the Trinity, especially in respect of its unity, is primarily influenced by Dionysius, this in no way leads to the suppression of the differentiation or distinction, the nonreversible characteristic nature, the individuality, and the particular personality of each of the three Persons. On the contrary, this Dionysian influence made possible an internally differentiated, relationally moved conception of Trinity in Eriugena. Divine unity constitutes itself as creative thinking, willing, and loving threeness (in the manner of self-explication). It comprehends and preserves itself as a whole. Thus, the trinitarian unity may be understood as an internally moving and relational network which begets, creates, or forms itself in an original self-unfolding.

This inner relationality is to be understood as an abiding one. In its steadfastness it may be investigated: (a) with regard to its inner "origin"; and (b) as it arises or is "caused" through the self-unfolding of the *principium* or *principalis causa* into that which is constituted by it—and hence as its own being:

(a) The sense of the inner relationality shows itself in the reciprocal total being-in-each-other of the three through which each characteristic (*proprietas*)[49] is not denied, but, in a distinct unity, the whole Divine Being first constitutes itself as steadfast motion or as moving steadfastness. It remains what it is. This is in accordance with the Dionysian thought that all predications about God's nature are appropriate for all three in common and wholly. The following key text expresses this indivisible kinship of the three in unity in a manner which is dialectically complete:

> The whole of the Father who begets (is) in the whole of the Begotten Son, and the whole of the Begotten Son is in the whole of the Father who begets, and the whole of the Father who begets and the whole of the Begotten Son are in the whole of the Holy Spirit who proceeds from the Father through the Son, and the whole of the Holy Spirit who proceeds from the Father through the Son (is) in the Father from whom he proceeds and (in) the Son through whom he proceeds and the Three are One through the Trinity understood in unity.[50]

While the thought of the trinitarian self-explication is developed only in a rudimentary way by Dionysius, Eriugena makes this into an essential element of his concept of the Trinity. Eriugena raises it to the level of the absolute self-constitution of the Godhead. Significantly, the image of this archetype is realized imperfectly in the threefold related acts of the human spirit.

(b) The thought of the timeless process of the divine self-constitution finds its culmination in Eriugena's attempt to see this very aspect of the self-unfolding of the Tri-Unity in the light of causality or being-caused: the "infinite depth" or the "fruitfulness" which is hidden in the *principium* or "Origin" proceeds as a "causal" or as an "essential" Cause that subsists within itself (*causa principalis, essentialis, substantialis*) from itself into itself.[51] Within this active procession it sets up a second Cause, which is "begotten," but in the infinite realm the second Cause is not less than the first; indeed, it is necessarily "equal." Thus the Origin causes, begets, or creates in the second Cause only himself. This self as emerged, begotten, and formed is at once the "other" of the First, which is to say that the self gives himself in the second Cause another property, different from the First, and therewith also another function. According to a central text for this issue, "the Father is the Cause of the Son and of the Holy Spirit, while the Son is the Cause of the creation of the causes in the Beginning whereas the Holy Spirit is the Cause of the distribution of the same [causes]."[52]

This aspect of the causal self-explication for the extratemporal and extraspatial ("non localiter, non temporaliter")[53] coming-to-itself of the Trinity is so significant that the trinitarian formula according to Greek and Latin theology is reformulated in the light of the causal aspect. From "una essentia in tribus substantiis (vel personis)," or "una substantia in tribus personis,"[54] it becomes "Essentialis *causa una* in tribus substantialibus causis et tres substantiales causae in una essentiali causa." That is, "One essential Cause in three in themselves subsisting Causes and three in themselves subsisting Causes in one essential Cause." Another formulation says "Una causa per se existens in tribus causis per se subsistentibus," or, "*One* through himself arising and subsisting Cause in three through themselves subsisting *Causes.*"[55] Theologically more specialized, speaking of the whole Trinity, Eriugena says,

There is a substantial Cause (which is) unbegotten and begets; and there is a substantial Cause (which is) begotten and does not beget;

(and) also there is a substantial Cause which proceeds and is not unbegotten nor begotten nor begetting; and the three substantial Causes are one, and one essential Cause.[56]

The concept of self-explication of the Trinity as a causal movement invites the danger of a lessening of being, a subordinationist hierarchical limitation of the might of the *principium*. Even the saying of Jesus: "The Father is greater than I" (John 14:28) could have been misleading. Fatherhood and Sonship are irreversible in their constitutive relationality. In opposition to the subordinationist threat, Eriugena insists that distinction and characteristic property do not imply a lessening of being when they form with each other one infinite nature which in itself is an equal-polar relationship.[57]

In the finite dimension the concept of cause implies a temporal and factual (ontological) priority of the cause to the caused, and hence, on account of this dependence, a certain subordination of the caused to the cause. The being of the caused is less than that of the cause. For the "essential Cause," however, which belongs to the realm of infinity, such a priority or precedence is unthinkable. That which language, itself a mode of difference, is forced to differentiate is in God, that is, in the undifferentiated Infinite, as one (*unum*), simultaneous (*simul*), equal (*aequale*), co-essential, co-eternal, pure identity: "All in God is God."[58]

Divine in-finitude as absolute causality excludes each real degree in itself. It is before and beyond all creative opening into the world, a circle-like relatedness to itself. It is naturally already the world in the sense that as the absolute causality it sublimates and unifies in itself the manifold differentiation of the causes which were known to Eriugena from the Aristotelian tradition.[59] The three substantial Causes as Tri-Unity are thought of as one essential Cause. Thereby the Aristotelian causal aspects and activities are telescoped into one Cause: action from itself as the ("material") presupposition for a transition into the shape or "form" of the unfolded causes (*causae primordiales, Verbum, Sapientia*) is at once the beginning and the goal (*finis* as *principium sui*).[60]

I do not wish to go into the controversies concerning the *filioque*, especially the question as to whether the Holy Spirit proceeds exclusively from the Father or the Son or from both in different ways—"from" or "out of" the Father "through" the Son, or from the Father "and" the Son in the sense of consubstantial.[61] I would like merely to offer the following consideration. Eriugena takes over certain aspects of the Greek option concerning language and subject matter from his perspective on the Trinity as absolute causality when he asks: "Does the Holy Spirit proceed from one or two causes?"[62] But in order to preserve the unity of the three and to avoid a subordinationist hierarchy in spite of maintaining the characteristics (*proprietates*) of the Persons, he still prefers the Latin doctrinal position to the Greek formulas. Thus he intends no separation into two causes for the procession of the Spirit, but assumes *una eademque causa*. The Spirit becomes himself out of this one essential Cause through the Son; "*a*" or "*ex* patre *per* filium," or "*a* patre *et* filio procedit," which is thoroughly compatible with the *filioque* formula.[63]

With this concept of the Trinity as absolute causality which constitutes its own being as an inner-interrelatedness, Eriugena adopted and decisively developed in his own mode of thought the modest starting points for an inner-trinitarian *theogonia* provided by Dionysius.[64] Since such a trinitarian conception of causality cannot be found in Augustine,[65] Boethius, Gottschalk, Hincmar, or Alcuin in an explicated theoretical form and in a similar systematic intensity, one tends to see precisely this aspect of Eriugena's theory as his particular contribution to the reflective approximation of the *mysterium trinitatis*. Notwithstanding this, one should consider the fact that Greek theologians like Basil or Gregory of Nazianzus developed speculative theories of an inwardly dynamic Trinity more intensively than Dionysius, but these theories were not directly available as a whole to Eriugena.[66]

When one considers the entire development of the problem, however, the initial apparent degree of Eriugena's originality seems to be objectively lessened. Perhaps it would be even less, if it could be demonstrated that his thought about absolute causality as the essence of the Trinity is not merely structurally analogous, but directly and historically linked, to the trinitarian thought of Marius Victorinus.[67]

I have described Eriugena as a productive mediator of eastern theology to the West, and in this mediation I have included speculation of the Trinity. Yet, it is not so much on the basis of his interpretation of the Greek trinitarian formulas—in this respect both Hilary and Augustine are forerunners—but rather in the acceptance, development, and innovative arrangement of the Dionysian concept of relationship between unity and Trinity that I see Eriugena's productivity. Through Eriugena's grasp of this very relationship one can realize also a connection with Augustine's trinitarian speculation. Thus in Eriugena we find the establishment of a powerful synthesis between Augustine's concept of the Trinity (which concentrates upon the immanent relationality of the Tri-Unity and the analogy of the threefold human spirit to its divine archetype) and the eastern Dionysian tradition. On the one hand, this makes Eriugena's concept of a Trinity as an inwardly moved network of causal and reflexive relations quite clear; on the other hand, it shows why he believed that the triads which Augustine analyzed as the structure of the human mind can also be seen as yielding differentiated insight into the Trinity itself.[68]

Translated by Douglas Hedley

NOTES

1. Compare Wolfhart Pannenberg, *Systematische Theologie* (Göttingen, 1988), 1:283 ff.; Karl Rahner, "Bemerkungen zum dogmatischen Traktat *De trinitate*," *Schriften zur Theologie* (Einsiedeln, 1960), 4:103 ff.; and F. Courth, "Trinität," in *Handbuch der Dogmengeschichte* (Freiburg, 1988), vol. 2 ("in der Schrift und Patristik"; "in der Scholastik").

2. St. Augustine, *Confessiones* XIII 11, 12 (PL 32:849).

3. See Werner Beierwaltes, *Denken des Einen* (Frankfurt, 1985), 135 ff., 147 ff.; and *Identität und Differenz* (Frankfurt, 1980), 49 ff.

4. See Kurt Ruh, *Geschichte der abendländischen Mystik* (Munich, 1990), 1:53 ff.

5. See Beierwaltes, *Denken des Einen*, 193 ff.; and the article "Hen," in *Reallexikon für Antike und Christentum* 14 (1987): 454 ff.

6. I have developed the "types of unity" with respect to the concept of harmony in early medieval thought in *Zeitschrift für philosophische Forschung* 45 (1991): 1–21.

7. Plotinus, *Enneads* V 3, 12, 52.

8. For the Neoplatonic characterization of the transcendence of the One in Plotinus and in later Neoplatonism, which has its source in Plato's *Republic* 509 b, see W. Beierwaltes, *Selbsterkenntnis und Erfahrung der Einheit* (Frankfurt, 1991), 129 ff., 218 ff. For Proclus, see Beierwaltes, *Proklos, Grundzüge seiner Metaphysik*, 2nd ed. (Frankfurt, 1979), 331 ff., 352 ff.; and *Denken des Einen*, 312 ff. (on the Hymn

ʾΩ πάντων ἐπέκεινα). Finally, also note my article "Epekeina: Eine Anmerkung zu Heideggers Platon-Rezeption," in *Transzendenz: Zu einem Grundwort der klassischen Metaphysik. Festschrift für Klaus Kremer,* ed. Lud gar Honnefelder and Werner Schüssler (Paderborn, 1992), 39–55.

9. E.g., *Enneads* III 8, 10, 1.

10. We shall not discuss the third hypostasis, the *psyche*. The Plotinian conception of the self-reflexivity of the *nous* as re-flection of that which has gone forth from the One in three phases was systematized by Proclus as the basic law of the intelligible realm: remaining, emergence, reflection. Despite the levels of the self-unfolding of the One into the *nous* and the *psyche,* in the sense of a subordinationism, this Neoplatonic triad or the three hypostases were seen as a prelude or analogy to the Christian Trinity. Consider Eusebius, *Praeparatio evangelica* XI 17, 20; and St. Augustine, *De civitate Dei* X 23, where he (mediated by Porphyry) refers to Plotinus's treatise V 1, "De tribus principalibus substantiis." Porphyry's attempt to telescope the rather sharp Plotinian distinction between both dimensions—that of the nonthinking One and the reflexively thinking Spirit—and, instead, to think of a single immanently differentiated absolute essence or superessence may have been a more precise philosophical starting point for the Christian trinitarian thought which excludes an immanent hierarchy. On this point, see W. Beierwaltes, *Denken des Einen*, 198 ff.

11. Compare note 5, above, and E. Corsini, *Il trattato 'De divinis nominibus' dello Pseudo-Dionigi e i commenti neoplatonici al Parmenide* (Torino, 1962).

12. F. C. Baur, *Die christliche Lehre von der Dreieinigkeit und Menschwerdung Gottes in ihrer geschichtlichen Entwicklung* (Tübingen, 1842), Part 2:234.

13. Courth, 212.

14. Bernhard Brons, *Gott und die Seienden: Untersuchungen zum Verhältnis von neuplatonischer Metaphysik und christlicher Tradition bei Dionysius Areopagita* (Göttingen, 1976), 89, 97.

15. Brons, 117 (Brons has, in fact, done much to enhance our understanding of the Dionysian concept of the Trinity). Further judgments are to be found in Otto Semmelroth, "Gottes überwesentliche Einheit," *Scholastik* 25 (1950): 209–234, especially 213; René Roques, *L'Univers dionysien* (Paris, 1954), 339; and Gerald O'Daly, "Dionysius Areopagita," *Theologische Realenzyklopädie* 8 (1981): 772–780.

16. Pannenberg, 31.

17. See the collected references in Brons, 99. For the following, see Beierwaltes, *Denken des Einen*, 211 ff.; *Identität und Differenz*, 49 ff.; and "Hen," 466–469.

18. *De Divinis Nominibus* (= DN) I.5: αὐτὸ δὲ οὐδὲν ὡς πάντων ὑπερουσίως ἐξῃρημένον. In what follows I shall quote the new edition of Beate Regina Suchla, *Corpus Dionysiacum I: Pseudo-Dionysius Areopagita De Divinis Nominibus*, Patristische Texte und Studien 33 (Berlin, 1991)—after the page and line I shall give the PG 3 column reference. This text is found in Suchla 117,4 (593C).

19. DN II.11, 136,10 ff. (649 C).

20. DN V.6, 184,19 (820 C). Cf. other uses of Ex. 3:14, e.g., DN I.6, 118,11 ff. (596 A); and II.1, 123,1 ff. (637 A).

21. Compare, e.g., DN VIII.5, 202,6 ff. (892C–D); 204,1 ff. (893C–D); DN XI.6, 223,11 ff. (956B).

22. DN VII.2, 196, 8 ff. (869 A–C). These "noetic" predicates are only conceivable in their paradoxical kinship with the other line of thought which sees the Godhead as "in the eminent and not the deprecating sense," which on the basis of God's superbrightness is untouchable and invisible darkness.

23. DN XIII.2, 227,12 (977 C): πρὸ παντὸς ἑνὸς καὶ πλήθους, in place of πρὸς. Further, see 227,16 ff. (980A); and 228,6 (980B): ἑνοειδῶς προείληφε. Also see 228,19 and 21 (980C): πρὸ παντὸς ἑνὸς καὶ πλήθους . . . πρὸ πάντων καὶ ὑπὲρ πάντα. . . .

24. The beginnings of a philosophical theory may be seen in the conception of the "being-One" as the inwardly differentiated locus of explication and web of relations of the *nous* in its different phases and forms or expressions of the original unity. For Proclus on this issue, compare my interpretation in *Denken des Einen*, 201 ff.

25. Dionysius refers to this in DN II.1, 122,11 (636C), as well as in 125,13 ff. (640B) and 130,15 (645A). All these references occur in connection with the Trinity.

26. DN II.4, 127,7 (641 B). See the similar formula in Gregory of Nazianzus, *Oratio* XXVIII.1 (PG 36:28A). Analogous expressions are found in DN II.6, 130,13 (644 D); and 135,16 (649 B)—the same formula for the creative unfolding of God within himself, who in this remains himself. Dionysius attempts to make the innertrinitarian aspect of this formula plausible through the one nondistinguished shining of three lights in one room, where each contributes its "own" light and is thus to an equal degree constitutive for the unity of the whole light (DN II.4, 127,4 ff. [641 A]). Compare Eriugena P V, 12 (883 C).

27. DN II.1, 123,9 (637 B); and 124,10 (637 C).

28. DN II.1, 122,15–124,15 (637 A–C).

29. E.g., DN II.3, 125,13 ff. (640 B).

30. DN II.4, 126,15 (641 A).

31. DN II.4, 126,17–127,4 (641 A): ταὐτότης . . . μονὴ καὶ ἵδρυσις ὁλικῶς ὑπερηνωμένη; cf. 134,11 ff. (648 C); 135,14 ff. (649 B). In DN

V.7, 185,16 ff. (821 B) and 189,7 (825 B) the Origin includes all polarity within itself in "an eminent way" (ὑπεροχικῶς). "Coincidence" of the opposites as being *above* the opposites is found in DN XIII.2, 227,18 ff. (980 A): . . . *καὶ ὅλα πάντα καὶ τὰ ἀντικείμενα καὶ ἐνιαίως προσυνειληφότος.*" Cf. 228,6–7 (980 B): "*πάντα γὰρ ἐν ἑαυτῷ τὸ ἐν ἐνοειδῶς προείληφέ τε καὶ περιείληφεν . . . πρὸ πάντων*; and 228,21 ff.

32. DN XIII.3, 229,8 (981 A): θεογόνον; 229,11: γονιμότης. Compare also II.5, 128,10 (641 D): θεογονίας; 14 ff. (641 D); and 135,13 ff. (649 B) in respect to the unity of both aspects of the "abiding-inwards" and the creative "turning outwards."

33. DN II.11, 137,5 ff. (652 A): *ἐπὶ τῶν θειῶν αἱ ἑνώσεις τῶν διακρίσεων ἐπικρατοῦσι καὶ προκατάρχουσι.*

34. For each οἰκεία and ἴδια, see the respective hypostases: DN II.4, 126,6 (640D); 127,14 (641B); 128,13 (641D).

35. DN II.3, 125,20 (640 C); 128,11 ff. (641 D).

36. DN II.4, 127,6 (641 B); 127,12 (641B); 128,9 (641 D).

37. DN II.4, 127,2 and 6 (641A–B).

38. DN II.4, 127,4 and 16 (641 A–C).

39. In analogy to the "lights" as in DN II.4, 127,12 (641B): *ὅλων ἐν ὅλοις ἀμιγῶς συγκεκραμένων*; cf. 127,16 (641C): *ἡ ὅλων πρὸς ὅλα παντελὴς ἕνωσις ἀμιγής.*

40. DN II.2, 125,6 (640 A): *οὔτε τὰ ἡνωμένα διαιρεῖν θεμιτὸν οὔτε τὰ διακεκριμένα συγχεῖν.*

41. DN II.7, 132,1–3 (645B): *βλαστοὶ θεόφυτοι καὶ οἷον ἄνθη καὶ ὑπερούσια φῶτα.* See II.5, 128,11 (641D): *πηγὴ τῆς ὑπερουσίου θεότητος*; and II.1, 124,8 (637C): *πηγαίαν καὶ ἀνέκλειπτον αἰτίαν.*

42. DN II.5, 128,10 (644A).

43. DN II.1, 123,5 (637 A): *ὁ παρὰ τοῦ πατρὸς ἐκπορεύεται*; cf. John 15:26.

44. Compare Brons, 103: "Nowhere is the shibboleth of orthodoxy (ὁμοούσιος) to be found!"

45. See on this above, note 25.

46. See Baur, Part 2:320 ff., and 344. Compare also the passage in W. Beierwaltes, " 'Duplex Theoria': Zu einer Denkform Eriugenas," in *Begriff und Metapher: VII. Internationales Eriugena-Colloquium,* Sitzungsbericht der Heidelberger Akademie der Wissenschaften, philosophisch-historische Klasse, 1990, 3. Abhandlung (Heidelberg, 1990), 39–64, esp. 55 ff.

47. Theodor Christlieb, *Leben und Lehre des Johannes Scotus Eriugena* (Gotha, 1860), 182, 264 (on the transfer of human concepts to the trinitarian God as anthropomorphism). Against these judgments of Baur and Christlieb, see Leo Scheffczyk, "Die Grundzüge der Trinitätslehre des Johannes Scotus Eriugena," in *Theologie in Geschichte und*

Gegenwart: Michael Schmaus zum sechzigsten Geburtstag (Munich, 1957), 497–518.

48. P II 34, 198,21–22. See P II 29, 164,31 ff.; and II 23, 94,16 ff. In this last passage Eriugena says (different from II 34, 198,19) that he did *not* find the formulation "MIAN HYPOSTASIN, id est unam substantiam" among the Greeks. There is, however, such a formulation in St. Augustine, whom Eriugena refers to at II 23, 198,16 ("unam substantiam in tribus personis"). Augustine translates the Greek formulation (μία οὐσία, τρεῖς ὑποστάσεις) in *De trinitate* V 8, 10 with "una essentia, tres substantiae." He uses *substantia* and *essentia* in a rather indiscriminate way; see *De trin.* IX 5, 8: "substantia vel essentia," or ibid. 5: "substantialiter, vel, ut ita dicam, essentialiter." Eriugena holds steadfast the unambiguity and distinctness of *essentia* and *substantia:* compare II 34, 200,17. The classification of *essentia* and *persona* remained clear for Eriugena even after *De divina praedestinatione* 9.4, as the above text demonstrates. (Courth, 214, appears to dismiss or question this.) In P II 22, 90,3 ff., for example, both concepts are used synonymously: "substantiae seu personae." V 27, 921A: ". . . una substantia est, et ut usitatius [!] dicam, una persona humanitas Christi et divinitas." IV 10, 786 C: "tres substantiae unius essentiae, vel ut usitatius Latini volunt, tres personae unius substantiae. . . ."

49. Compare, e.g., P II 21, 84,7 ff.; and 90,31 ff. Each *proprietas* belongs equally (*aequalitas*) to each trinitarian person: P IV 1, 741 C–D (Epiphanius as witness for this thought).

50. P II 31, 190,11–15: "totus pater gignens in toto filio genito et totus filius genitus in toto patre gignente et totus pater gignens et totus filius genitus in toto spiritu sancto a patre per filium procedente et totus spiritus sanctus a patre per filium procedens in patre a quo procedit et filio per quem procedit, et tres unum sunt per intellectam trinitatem in unitate." Cf. also 188,18 ff.

51. On the "ineffabilis ac supernaturalis divinae bonitatis foecunditas" as the inner origin of the trinitarian Godhead, see P II 33, 192,37 ff. For the concept of an absolute *causa:* P II 29, 164,28 ff.; 166,7ff.; 168,16ff.; 188,24 ff.

52. P II 30, 170,28–30: "Causa itaque filii pater est et spiritus sancti, filius uero causa est conditionis principaliter causarum, earundem autem causarum distributionis spiritus sanctus causa est." Cf. P II 32, 188,26–190,1: "ut cognoscamus patrem et filium et spiritum sanctum tres causas et unam causam—tres enim unum sunt—patrem autem causam gignentem nascentis de se filii sui unigeniti qui causa est omnium primordialium causarum in se ipso a patre conditarum, eundem uero patrem causam procedentis a se per filium sancti spiritus qui spiritus causa est diuisionis et multiplicationis distribution-

isque causarum omnium quae in filio a patre factae sunt in effectus suos et generales et speciales et proprios secundum naturam et gratiam. Et quamuis sanctum spiritum a patre per filium credamus et intelligamus procedere non tamen duas causas eundem spiritum habere debemus accipere sed unam eandemque causam, patrem scilicet, et nascentis de se filii et procedentis ex se per filium spiritus sancti."

53. P II 31, 190,28.

54. Compare note 48.

55. P II 29, 166,7–9 and 16–17. Compare also P II 27, 132,34—"per se subsistens" as the translation of $\alpha\dot{v}\theta v\pi\acute{o}\sigma\tau\alpha\tau o\varsigma$ in Maximus the Confessor's *Ambigua* XXII 29 (CCSG 18:154). For this concept see Stephen Gersh, "*PER SE IPSUM:* The Problem of Immediate and Mediate Causation in Eriugena and His Neoplatonic Predecessors," in *Jean Scot Erigène et l'histoire de la philosophie*, ed. René Roques (Paris, 1977), 374.

56. P II 30, 168,16–19: "Est igitur substantialis causa ingenita et gignens et est substantialis causa genita et non gignens, item substantialis est causa procedens et non ingenita nec genita nec gignens, et tres causae substantiales unum sunt et una causa essentialis." With respect to this logical aspect of the differentiation of the three *causae* through the active and passive forms, and the differentiation of *gignere* into affirmative and negative, one is reminded of the division of nature into four species through the analogous differentiation of *creare* at the beginning of *Periphyseon*.

57. P II 30, 168,21 ff.

58. Compare Beierwaltes, *Denken des Einen*, 352 ff.; *Eriugena und Cusanus*, 319 ff. (English version in *Dionysius* 13 [1989]: 123 ff.); and *Duplex Theoria*, 46 ff. For the Cusanus axiom "omnia in deo deus," which is already valid for Eriugena, see *De docta ignorantia* I 22 (45,16 in the Hoffmann-Klibansky ed.). Eriugena in P I 8, 50,11, says of the "causae rerum creandarum" . . . "aeternaliter in deo sunt et deus sunt."

59. E.g., P II 31, 178,17 ff.

60. P V 3, 866C. This formula is valid also for the trinitarian procession.

61. On the *filioque* compare Courth, 126–137; and H. G. Beck, *Kirche und theologische Literatur im Byzantinischen Reich*, Byzantinisches Handbuch im Rahmen des Handbuchs der Altertumswissenschaft, part 2, vol. 1 (Munich, 1977), 306 ff. For Eriugena's circle, see Jean Jolivet, *Godescalc d'Orbais et la Trinité* (Paris, 1958), 117 ff.; and Marta Cristiani, "Itinerari e potenzialità del pensiero cristiano in età carolingia: La teologia trinitaria di Giovanni Scoto," in *Giovanni Scoto nel suo tempo: L'organizzazione di sapere in età carolingia*, Accademia Tuder-

tina, ed. Claudio Leonardi and Enrico Menestò (Spoleto, 1989), 337–363, esp. pp. 339 ff. On *filioque* in Eriugena, see P II 33, 196,7 ff.; and II 24, 120,33. See Giulio d'Onofrio, "Giovanni Scoto e Remigio di Auxerre: A proposito di alcuni commenti altomedievali a Boezio," in *Studi Medievali*, 3rd series, 22 (1981): 587–693; concerning the doctrine of Trinity, esp. 657 ff.

62. For the discussion of this question, see especially P II 31, 172 ff.; 174, 22 ff. ("ex patre per filium") and 184,11–16. Cf. II 32, 188,26 ff.; and the *Omelia Iohannis* VIII (SC 151: 240.18–19). The *aequalitas* of the *filius* and *spiritus sanctus*, despite each one's *proprietates*, leads Eriugena to a *new* question which he found neither in the *symbolum* of the Greeks nor the Latins. This is the question of whether by way of analogy to the formulation that the Holy Spirit proceeds "a patre per filium" one might not speak of the "*Son* begotten *through the Holy Spirit*" (II 33, 192,32 ff.; 194,4 ff. and 31 ff.). This is primarily related to the immanent procession within the Trinity, but it is applied to the economic activity of the Spirit ("per spiritum sanctum") in the birth and baptism of Christ (194,11 ff).

63. Compare P II 32, 188,24. Discussions of the *filioque* also occur in II 33, 196,7 ff.; and II 24, 120,33.

64. DN II.5, 128,10 ff. (641D): "τὰ τῆς ὑπερουσίου θεογονίας οὐκ ἀντιστρέφει πρὸς ἄλληλα." Cf. DN II.7, 132,1 ff. (645B): πηγαία and θεόγονος θεότης, which begets Son and Spirit as "offspring, blossom, and light" from out of itself. Compare notes 42 and 43, above.

65. See, however, Augustine, *De diversis quaestionibus* 83, qn. 16: "Deus omnium quae sunt, causa est. Quod autem omnium rerum causa est, etiam sapientiae suae [= Filii] causa est: nec umquam Deus sine sapientia sua. Igitur sempiternae sapientiae suae causa est sempiterna: nec tempore prior est quam sua sapientia." Augustine also uses (rarely and not systematically) the concept *causa* for the begetting of the Wisdom (*sapientia*) of the Son, which does not exclude the Being-Wisdom of the Father. Wisdom is described as begotten, "caused in *one* direction," and not reciprocally causal in *De trinitate* VII 1, 2. For the thought experiment which reverses the causal movement from the Spirit to the Son, compare Eriugena's text quoted in note 62.

66. Maximus the Confessor is an exception. Eriugena's translation of the *Ambigua ad Iohannem* proves that he was familiar with Maximus's thoughts about the Father being the *cause* of the Son, and was also familiar with the refutation of Arian consequences from the syllogism "Si causa maior Pater Filio,/natura autem Pater causa Filii,/ natura itaque Pater maior Filio." Compare Maximus, *Amb.* XXI, 33–35. In general, see also XIX, XX, and XXII.

67. See further, Beierwaltes, *Denken des Einen,* 354; and *Identität und Differenz,* 74. G. A. Piemonte has initiated a deeply informative beginning of a detailed explication of this issue in " 'Vita in omnia pervenit': El vitalismo Eriugeniano y la influencia de Mario Victorino," *Patristica et Mediaevalia* 7 (1986): 3–48; 8 (1987): 3–38. See the same author's "L'expression 'quae sunt et quae non sunt': Jean Scot et Marius Victorinus," *Jean Scot écrivain,* ed. G. H. Allard (Montréal-Paris, 1986), 81–113.

68. This essay is a shortened version of a larger text in which I present Eriugena's doctrine of the Trinity. It will be published in German in my forthcoming book about Eriugena.

Isaiah Meets the Seraph:
Breaking Ranks in Dionysius and Eriugena?

Donald F. Duclow

Dionysius aptly describes himself as "a lover of angels," and his *Celestial Hierarchy* is the clearest and most influential legacy of this love.[1] Eriugena gives close attention to Dionysius's account of the angels in his translation of the *Celestial Hierarchy* and in the *Expositiones* on the same text. Yet while Dionysius's teaching has received frequent and thorough study, there has been little discussion of Eriugena's views about the angelic hierarchy.[2] As a modest corrective to this imbalance, I would like to compare the two thinkers' views on humanity's relationship with the angels. To focus the issue, I shall first examine Dionysius's discussion of Isaiah's encounter with the seraph. In the *Expositiones* Eriugena discusses this incident, and he refers to it during *Periphyseon*'s commentary on the cherubim placed before paradise after the fall. By comparing Dionysius's and Eriugena's handling of these events, we shall recognize important differences in their anthropology and Christology.

Isaiah and the Seraph

Dionysius's familiar scheme organizes nine ranks of angels into three triads. While members are equal within each triad,[3] Dionysius subordinates one triad to another. The Godhead and divine Word act directly on the first triad (seraphim, cherubim, and thrones), which transmits the knowledge received to the second angelic order, which in turn influences the third; and finally, beneath the lowest ranks of angels stands the human, ecclesiastical hierarchy.[4] With each step the initial revelation's power diminishes, yet it simultaneously lifts up each rank to the highest contemplation of its superiors and of the Godhead of which it is capable. Dionysius here adapts a familiar Neoplatonic device to describe an

233

"order" that unifies and differentiates God, the angels, and human beings. His universe is essentially hierarchical—that is, it arranges sacred realities in ranks of interlocking action and knowledge.[5]

Chapter 13 of *The Celestial Hierarchy* discusses a biblical text that challenges this hierarchical vision. Describing his prophetic call, Isaiah says, "One of the seraphs flew to me, holding in his hand a live coal which he had taken from the altar with a pair of tongs. With this he touched my mouth and said: 'See now, this has touched your lips, your sin is taken away, your iniquity is purged.' "[6] But as the highest angelic rank, the seraphim should not encounter human beings directly but only through the mediating lower levels of the hierarchy. Other prophets—Zechariah, Ezekiel, and Daniel—respect this hierarchical order.[7] So why does Scripture say that a seraph purges Isaiah's lips for his prophetic mission? As Dionysius notes, "Someone could well be puzzled by the fact that it was not one of the subordinate angels but someone from among the most senior beings who came to purify the interpreter."[8] Perhaps no one would be more puzzled than Dionysius himself, who argues for a strict chain of command along the ranks of the angelic hierarchy.

So Dionysius ingeniously adapts this inconvenient text to his own scheme. He offers two interpretations. The first is a functional and semantic analysis. In fact, an angel from the lowest rank approached the prophet, but "was *named* one of the seraphim since he had to wipe out the sins referred to by fire and he had to rekindle obedience to God in the one who had been purified."[9] The burning coal thus recalls the fire for which the seraphim are named, as well as their purifying activity.[10] Isaiah's angel thus acts *like* a seraph.

Dionysius's second explanation is typically hierarchical—indeed bureaucratic—with the higher-ups getting credit for their subordinates' work. Isaiah's angel "attributed to God and, after God, to the senior hierarchy his own sacred work of purification."[11] To support this attribution, Dionysius then discusses divine causality and disclosure. God's power is transcendent, yet omnipresent as it "manifests itself in due measure to every intelligent being." The key phrase here is "in due measure," which accents the principle of mediated, hierarchical transmission. Examples of light and heat illustrate the same law, since the sun's rays and fire's heat first encounter receptive media, through which they are communicated to increasingly opaque and resistant materials. As Dionysius therefore generalizes, "On each level, predecessor hands on to successor whatever of the divine light he has received and this, in providential proportion, is spread out to every being."[12] In particular, Dionysius highlights the first two sources of transmission: God who is light itself and thus the "Cause of being and of seeing"; and the seraphim who, as "the first ministers and teachers of divine things," mediate "the divine enlightenment to all other beings, including ourselves." Other angels thus honor the seraphim as "the source, after God, of all sacred knowledge of God and of all imitation of God."[13] It is therefore appropriate for Isaiah's angel to credit God and the seraphim for his purifying activity.[14] Isaiah's call thus confirms Dionysius's whole hierarchical scheme.

Further, Isaiah provides Dionysius with a model for hierarchical ascent to mystical insight, since the angel's action leads the prophet into the highest possible knowledge. The transmission of divine light aims to lift up lower beings—here, the prophet—to contemplation of the higher ranks and God. With the angel's guidance, Isaiah contemplates the seraphs with their six wings and song of praise, and he looks beyond them toward the Godhead itself, utterly transcendent and the source of all being. The description of the seraphim relies on Isaiah 6:1–4, while the vision of God recalls Dionysius's *Divine Names* and *Mystical Theology*. Not surprisingly, what the prophet learns reinforces the mediating role of the hierarchy. He discovers that "Purification consists of a participation in the transparent clarity of the Godhead," and that all beings partake of this clarity insofar as they conform to the divine. For "purification, together with all those other activities of the Deity which are reflected through the superior beings, is spread out among all the others in proportion to each one's participation in the divine operations."[15] God is seen in and through the celestial hierarchy, which filters the divine light in proportion to the capacities of each rank, down to and including the ecclesiastical hierarchy. Like Isaiah, the great human "hierarchs" may ascend to mystical vision, but only through the mediating action of the celestial hierarchy.

Dionysius's two readings of Isaiah's call thus preserve his principle of order. The seraphim remain in their privileged place around God. The lower angel can be named for the seraphs' fiery, purifying work; or this work can be attributed to them as its cause, after the Godhead itself. In both interpretations, there has been no break in the angelic ranks. Dionysius therefore leaves open the question of which reading best solves the problem. René Roques notes how questionable these interpretations are as exegesis but finds nevertheless that "they lack neither ingenuity nor coherence when one places them in the ensemble of the hierarchical doctrine."[16] We may even say that the second interpretation turns a problem passage into a prooftext for Dionysius's hierarchical vision.

Eriugena's *Expositio*

Eriugena responds to Dionysius's handling of this biblical text in two quite different ways. The *Expositiones in Ierarchiam coelestem* carefully respects its main lines, while *Periphyseon* suggests important disagreements with the master's account of our relation to the angels.

In the *Expositiones* John confirms Dionysius's view that "by God and through the seraphim, the angel is seen to purify the prophet"[17] (Ex 13, 584–585). And at several points Eriugena notes how divine activity is communicated "step by step" through the three levels of the celestial hierarchy into the fourth, human rank.[18] Yet while following Dionysius's text and scheme, his account also dwells at length on divine transcendence, participation, and the prophet's vision of the superessential God. The result is a richer, more dialectical reading of Isaiah's text than Dionysius presents. For John accents the basic paradox of God's utter transcendence and hierarchical self-disclosure: the hidden, superessential divine power nevertheless communicates itself to every intellect "according to the measured contemplation of each order."[19]

Of Dionysius's two interpretations of Isaiah's seraph, Eriugena briefly notes the first: the lower angel acts like the purifying fire and heat for which the seraphim are named.[20] The second, participatory account receives extended treatment because John considers it the "more probable" explanation, and "Blessed Dionysius follows and approves this sense as his own."[21]

Discussing mediating participation, Eriugena expands Dionysius's examples of light and heat into a detailed "physical" account of their penetrating motion. The sun's light moves easily through the ether and upper air; it is obscured by the increasingly dense, "watery" air, and finally stops at solid, earthly bodies. The limited capacity of the receiving materials, not a weakness in the light's rays, causes this progressive dimming. John discusses fire's heat in similar detail.[22] What in Dionysius had been quick, commonplace analogues here become topics for close scrutiny. Eriugena the naturalist is at work. Yet Dionysius's point remains intact, since these examples of "physical" diffusion illustrate communication through the hierarchies: "The first hierarchy distributes the divine illuminations to the middle, the middle to the third, the third to the fourth, which is among human beings."[23]

Eriugena the metaphysician responds when Dionysius describes God as "the source of illumination for those who are illuminated."[24] Exploring this illuminating source or *principium*, John first emphasizes God's causal presence: "Every light and everything illuminated subsists in him [God]," whose essence is light and who causes its being. Expanding on Dionysius's text, he then fuses the themes of being, illumination, and vision. "For God and for every rational and intellectual creature, it is not one thing to be and another to be light; nor is it one thing to be light and another to see. . . . For them it is one and the same thing to be, to give light, and to see; for their being is light and vision."[25] God, the angels, and humans are thus united in a reciprocal lighting and seeing.

Later in the chapter John becomes more specific about the divine, illuminating source. When Dionysius identifies purgation with participation in divine brightness or clarity, Eriugena none too subtly introduces themes from *Periphyseon*. For he identifies the divine clarity with "God the Word, namely, the Son, who in the most hidden recesses of his Father perfects all the holy intellects in their primordial causes."[26] John then expands on the light metaphor and describes how "the likeness [*instar*] of the brightest ray proceeds from the light of the inaccessible divinity" and communicates itself first to those nearest to it and thence to the others. "And this is their purgation, illumination, and perfection, namely, their participation."[27] Not only purgation, but all three of Dionysius's saving functions thus involve participation in the Word as the Father's *claritas*.

Commenting on Isaiah's vision of God seated "above the highest essences," John emphasizes transcendence by piling up superlatives and negatives to an extent that outdoes Dionysius himself.

Since the divine is superessential and radically set apart from all
things, not even the first essences can be like God. "For what essence," John asks, "can be like [*similis*] the superessential?"[28]

John likewise emphasizes transcendence in his commentary on
Isaiah's description of the seraphim. With Dionysius, he sees their
wings continually moving so as to imitate God. But Eriugena goes
farther to describe what the seraphs see: "the face of the Lord
seated above the sun, namely, his superessential height [which is]
above the highest celestial essences."[29] Trembling before this vision, the seraphs' wings conceal the divine face, which they fear to
look upon. The highest angels themselves thus see—and retreat
from seeing—the transcendent face of God. John then considers
the feet of the enthroned Lord. Here the seraphim gaze upon
God's footprints (*vestigia*) throughout creation.[30] They see how
God who transcends all things is also "poured forth in all and is
everywhere. Without Him nothing can be, since He is the essence
and substance of those things that are because He is superessential
and supersubstantial."[31]

With an exegetical ingenuity of his own, Eriugena thus finds familiar metaphysical patterns in Isaiah's and Dionysius's texts. Yet
the interpretation mainly serves his master's reading of the prophet's call and the hierarchical scheme that underlies it.

Cherubim before Paradise

In *Periphyseon*, however, Eriugena severely alters Dionysius's interpretation. Early in book V, John mentions Isaiah's call in his
bold commentary on the expulsion from paradise as an act of divine mercy. In Genesis 3:22 God does not command a punishing
exile, but puts a hopeful question: "And now, . . . may he not at
some time extend his hand and take of the tree of life?"[32] This text
promises us the happiness for which humanity was created, since
as John paraphrases, "It may be that he will put forth his hand,
that is, stretch his zeal for good conduct by practicing the virtues,
so that he may take of the fruit of the tree of life, which is the spiritual gifts of the Word of God, and eat the food of pure contemplation, by virtue of which he shall live forever."

Considering the cherubim that God places before paradise
(Gen. 3:24), Eriugena turns to Dionysius's *Celestial Hierarchy*. He
asks about three possibilities: Does the name *cherubim* indicate a

being from the first angelic triad? Or, "is the word used solely in the literal sense?" Or, "is that name intended to teach some other doctrine by a higher significance?"[33]

If Genesis means to indicate the angelic order, then paradise too must be spiritual, because so exalted a spiritual nature could not stand guard before "a local and physical paradise." If a physical place were in question, then "it was not really cherubim that was set before Paradise, but one of the lowest orders of the heavenly powers, which is properly called angelic, and . . . it is given the name of the *cherubim* because it is by the cherubim that he is ordered to place himself before Paradise."[34] Here John invokes Dionysius's argument that refers the actions of lower angels to their superiors. In confirmation he cites Dionysius's commentary on Isaiah's call, which attributes the purgation "not to the immediate purgator but to him who ordered that the prophet should be purged"—that is, to the seraphim.[35] Thus far Eriugena confirms Dionysius's hierarchical analysis and extends it to the cherubim before paradise. But he then notes that this analysis does not resolve Genesis's exegetical problem, since as a spiritual nature no angel—however lowly—occupies an earthly place. So John returns to book IV's argument that paradise is not a physical place but human nature itself and therefore "spiritual." He then has no difficulty envisioning the cherubim standing directly before the paradise of human nature, and says nothing about intermediaries between the cherubim and humanity as *spiritual* realities. John has thus redefined Dionysius's problem. Whereas Dionysius addresses a break in ranks between seraphs and prophets, John posits a gulf between angels' spiritual nature and an earthly paradise. Once paradise is interpreted spiritually, he dismisses both the problem and its Dionysian solution.

Turning to his second option, John concentrates on the semantic reading of the word *cherubim*, which Dionysius interprets as "the variety of knowledge" or "the outpouring of wisdom."[36] Significantly, Eriugena deliberately excludes any reference to the celestial hierarchy in this semantic analysis. He says, "If we accept in this context *only* the significance of the name *without relating it to the celestial essence* (to which that name belongs), we can say that God placed cherubim, that is, the variety of knowledge, or the pouring forth of wisdom, before the paradise of pleasure, that is to say, before the sight of rational human nature."[37] When Eriugena thus isolates the etymology of *cherubim* from its referent, the angelic hierarchy disappears from the story of the expulsion from paradise. What matters is no longer the mediating chain of angelic command, but semantics and allegory. Dionysius's etymology confirms John's account of God's saving compassion for humanity's intellectual nature: Genesis's *cherubim* becomes the knowledge and wisdom that restore human beings to self-knowledge and the tree of life. For Eriugena, humanity's exile and restoration seem to bypass the celestial hierarchy.

John departs still farther from Dionysius when he probes the third possibility of discovering "a higher significance" in Genesis's use of the term *cherubim*. His commentary here takes a christological turn, since "by the word *cherubim* is signified not inappropriately the very Word of God Itself." Dionysius's very etymology suggests this turn to Eriugena, since varieties of knowledge and an outpouring of wisdom characterize the divine Word. "For the Word of God, in Which are concealed the treasuries of science and wisdom, is always, without intermission, present to the powers of observation of human nature, advising, cleansing, and enlightening it, and eventually leading it back to the pure perfection of its nature."[38] In Eriugena's hands, Dionysius's semantics of upward attribution moves beyond the angelic ranks to the Word itself. Where Dionysius attributes Isaiah's angel's action to God and the seraphim as its source "after God," Eriugena deletes the cherubim's mediating role and emphasizes the Word's continual—and apparently direct—presence to the human mind. He reduces Genesis's narrative of exile to a drama between two players: God and humanity. The cherubim, the flaming sword, and the tree of life all symbolize the divine Word that "never recedes from human consciousness."[39] Within this context, John generalizes and sees all the angelic ranks as symbols for the second Person of the Trinity: "By a kind of wonderful metaphor the Wisdom of God is intimated in Holy Scripture by the names of all the heavenly essences."[40]

Dionysius's *Celestial Hierarchy* figures prominently in Eriugena's three analyses of the cherubim before paradise. The first invokes Dionysius's principle of hierarchical mediation, only to dismiss it along with the problem of an earthly paradise that it seems to resolve. The second uses Dionysius's etymology of *cherubim*, but detaches it from the angelic hierarchy in order to designate the knowledge and wisdom that God places before exiled humanity. The third interpretation uses Dionysius's semantics of upward attribution, but in a different way: instead of referring a lower angel's action to its superior, Eriugena refers the term *cherubim* to the Word itself. Especially in his second and third approaches, Eriugena suggests a more direct, unmediated relation between God and human nature than Dionysius's principle of hierarchy would allow.

Anthropology

Eriugena's exegetical differences from Dionysius reflect deeper discrepancies in their anthropology and Christology, areas which John developed in far greater detail than his master.

Eriugena's anthropology has received much attention of late[41] and so can be sketched briefly. By defining humanity as "a certain intellectual concept formed eternally in the mind of God,"[42] Eriugena places the human being among the primordial causes within the divine Word. He further describes humanity as created in God's image and likeness, with two basic features: (1) a self-ignorance whereby humanity knows only *that* it is, not *what* it is; and (2) a self-knowledge that embraces all creation, visible and invisible. In the first, the human being reflects God's unknowable transcendence.[43] In the second, the human being becomes—in Maximus's phrase—"the workshop of all things, *officina omnium*," and faithfully mirrors God's creative Wisdom.[44] Simultaneously transcending and embracing the whole created order, humanity thus becomes a precise image of its divine exemplar.

This anthropology significantly alters Dionysius's view of our relationship to the angels, since Eriugena presents a direct, unmediated relation between humanity and God. As Edouard Jeauneau has noted, a passage from Augustine highlights this theme: "Between our mind, by which we know the Father, and the Truth, that is to say, the inward light through which we know Him, no creature intervenes."[45] Eriugena often uses Augustine's phrase, *nulla interposita creatura,* to describe the human mind as God's image and its contemplative vision. He brings the phrase into his commentary on Gregory of Nyssa, who similarly locates God's image in the human mind, which "receives the cause of its formation, with no other creature intervening, from God."[46] Image and archetype

differ only "in relation to the subject"[47]—i.e., as creature and creator—but in all other respects are identical. For this reason nothing stands between the Godhead and its human image, and John
concludes that "man was created for the contemplation of his Creator, without any creature interposed."[48] This exalted status and
power of vision persist in our fallen state, so that even now "between our mind and Him [God] no nature intervenes."[49] For whatever estrangement it brings, sin cannot remove the dignity of the
mind's nature.[50]

In the *Expositiones* we find a properly Dionysian use of Augustine's phrase to describe the seraphim in their praise of God. As
the angelic rank closest to God, nothing mediates their vision
while they themselves communicate this vision to others.[51] It is
therefore interesting when John describes the human mind's contemplation of God in seraphic terms, as an unceasing circular motion around God—again "with no intervening creature."[52] By
associating the angelic and human motions, Eriugena suggests a
key consequence of his anthropology: as a result of the direct relation between the human mind and God, human beings become
peers of the highest angels.

Periphyseon's commentary on the creation of humanity spells
out this suggestion in detail. Eriugena flatly states, "By no law
of creation or method of precedence can it be rightly believed or
understood that angel is prior to man."[53] Rather, they are simultaneously created as equals. For when Genesis says, "God created
light," it describes the creation both of human beings and angels.[54]
In this beginning, nothing created precedes humanity in any way,
including dignity or rank.[55] Here John discerns not only an equality, but a rich mutuality between the angelic and human natures.
As intellectual natures that become one with what they know, angels and humans understand and are created in each other. "So
closely indeed were the human and angelic natures associated, and
so would it be now if man had not sinned, that the two would have
become one."[56]

As a result of the fall, human beings have temporarily compro-
mised their equality with angels. Instead of governing the entire
universe, they have become a part of the created world.[57] Earthly,
mortal bodies have been added to our spiritual, incorruptible bodies, so that we reproduce sexually rather than like the angels.[58]
With the animal body, our differences from the angels multiply:

the senses and *phantasiae* mediate knowledge; and reason encounters "difficulty and perplexity" as it struggles to understand the universe and make moral distinctions.[59] Considered as a rational, mortal animal, the human being becomes the negation of the higher, angelic order which is "neither a rational animal nor mortal."[60] Further, in this state we become subject to the angelic hierarchy. In a direct bow to the *Celestial Hierarchy*, *Periphyseon* describes the angels' administration of the world, including the lower angels' apparitions to the human mind in order to communicate providence's commands.[61] The *Expositiones* sum up this pattern. Speaking of the soul, John says, "No creature is closer to God, and if it had not sinned, it would not be administered by any higher order, just as it will not be when it will be restored to the pristine dignity of its nature."[62] The implications are clear: our fall places us beneath the celestial hierarchy, but our return will restore equality with the angels.

Hence, only in the once and future paradise of human nature do we equal and surpass the angels. It is therefore not surprising that many of *Periphyseon*'s texts exalting humanity occur in discussions of creation and eschatology. In contrast, the *Expositiones* speak mainly from the standpoint of fallen humanity and history. Here Eriugena attends more carefully to the weakness and limitations of human insight. Symbolism thus becomes essential to the *manuductio* and *anagoge* whereby the mind is led through sensible signs into equality with the angels, and thence into contemplation of the divine mysteries.[63] In this light, the mediating function of the celestial hierarchy is appropriate to humanity's current, fallen state, where even Isaiah needs angelic purification and guidance. Following Dionysius, John therefore places humanity beneath the celestial powers, which direct the ecclesiastical hierarchy toward its divine source.[64] From this perspective, equality with the angels becomes the goal of human effort and rational striving, which shall be fulfilled in the return to God.

This return will occur in two stages. First, in the general return, human nature as a whole will regain its original, angelic state.[65] Second, in the special return when the elect attain varying levels of contemplation, they will penetrate the entire celestial hierarchy so that "there will be no angelic order into which human nature . . . will not enter according to its intelligible degrees."[66] Similarly, discussing the "special sabbath of sabbaths" that will occur in both the angels and the saints, John says, "the House of God shall be filled, and each shall have its proper place, some below, others above, some at the very summit of their nature, others beyond every natural virtue in the presence of God Himself."[67] In the end, difference and hierarchy will thus remain, with the deified elect entering the Godhead itself.

Incarnation and Christology

Of course, this restoration requires Christ's incarnation. And Dionysius's and Eriugena's discussions of this event bring their differences into still sharper focus.

For Dionysius, the gospel narratives illustrate his view of the celestial hierarchy's mediating role in human salvation. Hence, he says that "the mystery of Jesus' love for humanity was first revealed to the angels and . . . the gift of this knowledge was granted by the angels to us."[68] The angel Gabriel announced the coming births of John the Baptist and Jesus; angels addressed the shepherds with a song of joy and instructed Joseph about fleeing to Egypt. Further, the angels govern Christ's own human actions, since "he obediently submitted to the wishes of God the Father *as arranged by the angels.*"[69] In virtue of his saving work, Christ himself "entered the order of revealers and is called the 'angel of great counsel.'" Using the Greek play on *angel* as "the one who announces," Dionysius therefore assimilates Christ to the angels, insofar as "he announced what he knew of the Father."[70]

In the *Expositiones* John respectfully follows Dionysius's account and highlights the celestial powers' mediating position between God and human beings.[71] At the end of the discussion, however, he introduces an important modification. Describing Christ's angelic function, he exalts humanity in ways that reflect *Periphyseon's* themes more than Dionysius's text. Jesus came not only to save humankind, but also to manifest "with what dignity and with what orderly arrangement [*ordinatio*] in the harmony of the universal creature, man is made in the image and likeness of God." There can, John says, be no stronger argument for the dignity of human nature than the fact that Christ unites it to himself in order to save it and to deify those worthy of this ultimate grace.[72]

In *Periphyseon*, Eriugena goes farther and reverses Dionysius's pattern of revelation. Instead of the angels leading human beings to see God in Christ, the Word's becoming man initiates the angels into knowledge of the hidden God. "The Incarnation of the Word of God was beneficial to angels no less than to man. For just as it conferred upon man the benefit of redemption and the restoration of nature, so it conferred upon the angels the benefit of gnosis."[73] And rather than viewing Christ in terms of angelic proclamation and mediation, Eriugena accords Christ's humanity the primary role in God's self-disclosure. Prior to the incarnation, divine transcendence had ruled out both angelic and human knowledge of God. Since all were in the dark, the angels had no privileged insight to communicate. Christ's humanity thus becomes the vehicle for the angels', as well as humankind's, enlightenment. As Eriugena says,

> Before the Word was made flesh It was incomprehensible in every visible and invisible creature whether intelligible or rational, whether angel or man. . . . But at the Incarnation It descended from Its secret place . . . into the knowledge of the angelic and human natures. . . . The inaccessible Light gave access to every intelligible and rational creature. This is the burden of the angels' song which the universal Church on earth and in heaven never ceases to sing in sensible and intelligible melody: "Glory be to God on high and in earth peace to men of good will."[74]

No longer the angels' privileged announcement to humanity on the hillside, this song now becomes an anthem of the universal church, at once angelic and human.

Finally, Eriugena envisions humankind's highest exaltation in Christ's own humanity. For by taking on human nature, Christ not only lifted it up "to a parity [*aequalitas*] with the angelic nature, . . . but also exalted it above all angels and heavenly powers, and in short, above all things that are and all things that are not."[75] This assertion thrusts humanity beyond the entire celestial hierarchy, and into the Godhead itself where it transcends nature's basic division into being and not-being. For in ascending to the Father, Christ's humanity becomes literally deified, and thus shares the unknowability of divine transcendence. Boldly extending his consideration of human self-ignorance as a reflection of divine unknowability, Eriugena argues that Christ's *humanity* is so united with his divinity that it too is "incomprehensible and inscrutable to every creature."[76] Christology thus completes Eriugena's apotheosis of humanity.

Conclusion

The examples of Isaiah's seraph and the cherubim before paradise have raised basic issues concerning humanity's relation to the angels. Where Dionysius insists that the angels mediate between God and human beings, Eriugena exalts human nature to a position equal to the angels, and his Christology lifts humanity still higher into the hidden depths of the Godhead. Eriugena thus breaks ranks with Dionysius concerning angelic mediation between human beings and God. Indeed, we might say that humanity, not the celestial hierarchy, plays the pivotal role in Eriugena's system.[77] For as God's image and the *officina omnium*, humanity mediates the entire process of creation and nature's divisions. And in virtue of the incarnation, human nature becomes the privileged vehicle for God's self-disclosure and the saving return of all creation.

John does not abandon the celestial hierarchy but, rather, redefines humanity's relation to it. First, he confines angelic mediation to humanity's earthly, historical life. This move relativizes Dionysius's systematic claims concerning angelic mediation, which fallen humanity may still require, but which will disappear when human nature attains its original perfection. Second, gradation, degrees of insight and blessedness persist in Eriugena's final vision. He justifies the inequalities among the elect by appealing to the angelic order: as "the angels are disposed according to their proper ranks," so after the resurrection shall the blessed "be disposed according to the different degrees of their virtues."[78] Here the Dionysian hierarchies are taken for granted, but with an important difference. For John, humanity ultimately is not a tenth rank beneath the angelic nine, but finds its place within—and in Christ, above—that hierarchy according to its own capacities and achievements of vision.[79]

While these differences may be clear to us, Eriugena does not seem to notice how sharply he deviates from his master. As Jeauneau remarks, he finds these divergent views harmonized in mystical theology. Immediately following Augustine's statement that "no creature intervenes" between our mind and divine truth, John says that "Dionysius teaches the same thing" when he summons Timothy to abandon all sensible and invisible things so as to "restore yourself as far as possible to the Unity of Him who is beyond

all essence and all knowledge."[80] At its summit, Dionysius's apophatic theology places no intermediary between the contemplative
and God. Yet even with this mystical turn, tensions remain in Eriugena's account of humanity's relation to the angels. To indicate
these last tensions, let us glance at his use of three models for contemplation: Paul, Dionysius, and John the Evangelist.

When Dionysius says that nothing can be more "deiform" or
closer to God than the first angels, Eriugena compares Paul's rap-
ture with angelic vision. He writes, "The human intellects of the
holiest theologians ascend to the height of their [the angels'] contemplation, *as Paul was taken up,* but they neither exceed their excellence, nor are more deiform than they."[81] Here Eriugena neatly
fits his anthropology to Dionysius's hierarchical scheme. For as
theologians and angels share a direct, unmediated contemplation
of God, the human mind attains equality with the highest angels;
it can, however, ascend no higher. As we have seen, Isaiah joins the
seraphim in their vision of God. A poem attached to John's translation of the Dionysian writings suggests that Dionysius himself
attained this height.[82] It sketches his legendary biography, culmi-
nating in the claim that "Finally, following St. Paul, he soared on
high above the stars / And saw the three realms of the heavenly
empyrean." The poem then lists the *Celestial Hierarchy*'s nine choirs
of angels and concludes, "These numbers, separated by a thrice
threefold division, are the subject of the mystical teachings of the
father." Dionysius's ascent to the third heaven thus authorizes his
account of the celestial hierarchy, and places it at the center of his
doctrine.

Yet we have seen that Eriugena envisions still higher contemplative flights. These find their model in John the Evangelist who,
soaring like an eagle above Paul, "passes beyond every created
heaven and every created paradise, that is, every human and angelic nature."[83] The comparative restraint of Pauline ecstasy here
yields to a powerful contemplative drive that carries the Evangelist
into the Godhead. Rising above equality with angels, he "enters
into God who deifies him." The author of the fourth Gospel thus
confirms Eriugena's exaltation of human nature and anticipates
the deification of the elect. In his most radical claims, Eriugena
follows John the Evangelist's path—a path that leads beyond
Dionysius, Isaiah, and the seraphim themselves.

NOTES

1. Abbreviations for editions and translations cited:
CH: Dionysius the Areopagite, *La Hiérarchie céleste*, ed. G. Heil, intro. R. Roques, French trans. by M. De Gandillac, SC 58b (Paris: Cerf, 1970). English trans. by C. Luibheid in Pseudo-Dionysius, *The Complete Works* (New York: Paulist, 1987). Cited by chapter number, column in PG 3, and page in Luibheid's translation, as here: CH 13 308B, 181.
Ex: John Scotus Eriugena, *Expositiones in Ierarchiam coelestem*, ed. J. Barbet, CCCM 31 (Turnhout: Brepols, 1975). Cited by chapter and line numbers.
P: Eriugena, *Periphyseon (De divisione naturae)*, books I–III, ed. I. P. Sheldon-Williams (Dublin: Institute for Advanced Study, 1968, 1972, 1981); books IV–V, ed. H. J. Floss, in PL 122; translation by I. P. Sheldon-Williams, revised by J. J. O'Meara (Montréal: Bellarmin; Washington: Dumbarton Oaks, 1987). Cited by book, with column numbers from PL 122.
2. For Dionysius, see R. Roques, *L'Univers dionysien* (Paris: Cerf, 1954 and 1983); I. P. Sheldon-Williams, "Henads and Angels: Proclus and Pseudo-Dionysius," *Studia Patristica* 11 (1972): 65–71; S. Gersh, *From Iamblichus to Eriugena* (Leiden: Brill, 1978), 167–177; and H. U. von Balthasar, *The Glory of the Lord*, vol. 2, trans. A. Louth et al. (San Francisco: Ignatius, 1984), 191–203. For Eriugena, see M. de Gandillac, "Anges et hommes dans le Commentaire de Jean Scot sur la *Hiérarchie céleste*," in R. Roques, ed., *Jean Scot et l'histoire de la philosophie* (Paris: CNRS, 1977), 125–134; and N. M. Häring, "John Scottus in Twelfth-Century Angelology," in J. J. O'Meara and L. Bieler, ed., *The Mind of Eriugena* (Dublin: Irish University Press, 1973), 158–169. Concerning Eriugena's later influence, see H. F. Dondaine, *Le corpus dionysien de l'Université de Paris au XIIIᵉ siècle* (Rome: Edizioni di Storia e Letteratura, 1952); in addition to Eriugena's translations and excerpts from *Periphyseon*, the Dionysian corpus included most of the *Expositiones*, with two lacunae (Ex 3, 84–7,220; and Ex 15, 616–1085).
3. CH 6 201A, 161.
4. CH 10 272D–273A, 173.
5. Dionysius, *The Ecclesiastical Hierarchy*, chap. 1; PG 3:373C; *Complete Works*, trans. Luibheid, 197.
6. Isaiah 6:6–7 (*Jerusalem Bible*).
7. CH 8 241A–C, 167–169.
8. CH 13 300B, 176.
9. CH 13 300B–C, 177; my emphasis. This reading raises problems on Dionysius's own terms, since he has previously denied that

the last rank of angels can be given "the title of . . . seraphim since they lack participation in these latter supreme powers" (CH 5 196C, 159).

10. CH 7, 205B–C, 162. Concerning fire's symbolism, see CH 15 328C–329C, 183–184; and Eriugena's commentary, Ex 15, 160–290.

11. CH 13 300C–D, 177.

12. CH 13 301C, 178.

13. CH 13 301D–304A, 178; see also CH 13 301A, 177.

14. CH 13 305D–308A, 181.

15. CH 13 305C, 180, translation modified.

16. Roques, *L'Univers dionysien,* 152. Roques also notes "l'exégèse laborieuse" (230 n.7) and "la subtilité embarrassée avec laquelle Denys explique Is VI,6" (211 n.1).

17. Ex 13, 584–585.

18. Ex 13, 325–338.

19. Ex 13, 92–103.

20. Ex 13, 46–47. Gregory the Great cites Dionysius's gloss of Is. 6:6–7 but leaves open the general question of whether the seraphim and cherubim act directly or through lower angels; *Homilarium in Evangelia* 2, 34, 12–13 (PL 76:1254B–1255A). See C. Straw, *Gregory the Great* (Berkeley: University of California Press, 1988), 35–36.

21. Ex 13, 650; and Ex 13, 79.

22. Ex 13, 144–195. Concerning fire's symbolism, see CH 15, 328C–329C, 183–184; and Eriugena's commentary, Ex 15, 160–290.

23. Ex 13, 218–220.

24. CH 13 301D, 178.

25. Ex 13, 254–258. See also Ex 1. 76–77, where Eriugena takes up the question, "Quomodo omnia quae sunt lumina sunt?"

26. Ex 13, 536–539; see Ex 1, 337–340.

27. Ex 13, 539–545.

28. Ex 13, 389–413.

29. Ex 13, 475–476.

30. See E. Jeauneau, *Quatre thèmes érigéniens* (Montréal, 1978), 33–34.

31. Ex 13, 487–489. See Ex 4, 133, and P I, 516C, where Eriugena discusses Dionysius, CH 4 177D: "Esse enim omnium est super esse divinitas"; and D. Duclow, "Divine Nothingness and Self-Creation in John Scotus Eriugena," *Journal of Religion* 57 (1977): 109–123.

32. P V, 859D, 860D–863A: Eriugena's argument is in part grammatical, as he criticizes "those who think that in this passage the particle *ne* has a negative rather than an interrogative meaning, expressing as it were a doubt."

33. P V, 863B–C.

34. P V, 863D; translation modified. Sheldon-Williams follows PL 122 in describing the lowest order of angels with the puzzling phrase "*prope angelicus*, near-angelic." I thank E. Jeauneau for informing me that the manuscripts read *proprie angelicus*, that is, "properly angelic" (Paris, Bibl. nat. Lat. 12965, f. 92v; and Cambridge, Trin. Coll. 0.5.20, p. 185B).

35. P V, 864A.

36. P V, 863C; see CH 7 205C, 162; Ex 7, 30–31; and Ex 13, 308–309.

37. P V, 864A–B, my emphasis.

38. P V, 864C.

39. P V, 865B–C.

40. P V, 864D.

41. See W. Otten, *The Anthropology of Johannes Scottus Eriugena* (Leiden: Brill, 1991); and D. Moran, *The Philosophy of John Scottus Eriugena* (Cambridge: Cambridge University Press, 1989), 154–211.

42. P IV, 768B.

43. See P IV, 771B–C; and B. McGinn, "The Negative Element in the Anthropology of John the Scot," in *Jean Scot Erigène et la philosophie* (Paris: CNRS, 1977), 315–325.

44. See P II, 530C–D; III, 733B; V, 893B–C; and Eriugena, *Homélie sur le prologue de Jean,* ed. E. Jeauneau, SC 151 (Paris: Cerf, 1969): 292–296 (294A–B); and Jeauneau's commentary, 336–338. On humanity as creation's "second essence," see P IV, 778C–779A. Concerning why God created human beings rather than the angels in his image, see P IV, 762B–764B.

45. Augustine, *De vera religione* 55, 113 (CCSL 32:259). See E. Jeauneau, "Pseudo-Dionysius, Gregory of Nyssa, and Maximus the Confessor in the Works of John Scottus Eriugena," in *Carolingian Essays,* ed. U. R. Blumenthal (Washington: Catholic University of America Press, 1983), 145.

46. P IV, 790D; translation modified.

47. P IV, 778A.

48. P V, 941C–D, where John also offers the following etymology: "The Greeks called humanity *anthropia* that is, *anotropia* a turning towards what is above or *ano terousa opia* that is, 'holding the gaze aloft.' "

49. P II, 531B–C.

50. Ex 4, 405–412.

51. Ex 7, 69; see Ex 6, 106–107.

52. Eriugena, *Commentaire sur l'évangile de Jean,* ed. E. Jeauneau, SC 180 (Paris: Cerf, 1972): 304–306 (336B). See also CH 7, 205B–C, 162; and Dionysius, *The Divine Names* 4, 8–9, 704D–705A, where

he describes the first movements of both the divine intelligences and the soul as circular but—unlike Eriugena (P IV, 754C–D)–says that the soul's movement joins that of the angelic powers before turning to the good and beautiful Godhead.

53. P IV, 780D.

54. P IV, 782B. See Gandillac, "Anges et hommes," 400.

55. P IV, 779D.

56. P IV, 780B. Eriugena goes on to say, "Even as it is this is beginning to happen in the case of the highest men, from whom are the firstborn among the celestial natures." We may suspect that he would number Isaiah among these firstborn.

57. P IV, 782B–C.

58. P IV, 798A–800B. See A. Wohlman, "La matière et le péché de l'homme," in *L'Homme et son univers au moyen âge,* ed. C. Wenin (Louvain: Institut Supérieur de Philosophie, 1986), 211–219; Moran, *Philosophy of Eriugena,* 174–177.

59. P IV, 772C.

60. P I, 444A–B, where John distinguishes his second mode of being and nonbeing within the hierarchy of created natures. See P IV, 768B–C, where he downgrades the definition of man as "a rational mortal animal capable of sense and learning" to a description of his attributes as part of created nature.

61. P IV, 773B–C.

62. Ex 7, 427–432.

63. Ex 1, 262–264, 506–508, and 639–661; Ex 2, 124–128 and 874–876. See R. Roques, "Tératologie et théologie chez Jean Scot Erigène," in his *Libres sentiers vers l'érigénisme* (Rome: Edizione dell' Ateneo: 1975), 13–43.

64. Ex 8, 562–565.

65. P V, 949A.

66. P V, 1005D; see P V, 1012D–1013B.

67. P V, 1016A. The elect who pass beyond human nature into God's presence undergo "deification"; see P. Dietrich and D. Duclow, "Virgins in Paradise: Deification and Exegesis in *Periphyseon* V," in *Jean Scot écrivain,* ed. G. Allard (Montréal: Bellarmin; Paris: Vrin, 1986), 29–49.

68. CH 4 181B, 158.

69. CH 4 181C, 158, my emphasis. See Hebrews 2:9: "But we do see in Jesus one who was for a short while made lower than the angels," glossing Psalm 8:6; and Eriugena, Ex 8, 410–419.

70. CH 4 181D, 159.

71. Ex 4, 558–560.

72. Ex 4, 676–682.

73. P V, 912C.

74. P V, 912C–913A. See P IV, 743B; Eriugena, *Homélie*, SC 151:256–258 (289D–290A); and Gandillac, "Anges et hommes," 395.

75. P V, 895B. See Eriugena, *Homélie*, SC 151:202–204 (283B–C); and Gregory the Great, *Homilarium in Ezechielem* 1, 8, 23 (PL 76: 864C–D). Like Dionysius, Gregory cites Psalm 8:6 and Hebrews 2:9 concerning Christ as "lower than the angels"; but like Eriugena, he emphasizes the postresurrection exaltation of humanity "above the angels" in Christ. See also Gregory's *Homilarium in Evangelia* 1, 8, 2 (PL 76:1104B–1105B); and Straw, *Gregory the Great*, 155–156.

76. P V, 921A–B. Concerning John's Christology, see D. Duclow, "Dialectic and Christology in Eriugena's *Periphyseon*," *Dionysius* 4 (1980): 99–118; and M. Colish, "John the Scot's Christology and Soteriology in Relation to His Greek Sources," *Downside Review* 100 (1982): 138–151. For a similar analysis of humanity and angels in a christological setting, see F. Tobin, "Meister Eckhart and the Angels," in W. McConnell, ed., *In hôhem Prîse: A Festschrift in Honor of Ernst S. Dick* (Goppingen: Kummerle, 1989), 379–393.

77. See Moran, *Philosophy of Eriugena*, 95; and Otten, *Anthropology of Eriugena*, 213–215.

78. P V, 1013B. Jeauneau notes that Eriugena considers difference and inequality as necessary for beauty; see "Le thème du retour," *Etudes érigéniennes* (Paris: Etudes augustiniennes, 1987), 391–392.

79. P V, 1005D.

80. P IV, 759C, citing Dionysius, *Mystical Theology* 1, 997B. See Jeauneau, "Pseudo-Dionysius, Gregory of Nyssa, and Maximus the Confessor," 145–146.

81. Ex 6, 146–151; my emphasis. See also P V, 887C–D; and B. McGinn, "Eriugena Mysticus," in *Giovanni Scoto nel suo tempo* (Spoleto: Centro Italiano di Studi sull'alto Medioevo, 1989), 257.

82. "Lumine sidereo Dionysius auxit Athenas," MGH, *Poetae* 3, 548; and PL 122:1037A–B/1038A–B, at the head of Eriugena's translation of the *Celestial Hierarchy*; MGH text and English translation in *Poetry of the Carolingian Renaissance*, ed. Peter Godman (Norman: University of Oklahoma Press, 1985), 304–306. For all his disguising, Pseudo-Dionysius makes no claim to this Pauline ecstasy. Eriugena's poem, however, found its way into the Dionysian corpus of thirteenth-century Paris; see Dondaine, *Le corpus dionysien*, 16.

83. Eriugena, *Homélie*, SC 151:218–220 (285C); translated by J. J. O'Meara, *Eriugena* (Oxford: Oxford University Press, 1988), 161. Concerning the symbolism of the eagle, see also Ex 15, 831–859.

Metaphysics and Christology
in Maximus Confessor and Eriugena

Eric D. Perl

Eriugena, as is well known, adopts from his Greek sources a cosmic, metaphysical understanding of the incarnation of Christ which is far less evident in the Latin Fathers. But because he is not familiar with the developments in Byzantine Christology in the sixth and seventh centuries, he does not completely appropriate the Greek vision. In Eriugena, the doctrine of the incarnation remains distinct from, although closely connected with, his Neoplatonic account of the world's procession from and return to God. It is rather in St. Maximus, the heir of both Neoplatonic metaphysics and Byzantine Christology, that we find the complete union, or rather identification, of the two. Maximus offers, not only an idea of a "cosmic Christ," but a fully integrated christological ontology, in which the mystery of Christ is itself the basis for understanding the metaphysics of the relation between God and world.

In his metaphysical account of creation, Maximus, basing his thought principally on the work of Pseudo-Dionysius, anticipates virtually the entire doctrine of theophany and of God's self-creation that we are familiar within Eriugena. Indeed, his ontology as a whole is far more like Eriugena's than is usually recognized. Maximus regards the act of creation not as the production of new or additional beings over against God, in such a way that God and the world would be two distinct things, but as the ontological participation of the creature in God.[1] God, who in himself is beyond being, and is thus, in Dionysius's and Eriugena's terms, Nothing, not any thing, becomes in creating the formal being of all things, the being in which they participate and in virtue of which they are beings.[2]

253

> God . . . is and becomes the life of things which live and are made
> alive, and all things to all things, through the very things which are
> and become; but through himself he neither is nor becomes any-
> thing in any way whatever. . . . [God] is naturally coordinated with
> none of beings at all; and therefore, it is more appropriately said of
> him that he is not, because he is above being. For it must be, since
> it is necessary for us truly to recognize the difference between God
> and creatures, that the affirmation of what is above being is the
> negation of beings, and that the affirmation of beings is the nega-
> tion of what is above being.[3]

God and creation, then, cannot be two beings. Rather, in the words
of Dionysius which Maximus here expands, God is "all things in all
things and nothing in any."[4] Not only is God both transcendent
and immanent, but his transcendence is his immanence and his
immanence is his transcendence. From this it follows that creation
is nothing but the self-multiplication and self-impartation of God
to the creature, and the creature's participation in or reception of
God. Thus to say that the creature comes to be by participating in
God is to say that in the act of creating, God gives himself to the
creature and the creature receives God as its being. As Maximus
says,

> God, who is one in himself . . . willed . . . to impart himself propor-
> tionally to all and to each, granting to each the power for being and
> continuing. According to . . . Dionysius . . . the One praised in
> God, by transcending all things, having brought into being by
> goodness the entire order of intelligible things and the beauty of
> visible things, without diminution exists in each of the created
> things. . . . And this . . . is [what it means that] the Good is poured
> out and progresses: that the one God, proportionally to the recip-
> ients, is multiplied by the impartation of goods.[5]

Although neither Dionysius nor Maximus goes so far as to say, as
Eriugena does, that God creates himself in the creature, the ontological content of Eriugena's doctrine is already present in their
idea of creation as participation, as God's self-multiplication and
self-impartation.[6] Since the creature is nothing save what it receives from God, and this is God himself, creation can only be understood as such a self-creation.

This act is the motion of procession and reversion, in which God
creates by both extending himself to the creature and drawing the

creature to himself, and the creature comes to be by at once coming out of God and moving into him. "It is granted that out of God [ἐκ θεοῦ], who is forever, all things come to be out of non-being . . . wisely brought forth as from an infinitely knowing and infinitely powerful cause, and in him all things consist, guarded and held fast as in an almighty foundation, and to him all things revert, as each to its proper limit, as Dionysius the great Areopagite somewhere says."[7] And since this movement of participation is not only the creature's coming into being but also its return to God, it is not only the act of creation but also that of deification.[8] Thus Maximus says of deification that the creature which loves God hastens towards its beloved, and "does not rest until the whole comes to be in the whole beloved and encompassed by the whole, willingly receiving the whole saving circumscription . . . so that the whole is qualified by the whole circumscriber, so that it wishes no longer at all to be able to be characterized from itself, but from the circumscriber."[9] Again, he says that in being deified man "enters into God himself, and the whole is qualified and transqualified."[10] This is perfect participation, in which the creature possesses God as its determination, its very identity. God deifies the world, Maximus says, by imparting or distributing himself to it.[11] But since according to the Neoplatonic theory of participation the creature is nothing save what it has or participates in, and this is God himself, the creature *is God* by participation.[12] This is the meaning of St. Maximus's frequent statements that the deified creature is "identical with God in all but nature."[13] The only difference is the fact of participation itself, the fact that what God is in himself, the creature is *ab extra,* by reception or impartation from God. Thus the creature is both ontologically identical with, and absolutely other than, God, in an identity of difference and identity, of transcendence and immanence, precisely the same as that which we find in Eriugena.[14] The deified creature is, as Maximus says, "another God,"[15] not of course in the sense of being an additional God, but by being God-in-otherness, the self-impartation or self-creation in which God makes himself to be other and makes the other, the creature, to be himself.

Since Maximus regards both creation and deification as God's making himself other, it follows that they must ultimately be the same act. The only reason for any interval between them is the fall of man, that is, of the creation. For the creature to be created, that is, for it to be, is for it to participate in God and thus be deified. Since the creature is not an additional being alongside of God, since it is nothing but a participation of God, no creature can be without being God by participation. The only alternative to deification is the fall, which Maximus for this reason frequently describes as a fall toward non-being.[16] The fall is a diminution of the creature's participation in God[17] and hence of its very existence. Conversely, deification is nothing but the fullness of being, so that it is not a separate act, but simply the fulfillment of creation.

The central feature of Maximus's ontology, however, is that he regards this single motion of procession and return, creation and deification, as the incarnation of God.[18] For Maximus, the deification of the world, the purpose for which it is made, is simply the reverse side of the incarnation. In becoming incarnate, God makes himself the creature and thus makes the creature himself. Consequently, creation itself is not complete until all the cosmos, in man, is hypostatically identified with God the Word. The mystery of Christ, the hypostatic union,

> is the blessed end, on account of which all things were constituted. This is the foreknown divine purpose of the beginning of beings . . . on account of which all things are, but itself on account of nothing. Looking toward this end, God produced the essences of beings. . . . God the Word become man . . . makes apparent the inmost foundation of the paternal goodness, and reveals in himself the end on account of which the things that are made . . . received beginning in being. For on account of Christ, that is the mystery of Christ, all the ages, and the things in the ages, take in Christ their beginning and end of being.[19]

Since the incarnation is the fulfillment of creation, of God's self-manifestation and creation's participation in him, the world can fully and perfectly be only by being united with God in hypostasis, and any failure of such union is the creature's fall toward non-being.

This is why Maximus speaks of the act of creation itself as the incarnation of God. Expounding St. Gregory Nazianzen's statement that "the Word became thick," Maximus says that this refers first to Christ's "enfleshed presence" and secondly to the creative self-multiplication of God the Logos to be the many logoi, the divine ideas which are the causes and formal principles of creatures.

Hiding himself ineffably in the logoi of beings for us, he is signified appropriately by each visible thing as by certain letters, whole in wholes, at once most full, and complete in the particular, whole and undiminished, in different things he who is without difference and always the same, in composite things he who is simple and incomposite, and in things subject to beginning he who is without beginning, and the invisible in visible things, and in tangible things he who is intangible.[20]

Maximus intends not merely a parallel but an inner identity between God's self-incarnation and his creating the world by making himself present to it and in it. This identity between incarnation and metaphysical participation, God's creative and deifying self-impartation to the world, is the basis for Maximus's well-known doctrine of reciprocity between God and man: "God is hominified to man . . . so far as man . . . deifies himself to God,"[21] and man "is made God as far as [God becomes] man."[22] For God to create and deify the world by making himself other and the other himself is for him to become incarnate, to become the creature, and for the creature to become God by hypostatic union. Maximus thus summarizes his entire ontology when he says that man is deified by

emplacing himself wholly in God alone, having wholly impressed and formed God on himself, so that he is and is called God by grace, and God is and is called man by condescension; and the power of the reciprocal disposition is shown in this, which both deifies man to God . . . and hominifies God to man, by a fair inversion, and makes man God by the deification of man, and God man by the hominification of God. *For always and in all the Word of God and God wills to effect the mystery of his embodiment.*[23]

"Always and in all": all creation and deification is simply the working out of God's will to make himself incarnate, and this will is thus the very heart of his act of creating.

St. Maximus was able to achieve this integration of the Neoplatonic ontology of participation, of procession and reversion, with the mystery of Christ, on the basis of a very precise Christology which he inherited from the so-called "neo-Chalcedonian" theologians of the sixth century.[24] The Council of Chalcedon had defined Christ to be one person, or hypostasis,[25] in two natures. But only a hypostasis is an actually existing thing. A nature is merely a generality or kind, while a hypostasis, a nature with properties, has the individual determinations whereby it is itself and no other, and so actually exists. Human nature, for instance, cannot exist except as the human nature of Peter, Paul, or James, having the hypostatic determinations which make it to be this particular human being. Hence the Nestorians argued that since there can be no nature devoid of hypostatic determination, no nature which is not a hypostasis, to deny a second, human hypostasis in Christ, in addition to the divine hypostasis, God the Word, is to deny the reality of Christ's human nature and thus fall into monophysitism. The monophysites, on the other hand, contended that since there can be no nature which is not a hypostasis, the Chalcedonian definition of two natures in Christ necessarily implies two hypostases and thus leads to Nestorianism.

To defend the Chalcedonian dogma of one hypostasis and two natures, the neo-Chalcedonians, above all Leontius of Jerusalem, developed the crucial doctrine of enhypostasization. This Christology agrees that there can be no nature which is not a hypostasis, that only a hypostasis is a real thing. But it explains that the humanity of Christ is not its own, human hypostasis, but that it is rather *enhypostasized* in God the Word. That is to say, the hypostasis, the actual thing or self whose human nature it is, is the Word, who is thus the subject of all that pertains to Christ in the flesh, including suffering and death. One of the Holy Trinity, one hypostasis of the divine nature, becomes in the incarnation also the hypostasis of human nature, which is not in itself hypostatic. As we have seen, the nature is not another thing which is united to the hypostasis. A nature, when it has hypostatic determination, *is* that hypostasis, and apart from such determination it does not exist at all. Thus Maximus can say that Christ is his two natures, and that each nature is Christ.[26] The humanity of Christ is God the Word in person, although it continues to be human nature. It can be God without ceasing to be human because it is a divine hypostasis, one of the Holy Trinity, but not the divine nature.[27]

For Maximus, even the expression "hypostatic union" is inadequate to describe what happens in the incarnation. He insists rather on hypostatic *identity*. The two natures of Christ are one and the same thing, that is, one and the same hypostasis. "We confess . . . hypostatic identity, for the flesh is clearly the same in hypostasis with the Word,"[28] and conversely, "God the Word is the same with his own flesh."[29] For the human nature of Christ to be enhypostasized in, that is, to be the Word, is for it to have as the hypostatic determination by which it exists the personal determinations of God the Word himself, by which he is differentiated from the Father and the Holy Spirit. The two natures of Christ are the same hypostasis because they are determined by the same properties:

> For it is not by the properties by which it is marked off from the rest of men that the flesh [of Christ] maintains its difference from the Word; nor again, by the properties which differentiate it from the Word, is it marked off from us. But by those by which it is marked off from us, by these it preserves the union, that is, identity, in hypostasis with the Word; and by those by which it is naturally united to us, by these . . . it has its essential difference from the Word preserved. So, too, the Word, by the properties by which he is marked off from what is common to the Godhead as Son and Word, by these he preserves the union, that is, identity, in hypostasis with the flesh.[30]

There is one hypostasis of the flesh and the Godhead, the Word, because there is only one set of determinations. "For by the properties by which the flesh, being distinct from us, differs, by these it has identity in hypostasis with the Word; and by the properties by which the Word differs from the Father and the Spirit, being distinct as Son, by these he maintains . . . [the identity] in hypostasis with the flesh, differentiated in no way whatever."[31]

This understanding of incarnation as the enhypostasization of human nature in God the Word allows us to see how Maximus is able to identify metaphysical participation with incarnation. For the creature to participate in God, to be and be deified, to be God in all but nature, is for it to receive from without the determinations or perfections which God is in himself. But now we find that this is exactly what christological enhypostasization is: the human nature is enhypostasized in the Word, becomes God the Word in hypostasis, by receiving him as its self, its hypostatic determination, and this guarantees at once the identity in hypostasis and the difference in nature. This is why Maximus describes deific participation and enhypostasization in precisely the same terms. For instance, in both cases he uses the idea of *perichoresis,* or mutual interpenetration between God and man, and the associated images of air suffused with light and iron enflamed by fire, and he uses them in precisely the same way. In participation, the whole man receives all that God is, so that God is wholly taken into man and man into God, "as air illumined through the whole by light, and the whole iron enflamed by the whole fire."[32] The fire pervades the entire volume of the iron, and conversely the iron encompasses the fire in itself. As a result, the iron receives all the properties of fire throughout its entire substance, so that it indeed becomes fire, all that fire is. And yet iron and fire remain different in kind, for the iron has its fiery properties not in its own nature but by being enflamed. This represents perfect participation, the union of difference and identity. But Maximus illustrates enhypostasization too by explaining that the Word, the divine hypostasis, deifies his human nature "in the manner of enflamed iron, as penetrating it (περιχωρήσας) throughout . . . and becoming one thing with it without confusion, as one and the same hypostasis."[33] And this, he says, does not remove the human nature from what is essential to it, "as neither does . . . the mingling and union with fire [remove] iron from what is proper to it; but it receives what is proper to fire, since it has become fire by the union."[34]

Thus it is no surprise that Maximus explicitly refers to deification as our enhypostasization in God and calls the deified cosmos the body of God: "The things which are by nature far[35] separated from each other return into one, converging with each other in the one nature of man, and God himself becomes all things in all things, embracing and enhypostasizing all things in himself . . . whereby we are and are called Gods and children and body and limbs and parts of God."[36] Maximus says that in being deified, man, "uniting created to uncreated nature through love . . . shows it one and the same . . . the whole wholly interpenetrating [περιχωρήσας] the whole God, and becoming all that God is except for identity in essence, and receives the whole God himself instead of himself."[37] In deification the creature receives God the Word as its hypostasis, its very self. Perfect participation in God, the fulfillment of creation, then, is enhypostasization in him, and this is what enables Maximus to see the incarnation of God as not only the purpose but the very content and meaning of creation itself.

For the creature to be God by participation, then, is for it to be the body, or the human nature, of Christ. The doctrine of enhypostasization allows us to see how all creation can be that same, unique body. It is, in eschatological perspective, the same body because it is the body of the same person or hypostasis, and therefore is that hypostasis, God the Word. The deification of the world is "the mystery hidden from the ages and from the nations, and now made manifest through the true and perfect hominification of the Son of God, uniting our nature to himself in hypostasis . . . and . . . through his . . . flesh [taken] from us, as through first-fruits, conjoining us to himself and granting us to be *one and the same with himself* according to his humanity."[38] In the eschaton we are to be that humanity, that very body. There is no distinction between the historical and the mystical, eschatological, or cosmic body of Christ, for they are one and the same hypostasis, that is, the same thing. All creation is deified, and thus fully exists, only by being that unique body.

> If, then, Christ, as man, is the firstfruits of our nature with God the Father . . . , and is with God the Father according to the idea of humanity . . . let us not doubt that we shall be where he is, the first-fruits of our race. For as he came to be below . . . thus we too . . . will come to be above . . . and Gods as he is by the mystery of grace, changing nothing at all of our nature. And thus . . . the members of the body are drawn together to the Head . . . each member . . . filling the body of him who fills all in all, which fills all and is filled out of all.[39]

The cosmos, deified by perfect participation in God, is the created nature of God the Word himself, the creature which God has made himself to be and made to be himself, in accordance with his will for self-incarnation which is the very basis of the creative act.

St. Maximus's ontology is not mere pantheism, for while it maintains that whatever fully is, is God, it is not simply God, but God-in-otherness. But it would be accurate to describe this doctrine as a pan-Christism, in which to be is to be Christ by enhypostasization. It is in this intensely literal and christological sense that Maximus understands St. Paul's assertion, so important in the ontology of Dionysius and Eriugena as well, that God will be "all in all." All creation is made to be, and in eschatological perspective is, one macrocosmic man, God the Word Incarnate. Whatever is not the body of Christ is fallen toward non-being and to that extent fails to be. If for Maximus all creation, as Hans Urs von Balthasar suggested, is a cosmic liturgy,[40] then its center, purpose, and in the end its entirety can be nothing less than a cosmic Eucharist.

Eriugena's ontological vision is subtly but vitally different. He too makes the Dionysian principle that God is "all things in all things and nothing in any" the central tenet of his ontology[41] and regards creation as the theophany and self-multiplication of God.[42] Indeed, it is Eriugena who works out most fully the metaphysical consequences of the principle of creation as participation and arrives at the idea that creation is God's self-creation. This had remained unexpressed in Dionysius and Maximus, although it is clearly implied by their ontology and is of a piece with their incarnational metaphysics. In what is perhaps Eriugena's most explicit statement about this, he says,

> We ought not to understand God and the creature as two things distinct from one another, but as one and the same. For the creature is subsisting in God; and God, manifesting himself, in a marvellous and ineffable manner is created in the creature, the invisible making himself visible and the incomprehensible comprehensible and the hidden revealed . . . and the simple composite . . . and the infinite finite and the uncircumscribed circumscribed . . . and creating all things he is created in all things and making all things is made in all things . . . and . . . he . . . becomes all things in all things.

This passage paraphrases and expands Maximus's account of the incarnational "thickening" of the Logos in becoming the logoi of creatures. But in contrast to Maximus, Eriugena goes on to insist that this self-creation is *not* the incarnation of God: "And I am not saying this of the incarnation and hominification of the Word, but of the ineffable condescension of the Supreme Goodness, which is Unity and Trinity, into the things that are in order that they may be."[43] Thus Eriugena separates creation and incarnation into two distinct acts.

His separation of deification from incarnation is still more striking. Eriugena remarks, with reference to Maximus, that "he says that theophany is effected from none other than God, but it happens by the condescension of the Divine Word . . . downwards, as it were, to human nature, created and purified by him, and the exaltation upwards again of human nature to the aforesaid Word through divine love." Here, it would seem, Eriugena adopts Maximus's doctrine of the reciprocity, indeed the identity, between the incarnation of God and the deification of man. But Eriugena goes on to make his meaning clearer: "By condescension here I mean not that which has already taken place through the incarnation but that which comes about by *theosis*, that is, the deification of the creature."[44] In this way he does away with the Maximian reciprocity, in which man becomes God precisely insofar as God becomes man, that is, becomes incarnate, so that there is only one condescension of God and exaltation of man. Thus, while Maximus overcomes the apparent distinction among the "types" of incarnation, that is, creation, historical incarnation, and deification, by understanding them all as the same ontological process, Eriugena clearly differentiates them. As a result, while for Maximus nothing can truly be without being the body of God, enhypostasized in the Word, for Eriugena there can be fully existent creatures which are not themselves that body.

Eriugena's metaphysics of creation and deification, of the relation between God and the world, then, is in principle independent of the mystery of Christ. For Maximus, the idea of incarnation, of hypostatic union, is the key to understanding the ontology of this relation. In Eriugena's system, on the other hand, it is possible to understand the metaphysical nature of creation and deification without reference to specifically christological doctrines. The fact of the incarnation is therefore additional, not intrinsic, to his ontology. Consequently, unlike Maximus, Eriugena sees the incarnation not as the very heart of creation, but only in instrumental terms, as a means to save the fallen world. We find many passages indicating this view of the incarnation,[45] but we do not find any statements parallel to St. Maximus's doctrine that "always and in all" God wills to be incarnate, that the incarnation is itself the original purpose and essence of the act of creation. In one of his most remarkable passages on the purpose of the incarnation, Eriugena says,

> Why did he descend? . . . For no other cause, as I believe, than that according to his humanity he might save the effects of the Causes which according to his Divinity he possesses eternally without change; and that he might call them back into their Causes that they, and likewise the Causes themselves, might be preserved in a certain ineffable unification. . . . If the Wisdom of God did not descend into the effects of the Causes . . . the principle of the Causes would perish. For if the effects of the Causes should perish, no Cause would remain, just as if the Causes should perish, no effects would remain.[46]

The salvation effected in Christ is certainly an ontological return of all the cosmos to God, so that both creatures and their Causes, the divine ideas, may not fall into non-being. But the ideas and the creatures themselves evidently have an existence of their own apart from the incarnation, which is needed only to preserve them from the effects of the fall. In Maximus, on the other hand, the very existence of the ideas or logoi in their multiplicity is the cosmic incarnation of the Logos. When Maximus ascribes an instrumental role to the incarnation, he does so because the purpose of creation, the hypostatic identity of God and the cosmos, is realized only in the historical incarnation,[47] not merely because the incarnation was needed to heal the fall of man.

As a result, while for Maximus the deified cosmos is not subordinate to but is the body or humanity of Christ, Eriugena sets that body apart from and above the rest of the deified creation: "In none but in himself alone is humanity joined to the Deity in unity of substance [i.e., hypostasis], and changed into Deity itself transcends all things. For the Head of the Church reserved this property for himself alone, that his humanity should become not only . . . a participant in Deity, but indeed Deity Itself." In what follows, Eriugena distinguishes yet more clearly between hypostatic union and deific participation: "He alone has brought his humanity into this unity, but the others whom he deifies he establishes after himself in a mere participation in his Deity."[48] This is quite different from Maximus, where, as we have seen, perfect participation in God is hypostatic union, that is, enhypostasization in Him. And while Maximus uses the concept of *perichoresis* indiscriminately to describe both incarnation and deification, because they are ontologically the same, Eriugena uses it with reference only to deifying participation, not to the incarnation.[49] Eriugena thus locates the incarnation of the Word as one moment within the larger ontological context of God's theophanic procession to the world and the world's return to God, while for Maximus that motion is the incarnation.

And yet, despite this difference, Eriugena also seems to follow Maximus in treating deification not merely as union with God, but specifically as union in Christ. Thus he says, for instance,

And thus ineffably and supernaturally is the harmony of our Head adapted, to which all his members, being united with each other, shall return, when they "shall come together into the perfect man in the fullness of the age of Christ," and he shall be and shall appear One in all, and all shall be and shall appear one in the One.[50]

This strongly recalls Maximus's christological understanding of deification. Again, he can say that "the perfect man is Christ, in whom all things are consummated,"[51] and that deification "shall be perfected in Christ and through Christ, who is the end and consummation of our nature."[52] Still more precisely, Eriugena repeatedly asserts that "that which he perfected in himself particularly, he shall at the time of our resurrection perfect generally in the whole of human nature."[53] This is a direct adoption of Maximus's teaching that in the eschaton all creation will be incorporated in the hypostatic union. In such passages Eriugena indeed presents a pan-Christic ontology like that of Maximus. What is missing in Eriugena is not this doctrine itself, but the precise Christology which enables Maximus to explain how it is true, and to understand the Neoplatonic metaphysics of participation in christological terms. All the elements of Maximus's doctrine are present in Eriugena, but they are not fully integrated in a single coherent christological ontology. As a result, there is an unresolved tension in Eriugena between the view that all creation is to undergo the same union with God that is realized in Christ, and the claim that the humanity of Christ is and remains different and set apart from the rest of the deified creation.

The reason for this tension is that Eriugena simply did not have access to the sophisticated Byzantine Christology which made Maximus's synthesis possible; above all, he was not aware of the meaning of enhypostasization. He betrays his unfamiliarity with this concept when, more than once, he fails to recognize and consequently mistranslates the term.[54] In the crucial passage where Maximus says that God deifies the world by enhypostasizing it in himself, Eriugena, not knowing the term ἐνυποστήσας, evidently reads instead ἕν ὑποστήσας ἑαυτῷ, and accordingly translates it as "unum substituens sibimet."[55] The sense remains much the same ("rendering one with himself"), but the vital christological significance of Maximus's term is lost.

More generally, Eriugena does not seem to be fully aware of the distinction between nature and hypostasis as ontological categories which is the basis of all orthodox Byzantine Christology. He sometimes speaks of Christ's human nature as though it were a hypostasis, an existing created being in its own right, distinct from

God the Word. Thus he can say that Christ "alone of all, by no previous merits, was joined in unity of substance [i.e., in Eriugena's terms, hypostasis] to the Word of God,"[56] or again, that "no creature besides the humanity of the Word could ascend beyond all the theophanies."[57] Such expressions seem to imply that the human nature of Christ, *qua* nature, is a created thing, distinct from, although joined to, a divine thing or hypostasis, God the Word. Eriugena's words would sound dangerously Nestorian to a Byzantine like Maximus, for they suggest that the incarnation is the union of two things, or hypostases, one divine and the other created, rather than the assumption into God of a human nature which is not a human hypostasis and which has no existence save that of God the Word himself. Conversely, Eriugena can also say that the humanity of Christ is deified by being "translated," "converted," or even "changed" into divinity.[58] Here again is the confusion between nature and hypostasis. "Divinity," *divinitas* or *deitas*, Greek θεοτής, refers not to any one hypostasis of the Trinity, but to the divine nature. Human or created nature deified in this way would be God, not by becoming God the Word through enhypostasization, but by ceasing to be human nature and becoming the divine nature. But as the Chalcedonian definition insists, human nature is assumed without change into the Word. A Byzantine theologian would thus reject Eriugena's idea of its being changed into divinity as monophysite. Both this and the Nestorian error spring from a failure to appreciate the distinction between nature and hypostasis, which alone allows us to say that the humanity of Christ is God and yet remains human, created nature.

Eriugena is not in any strict sense either a Nestorian or a monophysite, and he is quite capable of terminologically orthodox formulations of christological doctrine.[59] But his imprecise expressions show that he is not greatly concerned with technical Christology, and above all that he has not wholly appreciated its ontological significance. Lacking the full and precise account of the relation between nature and hypostasis in Christ which the Byzantines elaborated in the course of the "christological centuries," he does not have the means to understand the hypostatic union as the first principle of all ontology and to assimilate all theophany and all deification, every act of participation in God, to that union. He has no way of explaining how all creation can be the one body of Christ, can be God the Word, while remaining created in nature.

As a result, Eriugena's understanding of the incarnation is in fact less cosmic and ontological than that of Maximus, and in this respect more like that of his fellow Latins. Already in the ninth century, western theologians were distinguishing between the "historical" body of Christ and the body which is the Church or redeemed humanity.[60] In setting the humanity or body of Christ apart from the rest of the deified creation, in distinguishing as he does between the particular humanity of Christ and his body which is the Church,[61] Eriugena reveals the same tendency. In Byzantine thought, as exemplified by Maximus, there is no room for such a distinction. The Holy Eucharist, says Maximus, "transforms into itself . . . those who partake,"[62] with the result, as we have seen, that the world becomes that unique body. Only in the West was it found either possible or necessary to distinguish between the historical and eucharistic body of Christ on the one hand and the ecclesial and eschatological body on the other, and in this respect Eriugena remains a child of the West.

St. Maximus sums up his view of the relation between philosophical metaphysics and Christology when he says, "The mystery of the embodiment of the Word contains the power of all the riddles and types in Scripture, and the understanding of creatures, visible and intelligible."[63] Maximus sees all ontology summed up in that mystery, which is itself therefore the first principle of metaphysics. Eriugena undertakes a similar synthesis of philosophy and theology, but he is limited by the Christology available to him and lacks the resources needed to develop it into an all-embracing metaphysics. Thus it is in Maximus, not Eriugena, that we find a fully articulated pan-Christic ontology, in which every deified creature must say with St. Paul, "I live; yet not I, but Christ lives in me."

NOTES

1. For creation as participation in Maximus, see, e.g., *Capita* 15, 2 (PG 90:1177A–B); *Capita* 15, 7 (PG 90:1180C–81A); *Epistola* 6 (PG 91:428C–29A).

2. See, e.g., *Capita theologica et economica* I.4 (PG 90:1084C); *Ambiguum* 7 (PG 91:1073C); *Quaestiones ad Thalassium* 44, ed. C. Laga and C. Steel, CCSG 7:301 (PG 90:416C); *Capita de Charitate* III.27, ed. A. Ceresa-Gastaldo (Rome, 1963), 156 (PG 90:1025A).

3. *Mystagogia,* proemium (PG 91:664A–B).

4. *De divinis nominibus* VII.3 (PG 3:872A).

5. *Ambiguum* 35 (PG 91:1288D–1289B).

6. Cf. Stephen Gersh, *From Iamblichus to Eriugena* (Leiden, 1978), 188–189: Eriugena has "an idea of self-creation which is not to be precisely paralleled in the Greek sources, but which is clearly a consistent development of the earlier thought."

7. *Ambiguum* 10 (PG 91:1188B–C). For other expressions of creation as the Neoplatonic cyclical pattern of procession and reversion, διαστολή–συστολή, in Maximus, see, e.g., *Ambiguum* 23 (PG 91:1257C–60A); *Ambiguum* 10 (PG 91:1177A, 1177B–1180A).

8. For Maximus, as for Eriugena, there is no distinction between the creation and deification of man and that of creation in general, for human nature is not only microcosm but macrocosm, containing all creation in itself. See *Ambiguum* 41 (PG 91:1304D ff.); *Mystagogia* 7 (PG 91:684D–85C).

9. *Ambiguum* 7 (PG 91:1073D–1076A).

10. *Ambiguum* 10 (PG 91:1141B).

11. *Ambiguum* 10 (PG 91:1172C).

12. *Quaestiones ad Thalassium,* introductio, 37 (PG 90:257D); *Capita theologica et economica* II.88 (PG 90:1168A–B).

13. *Epistola* 25 (PG 91:613C–D); *Ambiguum* 41 (PG 91:1308B).

14. See Dermot Moran, *The Philosophy of John Scottus Eriugena* (Cambridge, 1989), 89, 100, 236–238.

15. *Quaestiones ad Thalassium* 6, 69–71 (PG 90:281A); *Epistola* 1 (PG 91:326A–B).

16. *Mystagogia* 1 (PG 91:668A–B); *Ambiguum* 7 (PG 91:1084D); *Ambiguum* 41 (PG 91:1308C). Hence Maximus says that the fall occurs ἅμα τῷ εἶναι, *Quaestiones ad Thalassium* 59 (PG 90:613C). There can be no temporal interval between creation and fall, since the creature must either exist by being deified or fall toward non-being. The doctrine that creation is nothing but theophany excludes any notion of "pure" or "autonomous" nature, creation fully existent but not yet deified by grace. Grace is participation and is therefore involved in the act of creation itself. See *Capita de Charitate* III.27, 156 (PG 90:1025A).

17. *Ambiguum* 42 (PG 91:1329B).

18. This is in fact already strongly implied in Dionysius, *De divinis nominibus* I.4 (PG 3:592A–B); *De Ecclesiastica Hierarchia* III.3.12 (PG 3:444A–B); *Epistola* III (PG 3:1069B).

19. *Quaestiones ad Thalassium* 60 (PG 90:621A–B).

20. *Ambiguum* 33 (PG 91:1285C–1289A).

21. *Ambiguum* 10 (PG 91:1113B–C).

22. *Ambiguum* 60 (PG 91:1385B–C).

23. *Ambiguum* 7 (PG 91:1084C–D).

24. The expression "neo-Chalcedonian" is here used purely descriptively, without the pejorative connotations which originally belonged to it.

25. The transliteration "hypostasis" is preferable to the inadequate translation "person" for ὑπόστασις, since the latter term refers simply to any actually existing thing, whether it be a man or merely a stone. In the case of God, angels, and men, however, the hypostasis is also the person.

26. *Epistola* 15 (PG 91:573A).

27. For more thorough accounts of this Christology, see John Meyendorff, *Christ in Eastern Christian Thought* (Washington and Cleveland, 1969); Patrick Gray, *The Defense of Chalcedon in the East* (Leiden, 1979); and Kenneth W. Wesche, *The Defense of Chalcedon in the Sixth Century* (Diss. Fordham University, 1986).

28. *Epistola* 15 (PG 91:572C).

29. *Epistola* 15 (PG 91:565D).

30. *Epistola* 15 (PG 91:557A–B).

31. *Epistola* 15 (PG 91:560A–B).

32. *Ambiguum* 7 (PG 91:1076A).

33. *Opuscula theologica et polemica* (PG 91:60B–C).

34. *Opuscula theologica et polemica* (PG 91:189C–D).

35. Reading, with Eriugena and with Polycarp Sherwood, *The Earlier Ambigua of Saint Maximus the Confessor and His Refutation of Origenism* (Rome, 1955), 24, πολλῷ, for PG (Oehler), πολλά.

36. *Ambiguum* 7 (PG 91:1092C).

37. *Ambiguum* 41 (PG 91:1308B). For the idea that the deified creature receives God as its self instead of itself, see also *Mystagogia* 5 (PG 91:676B), and *Mystagogia* 23 (PG 91:701B–C).

38. *Ambiguum* 7 (PG 91:1097A–B).

39. *Ambiguum* 31 (PG 91:1280C–1281B).

40. Hans Urs von Balthasar, *Kosmische Liturgie*, 2nd ed. (Einsiedeln, 1961).

41. E.g., P I 68 (512D–513A), 196, 20–21; P III 4 (632D–633A); P III 19 (681A).

42. E.g. P I 12 (454C), 64, 28–29; P I 13 (455A–B), 66, 21–25; P I 71 (516C), 204, 27–30; P III 4 (632D–33A); P III 9 (643B).

43. P III 17 (678C–D).

44. P I 9 (449A–B), 52, 22–31.

45. E.g., P II 9 (536C–D), 30, 6–8; P III 20 (684A); P IV 9 (777B); P IV 16 (823C).

46. P V 25 (912A–B).

47. See esp. *Ambiguum* 7 (PG 91: 1097B–D).

48. P V 25 (911B–C).

49. E.g., P I 10 (450A–B), 54, 21–31; P V 8 (879A).

50. P V 38 (994B).

51. P IV 1 (743B).

52. P V 37 (990B).

53. P V 38 (995B); cf. P II 11 (539C), 36, 8–10; P II 14 (545B), 46, 32–35; P II 23 (575C), 112, 21–24.

54. E.g., P II 35 (615C), 202, 29.

55. *Maximi Confessoris Ambigua ad Iohannem iuxta Iohannis Scotti Eriugenae latinam interpretationem,* ed. E. Jeauneau, CCSG 18:35 (PG 91:1091C).

56. P IV 9 (777C).

57. P V 23 (905C).

58. P II 11 (539C), 36, 2–3; P V 8 (877A); P V 25 (911B).

59. E.g., P V 26 (920D–21A); cf. P V 38 (1018B).

60 See Jaroslav Pelikan, *The Christian Tradition,* vol. 3: *The Growth of Medieval Theology (600–1300)* (Chicago, 1978), 78; Henri de Lubac, *Corpus Mysticum* (Paris, 1949), 87–88.

61. P II 22 (565A), 88, 25–27.

62. *Mystagogia* 21 (PG 91:697A).

63. *Capita theologica et economica* I.66 (PG 90:1108A).

Russian Scholarship on the Interrelation of Eastern and Western Thought in John Scottus Eriugena

Oleg Bychkov

THIS ESSAY WILL BY NO MEANS attempt to make any revelations in Eriugenian studies. It is, rather, a survey of characteristic views of prerevolutionary Russian scholarship on Eriugena and the problem of the interrelation of eastern and western ideas in his writings. The reason we have to deal here with such a remote period of time is simple and at the same time tragic: the whole of the Russian tradition of studies in western medieval philosophy was completely destroyed by the ideology of the Communist revolution, and the names of western medieval philosophers and theologians have since virtually disappeared from scholarly literature.[1]

I should like to start by mentioning a curious episode which occurred right on the border of the nineteenth and twentieth centuries in connection with the edition of Eriugena's Latin translation of the *Ambigua ad Iohannem* of Maximus Confessor. This episode is described by Edouard Jeauneau in volume 18 of the Greek series of Corpus Christianorum.[2] One folio was missing from the manuscript (Bibliothèque Mazarine 561 in Paris) which contained Eriugena's translation of the *Ambigua*. As it turned out, the missing folio was somehow placed into another codex (Vatican, Reginensis Latinus 596, fol. 9). This folio was published in 1838 by C. Greith as a fragment of some enigmatic work, *Liber de egressu et regressu animae*. Moreover, as it also turned out, it was published in the wrong order so that the content made little sense.

In November of 1903, the German scholar Johannes Dräseke received a letter from a Russian scholar in which the latter referred to his recent book published in 1898. In that book the scholar had identified the text of folio 9 as an extract from the

271

Latin version of the *Ambigua* which fitted perfectly between folios 215 and 216 of the Paris manuscript. Moreover, he had discovered that that text should have been read in reverse order (verso first, and then recto). The title of the book was *The Influence of Eastern Theology on Western Theology in the Works of John Scotus Eriugena*,[3] and the name of the scholar was Alexander Brilliantov.

In 1904 Dräseke published Brilliantov's letter, and in 1917 Paul Lehmann corrected the edition of Eriugena's translation taking into consideration Brilliantov's discovery. That is how Russian Eriugenian studies first became known in the West. This episode is remarkable not simply because it shows us what a brilliant scholar Brilliantov was. It is perhaps chiefly remarkable in that this letter from a Russian addressed as it is to a German concerning the work of the medieval western thinker interested in eastern ideas has a deeper, symbolic meaning. It is a perfect example of East-West relations, a proof of the living tradition and of the mutual attraction of two opposite poles which has existed since the time of Eriugena.[4]

But let us look first at the preceding period and try to trace the beginnings of Eriugenian scholarship in Russia. Its history dates back to the year 1885, when Professor Ierophey Tatarsky published his book entitled *Essence and Origin of the Philosophy of John Scotus Eriugena*.[5] It is a general work which was meant only to familiarize the Russian reader with Eriugenian philosophy. Nevertheless, Tatarsky already puts definite stress on the notion that the Eriugenian system is a combination of different strands, sometimes almost opposite trends, that originate in the eastern and western patterns of theological thought. Though this Russian scholar admits all the merits of Eriugena's system, he denies it originality and views it as a collection of many different ideas put together in a rather eclectic way. Such an attitude determines Tatarsky's approach towards Eriugenian philosophy: he endeavors to identify Eriugena's eastern and western sources as well as the ideas that were most influential in his mind. According to Tatarsky, Eriugena's translations of Dionysius and Maximus Confessor inspired the creation of his philosophical system. While Tatarsky points out that Eriugena's sources were both Greek (Basil the Great, Gregory of Nazianzus, Gregory of Nyssa) and Latin (Ambrose and Augustine) Fathers, he holds that "Eriugena preferred Greek Fathers to Latin ones because of the simple reason that his contemplative spirit tallied rather with the speculative way of thinking of the former than with the practical attitude of the latter."[6] And also, since it was the Neoplatonism of the Fathers that determined the main trend of ninth-century Christian philosophy, Tatarsky concludes that Eriugena's system is essentially Neoplatonic. Though Eriugena tries to bring his philosophy into conformity with Christian revelation, Tatarsky nevertheless argues that Eriugena still gives primary position to reason, thereby making use of Augustine's conviction that true philosophy can be as deep as true religion. Thus he concludes that the Eriugenian system remains pantheistic, with no essential distinction between God and nature but only a distinction of degree.

Tatarsky's book itself, however, was to a great extent eclectic and it left many issues in Eriugenian teaching without sufficient explanation. No wonder there was need for a more critical and comprehensive work—and such a work was written in 1898 by Alexander Brilliantov.

We should say something more about the author himself. Brilliantov was a broadly educated, outstanding scholar, professor of the Theological Academy in St. Petersburg. A man whose interests lay in the East as well as in the West, he knew both cultures well enough to make a substantial contribution to the studies of both (the episode concerning the letter noted above proves this). It is symbolic that a man such as Brilliantov decided to write a book on Eriugena. An "East-West" type of scholar, Brilliantov was a perfect parallel to Eriugena himself. Being a true representative of eastern Orthodox culture, this Russian professor meanwhile had studied the western tradition so profoundly that it influenced not only his ideas but his whole mode of life, his very convictions, and even, what is almost unbelievable, his approach towards his "eastern" Orthodox belief. In the notable dispute in Russian Orthodoxy in the beginning of our century about the nature of ecclesiastical dogma, when most of the traditionalists denied any possibility of its development or change, Brilliantov decisively supported the opposite point of view. According to Brilliantov, "Christian revelation is addressed to human reason and therefore subject to variations in its interpretation."[7] Brilliantov was firmly convinced that different minds enjoy different degrees of clarity in apprehension of the truth, and that different epochs created different schools of theology. What a typical example of a western approach, though taken by an eastern scholar!

What, then, does Brilliantov have to say about Eriugena, another scholar of the "East-West" type, and about the interrelation of eastern and western ideas in his works? Brilliantov points out at the very beginning that the key question in the analysis of both the origin and meaning of Eriugena's system is the question of the relation in it between eastern and western theologies. Eriugena's main eastern sources, according to the scholar, were works of Dionysius, the *De ambiguis* of Maximus Confessor, and the *De imagine* of Gregory of Nyssa. The main western source was Augustine. From the very beginning, Brilliantov outlines western and eastern features of Eriugenian theology. Thus, Eriugena has acquired from the West the rational approach towards the object of faith, the possibility of understanding the latter more profoundly through the light of reason. An example of such an approach is the construction of trinitarian dogma by western theologians through bringing in insights from psychology: since the human being is made in the image of God, there must be some resemblance between God and the human spirit, and so we can build our notion of God by proceeding from the human being. This approach, according to Brilliantov, presupposes attention to the inner life of the human spirit.

From the Eastern sources, however, Eriugena, following Gregory of Nyssa, acquires an almost opposite approach which derives the notion of human nature from the notion of God, though it nevertheless bases itself on the identical teaching of the image of God in the human being. This path of inquiry is characterized by its attention to the external relations of humanity with God and the world. And so the type of speculation which is used by Eriugena shows that he is first of all a philosopher who consistently follows the western principle of free philosophical investigation of truth. But because of his faith in revelation, Eriugena also wants to be a philosopher with his feet firmly planted on the ground of revelation and is therefore concerned to base his theory on the ideas of Christian theologians, particularly the theologians of the East.

But if Eriugena had such admiration for eastern theology, why did he seek philosophical methods at all? According to Brilliantov, the appearance of the western rational method in Eriugenian works was by no means fortuitous. The reason for applying rational criteria to the teachings of theological authorities arose out of contradictions between eastern and western thinkers which became obvious to the medieval scholar. And reason was called upon to judge these contradictions.

Brilliantov appears to consider the contradiction between two different approaches towards the question of the image of God in the human being to be of major importance for Eriugena. So let us concentrate on this particular subject and look closer at the essence of the question.

In general, it is quite common for the theologians of eastern and western traditions to approach certain theological matters in a different way. For example, according to the prominent Russian Orthodox theologian Vladimir Lossky and his *Mystical Theology of the Eastern Church*, western thought in its exposition of trinitarian dogma proceeds from one nature in order to come to the three Persons, while the Greek Fathers first consider the three Persons and then come to one nature.

A similar reverse order is observed concerning the question of the image of God in the human being. "The theological interpretation of this revealed truth in eastern and western traditions is often different," Lossky writes.

> Augustine tends to form the notion of God based on the likeness of our image to God's image and tries to discover in God what we ourselves find in our soul, which has been created in God's image. This is the method of psychological analogies applied to the cognition of God, to theology. However, St. Gregory of Nyssa, for example, on the contrary, proceeds from what the revelation tells us about God in order to find then in man something that would correspond to the image of God. This is the theological method applied to human science, to anthropology. The former tends to cognize God proceeding from man who has been created in God's image; the latter tries to establish the true nature of man proceeding from the notion of God, in whose image man was created.[8]

Similarly, Brilliantov points out that eastern and western approaches towards the interpretation of the problem of the "image of God" are opposite. (It will be necessary here to point out that we personally do not claim that the two approaches diverge as clearly as Brilliantov puts it. He himself may well have exaggerated the discrepancies in order to stress further the merit of

Eriugena in trying to reconcile them.) Thus, according to Brilliantov, when Eriugena studies the divine, he takes a western approach. The psychological method thus involved leads from human psychology to the God of revelation and assumes that the divine can be cognized through deep self-cognition since one cannot conceive anything related to the divine nature if he does not know human nature first. Moreover, in this approach the similitude, or likeness between God and the human soul, is understood as essential, and not simply analogical. Since the most essential characteristic of the human soul is its self-consciousness, it follows, according to the theological tradition of the West, that God must be an absolute self-consciousness. Since we think by means of inner words, God must also have his inner word, or *logos*. And, finally, since will, or love, is also essential for humans, God also has will, or spirit. And in this way we come to the revealed concept of Trinity.

Eriugena does not hesitate to introduce a number of other parallels with human nature. According to him, "God not only creates everything but also manifests himself in all created things." This idea was often interpreted as pantheistic. Brilliantov claims, however, that it should be understood as a pure analogy to the operation of the human spirit. In this case it means that God manifests himself not *as an essence*, but as thought and will of an absolutely personal divine spirit. Similarly, when man creates something he does not insert himself into these things; rather he manifests therein only his ideas.

Brilliantov thinks also that we should understand in a similar manner another Eriugenian idea—that "God does not know what he is" (*quid sit*). It means simply that God "does not know what he is" in anything created; he is not part of the creation. God, for Eriugena, as absolute, infinite, personal, self-conscious, and willing spirit, is always distinct from the finite world. As Brilliantov points out, this is a theological idea which does not have anything to do with pantheism.

While Eriugena takes a western approach in his theology, Brilliantov holds, he takes an opposite, eastern, approach in his anthropology. The essence of the eastern approach, according to Gregory of Nyssa, who uses the same doctrine of the image of God in humanity, is that we conceive of the properties of human nature by looking at what is known about God from revelation. So if God is good, then the human being should also be good in a certain manner. As is the case with God, the human being also has by way of parallelism a self-conscious mind and inner word, etc. So Eriugena builds his anthropology "downwards." The divine is reflected in the human soul. As a "perfect image [*perfecta imago*] of the Creator," human nature should possess *all* that the Creator possesses. The difference lies only in the subject itself—for example, the human being, as opposed to God, is dependent, finite, etc.

Together with Maximus Confessor, Eriugena thinks that humanity is the center of the finite world and is predestined to unite in itself all created things. All the world is contained not only in God's, but also in our mind. Since our consciousness is obscured in the material world, we need to return to our true nature. And that is why one of the most important Eriugenian ideas is the idea of the restoration of the ideal world through the human spirit—the spiritualization of human nature and its reunification with absolute spirit, a process which was first performed by Christ. All these ideas, though they in general resemble the mainstream of most of eastern spiritual theories and practices, have definitely been acquired by Eriugena through eastern Christian theology.

Now we come to the key point of Brilliantov's explanation of Eriugena's system. The essence of Eriugena's outlook is the analogy between divine and human spirit which was worked out by the Fathers and is based on the biblical notion of the image of God in the human being. This analogy, as we have already seen, was treated differently in the West and in the East, and it was also presented alternatively as an ascent from humanity to God or as a descent from God to humanity. According to Brilliantov, the main fact which determines the whole system of Eriugena is his acceptance of *both* points of view. His theory thus incorporates two directions: on the one hand, his teaching about *God* and the origin of everything from him; and on the other, his teaching about *humanity* and the returning of everything to God through human nature. As we see, what on first glance appears as no more than a simple combination of eastern and western theological approaches towards the question about the "image of God" in fact forms the essence of *Periphyseon*. Brilliantov then draws two important conclusions. First, since the Christian idea of the "image of God" pertains to the very essence of Eriugena's system, his teaching is essentially Christian. And second, since the structure of Eriugena's teaching is determined by acceptance of two different approaches towards the problem of the image of God in humanity, his system is essentially "eastern-western," though Brilliantov by no means claims that Eriugena's attempt to reconcile the two approaches was always successful.

Brilliantov's book could not, of course, pass unnoticed. Almost immediately after its publication, the Russian professor Serebrenikov published a review of the book.[9] In it, he praises Brilliantov's knowledge of the subject but completely disagrees with all of his conclusions. Two main questions become a matter of discussion. The first is about the meaning of the Eriugenian system. In company with some western scholars, Serebrenikov claims that, though Eriugena himself was a Christian, which is quite clear from the Christian orientation of his works, his philosophical system on the whole cannot be called Christian.

According to Serebrenikov, the Christian elements are fortuitous in Eriugenian works. There is no theism there, but only pantheism; Eriugena takes Neoplatonic ideas from the sources which he translated, and he revivifies Neoplatonism. The second question is about the origin of Eriugena's system. Serebrenikov thinks that its one and only origin is Neoplatonism, and all the eastern features in Eriugenian teaching can be reduced to it. The role of the doctrine of the "image of God" is rejected.

In 1899 Brilliantov published his refutation of Serebrenikov's review.[10] In it, he stressed the important role of revelation, divine grace and supernatural power in the Eriugenian system. According to Brilliantov, Eriugena has made an attempt to reconcile monism and Christian theism. God in Eriugena's system distinctly stands above all created things. Brilliantov argues also that Eriugena's system was first of all an acquisition of eastern Christian *theological* thought. Even if Serebrenikov contends that Eriugenian teaching is of a "nontheological" character, this should not necessarily imply that it is not *Christian*. After all, the Neoplatonism of the Fathers itself was influenced by Christian ideas to such an extent that it could hardly be called pagan anymore. Moreover, there is no way to deny the significance of the analogy between divine and human spirit for Eriugena, and this is an essential component of theism.

We can sum up Brilliantov's main views on Eriugena in his own words. Eriugena's system, Brilliantov writes, "cannot be acknowledged as having a purely external relationship with Christian teach-

Russian Scholarship

279

ing. . . . The Christian theistic element, which was borrowed from theologians, is not entirely alien to his system, . . . but belongs to its very essence,"[11] no matter whether it was incorporated successfully or not. Eriugena's system, according to Brilliantov, appeared as a result of the "impact of eastern theology on western theology," as well as of the "acquisition and independent clarification of eastern theological speculation on the ground of the principles of western speculation."[12] Brilliantov holds that although Eriugena, with his striving towards the Greek East, was an anomaly for his time, his attempt to unite the results of eastern and western speculation upon Christian grounds, on the contrary, is something very natural to the whole tradition of European thought.

The burden of this essay has been to show that Eriugena and his works were not completely unexplored by prerevolutionary Russian scholarship. This controversial figure caused discussions and disputes in Russia as everywhere else in the European world. Moreover, we believe that Eriugena was of even greater importance to Russian scholars because of the intermediary, controversial position of Russian culture itself, placed midway between the East and the West—a fact which always led to the appearance of devotees of both eastern and western trends among the Russian intellectual elite.[13] And, as usual, the approach of the Russian school towards the subject of Eriugena, was global, universal, almost "cosmic." Eriugenian teaching became not only the basis for an encounter of scholarly ideas, but also a ground for the collision of philosophical and religious outlooks, beliefs, and devotions of scholars themselves.

NOTES

1. In fact, Eriugena was one of the few medieval philosophers who enjoyed a rather favorable attitude in the Soviet manuals of the history of philosophy because of his having received condemnation for (according to the same manuals) pantheistic and therefore anticlerical ideas!

2. CCSG 18:xxi.

3. A. Brilliantov, *Vliyaniye vostochnogo bogosloviya na zapadnoye v proizvedeniyakh Ioanna Skota Erigeny* (St. Petersburg, 1898).

4. The interest towards western, and particularly Roman Catholic, culture was so strong in Russia at the beginning of this century that

some prominent scholars (like Karsavin) not only studied it profoundly, but even were finally converted to the Roman Catholic faith.

5. Ierophey Tatarsky, *Sushchnost' i proiskhozhdeniye filosofii Ioanna Skota Erigeny* (Khar'kov, 1885).

6. Tatarsky, 7.

7. N. Zernov, *The Russian Religious Renaissance of the XX Century* (New York, 1963), 94.

8. V. Lossky, *Essai sur la théologie mystique de l'Eglise d'orient* (Paris: Aubier-Montaigne, 1944), 109–110.

9. Serebrenikov's review was published in the *Journal of the Ministry of People's Education* (St. Petersburg, 1898).

10. A. Brilliantov, *K voprosu o filosofii Erigeny. Otvet prof. Serebrenikovu* (St. Petersburg, 1899).

11. A. Brilliantov, "Vliyaniye vostochnogo bogosloviya na zapadnoye v proizvedeniyakh Ioanna Skota Erigeny," M.A. Dissertation Theses (St. Petersburg, 1898), thesis 11.

12. Ibid., thesis 10.

13. The nineteenth century in Russian cultural history was marked by the long controversy between "zapadniks" ("Westerners") and "slavyanophils," the former trying to establish firm links with the West, and the latter standing for the purity of the Old Church Slavonic tradition. This controversy finally has led Russian intelligentsia to the discovery of the most profound paradox of Russian culture, namely, that this culture, although it is deeply rooted in the eastern tradition, is nevertheless always open to contacts or borrowings from the West. As far as Eriugena's system in particular is concerned, it has continued to influence some Russian philosophers and theologians. For example, S. Bulgakov's cosmology definitely has parallels with Eriugenian philosophy. See V. Zen'kovsky, *A History of Russian Philosophy* (London: Routledge and Kegan Paul, 1953), vol. 2, chap. 6. V. Lossky studied Eriugena extensively before he started his work on his original treatise on negative theology. See V. Lossky, "La théologie négative dans la doctrine de Denys l'Aréopagite," *Revue des sciences philosophiques et théologiques* 28 (1939): 204–221.

Index of Names

Index of Names prepared by Otto O. Mellink.

Index of Subjects

Index of Subjects prepared by Willemien Otten.

DATE DUE
